Living in the Spiritual World

A Study of the Other World We Live In

For Chris

¡ Con Mucho Aloha !

IanB

Living in the Spiritual World

A Study of the Other World We Live In

Michael and Laura Bagby
Randall Smith

Pleasant Word
A Division of WINEPRESS PUBLISHING

All photos by Michael Bagby, and David Melrose. Editorial Assistance: Carmel Gabrial and Beth Ferguson.

Cover design by Leesa Brinkley.

"LMB" indicates the author's own literal translation from the original language.

ISBN 1-4141-0113-9
Library of Congress Catalog Card Number: 2004100194

Dedication

It has often been said that the most effective people in this world are the ones who have their hope in the next.

One such person was Mabel Bagby, a woman who understood the key to living a successful life in this world and in the spiritual world. Her life (growing up on a farm in Kentucky and living as a military wife in Germany, Turkey, and the United States) was an example to many. While she raised her children, served as a Red Cross Auxilary Nurse, worked with her sister in a beauty shop, and even in her latter years when her body was not fully functioning, her words, her actions, and finally, her smile communicated love to all she encountered. She touched many for the kingdom and continually changed her world for the better. We all will miss her.

Mabel was also famous for saying: "You should read my son's book. He is a nice boy."

This book is dedicated to Mabel: a loving mother, a sweet sister, and a famous literary critic.

Welcome to *Living in the Spiritual World*!

Join a roundtable discussion of many aspects
of life in the spiritual realm!

Around the table you will find:

Laura Bagby—an honors graduate from the University of Hawaii with a degree in social work who has spent the past sixteen years working with the Miskito Indians in the jungles of Honduras and Nicaragua. Laura also holds a degree in cosmetology, is a certified aerobics instructor, and the mother of four children. Laura brings a unique

Michael, Laura, Dottie & Randy dining in Jerusalem

perspective and practical experience to our table.

Dr. Randall Smith—an archeologist and Bible professor who has resided in Jerusalem for most of the past fifteen years. Randy holds degrees in Near East archaeology and a doctorate in comparative religion and is respected as one of the foremost Bible teachers in the Land. He has a profound understanding of biblical culture, history, geography, and especially rabbinical teachings, yet focuses on the practical steps of our faith. Randy will help us understand what that first-century person was thinking when he heard the words of Jesus. His comments will be preceded by "**RS.**"

Michael Bagby—a missionary pilot, historian, and former ice cream "scooper" who is an honors graduate from Miami University with a degree in history and graduated from the University of Hope Bible School. Michael flew A-6 Intruders in the US Navy before becoming a skier in Colorado. He has been working in Central America with the Miskito Indians since 1984 and was one of the founders of Project Ezra, a Christian primary education project along the Coco River in one of the most remote regions in the Western Hemisphere. Michael's thoughts will be noted by "**MB.**"

Mikaela, Lukas, Arielle, and Moselle Bagby— These young believers will pop into our conversations to ask pertinent questions and make comments.

And most importantly,

The Holy Spirit—the Author of the Bible and the most profound teacher in the cosmos. It is only His teaching and His empowering that will make any difference in our lives. *Our comments are only an effort to provide a framework through which He will speak.*

This is not meant to be a theological treatise but simply the offering of some practical perspectives on spiritual life.

NOW, PLEASE, PULL UP A CHAIR AND TURN THE PAGE!

Table of Contents

Preface

WHEN WORLDS COLLIDE

We go through days of living in this world, dealing with problems, enjoying moments with family and friends, and getting caught up in the events around us. This is life in our natural world. Then out of the blue, we collide with another world and something special happens.

God often surprises us in the middle of mundane events. For me, today is just another warm morning here in Waspam, Nicaragua. Over the past two decades, I have experienced many similar sunrises, the same early conversations between the chickens, cows, pigs, parrots, and dogs, and the feel-

Rio Coco Nicaragua / Honduras

ing of tranquility that goes with a fourth-world environment. Often, as these warm mornings turned into hot days, I have seen God do some incredible things. I have learned that He likes to show up in places such as this. I live for those days when my natural world collides with His spiritual world.

Waspam is the largest "city" on the Rio Coco, the longest river in Central America and the border between Honduras and Nicaragua. The Coco River is the main highway through the center of Miskitia, the region on the Atlantic Coast side of Honduras and

Nicaragua, where the Miskito Indians live. Christianity first came to this river valley only eighty years ago. The Miskitos rapidly accepted Christianity and mixed Christian beliefs into their already-developed spiritual belief system. The spiritual world has always been very real here in Miskitia. Jesus became just another face in the heavens, another force to deal with. Hopefully, He would help the Miskitos where other spirits have harmed and taken from them.

I came here in 1984 with a relief team to help Miskitos who were refugees in villages across the river because of the Sandinista war in Nicaragua. In 1986, we began a primary school project in the villages along the lower Coco River. We also began teaching the students, as well as the adults, about relational Christianity—a personal relationship with God. As we taught the basics of our Christian beliefs, we ourselves began to learn some fundamentals of cross-cultural communication.

In 1997, we took three of our Miskito leaders of the school project to Israel for a study course on the life of Jesus. How we got there is one of those God-really-surprises-us things. It all began with a desire

Truman Cunningham, Onofre Zamora, Karthy & Craig Englert with Randy Smith, Jerusalem 1997

of our project director to see the land that Jesus lived in since nobody from the Miskito culture had ever been to the Holy Land. He told me this on one bug-infested night, sitting on his porch, down river in Sawa. Suddenly, after a few years of prayer, four different friends in Hawaii, in less than a week, gave us money for airfare. A few weeks later, a friend in Jerusalem provided us an apartment for a month rent-free. Another friend sent us thousands of dollars for "whatever else we needed." What he sent was almost exactly what we needed to take a course of study called *The Life of Jesus* offered by Christian Travel Study Programs.

Our teacher was archeologist/Bible scholar, Dr. Randall Smith, who turned out to be one of the most noted experts on biblical culture and history in Israel. During our twelve-day study tour, Randy communicated to our "three amigos" (Truman, Augusto, and Onofre) and us much of the background of the Bible. Along with this, he taught us what many of the Jews were thinking when they heard Jesus teach. As I verbally translated from English into Spanish for this course, I began appreciating the fact that these three believers from a culture where Christianity was relatively new were literally bypassing centuries of theology and Western interpretation of the Scriptures. They were right where those first-century believers were, sitting in the same places, listening with culturally-attuned ears to the message that Jesus was communicating within the context of first-century culture and language.

It dawned on me that these three Miskito men were beginning their spiritual walk right where those first disciples began. I didn't have to explain systems of theology, discuss heresies and other controversies that have sprung up over the centuries, or explain the Bible through my own American cultural heritage. These guys were getting the message straight from the first-century Jewish and Greek cultures right into their own Miskito culture.

What a concept! It was revolutionary! The Bible became alive to these three Miskito Indians, and they returned to their homeland much better able to communicate the essence of Christ's message.

Since then, Dr. Smith and I have had many discussions on the challenges facing our own culture to understand the message of the Bible and apply biblical truths to our own lives. We both realized that the key to any understanding of the Bible is an intimate relationship with the Holy Spirit. He is the one who makes the Bible come alive, who makes the words jump off the page into our lives. Having worked with third—and fourth-world cultures, we are well aware of the powerful effect that the Bible has on any person who reads it. Without the guidance of the Holy Spirit, history has proven that intellectual pursuits of biblical understanding are in vain.

One of Randy's favorite stories is of the two Chinese women whom he had on one of his *Life of Jesus* study tours in Israel. These ladies became Christians in the underground church in China, and the only "Bible" they had was the first two chapters of Philippians. Because of their relationship with the Holy Spirit, these two chapters gave them the guidance they needed to live a life pleasing and useful to God. When they discovered that there were sixty-five more books in the Bible, they were overjoyed. When they walked in the footsteps of Jesus in Israel and began to understand the cultural, his-

The authors

torical, political, and geographical background of the Bible, the message of the Scriptures became richer still.

This is our goal for *Living in the Spiritual World*, to open up the richness of the Scriptures as well as to provide a basis for accurately understanding the intended message of the writers.

In the summer of 1999, we began a project together to communicate first-century Christian cultural understanding to our own first world churches, as well as to other Christians around the world. Since then we have been compiling notes; recording conversations; taking photographs; filming on location in Israel, Greece, Nicaragua, and in the Caribbean; and organizing the material presented in the following pages. Much of what follow flows from a five-hour spontaneous conversation that was recorded at the International Christian Embassy in Jerusalem on Sept. 14, 1999. We hope that you will find our somewhat unorthodox roundtable presentation engaging and easy to assimilate.

Most of us have learned how to live in our natural world though our own education and life experiences. The most important challenge of our lives is the understanding of how we are to live in the spiritual world. We hope that *Living in the Spiritual World* will help you live a rich, satisfying, and productive life here in this world and the next.

—Michael Bagby

If we are searching about information on the spiritual world, we could begin with any of those magazines found at the checkout counter at your local supermarket. Another source would be some of the talk shows featuring the latest "gurus" that are aired daily on television. We might even call one of the psychic hotlines numbers for some inside information. However, the most accurate source for information on the spiritual world is a book found in many homes on the planet. The Bible contains many stories of men and women who suddenly found themselves faced with the reality of "living in the spiritual world."

Introduction

The Bible records that as a well-known Pharisee named Saul of Tarsus was on his way to Damascus to arrest the followers of Jesus, his journey was interrupted. Suddenly, a bright light, brighter than the noon sun, appeared, and a voice from an invisible source came with a message to Saul. He later described this event to King Agrippa.

One day I was on such a mission to Damascus, armed with the authority and commission of the leading priests. About noon, Your Majesty, a light from heaven brighter than the sun shone down on me and my companions. We all fell down, and I heard a voice saying to me in Aramaic, "Saul, Saul, why are you persecuting me? It is hard for you to fight against my will."

"Who are you, sir?" I asked.

And the Lord replied, "I am Jesus, the one you are persecuting. Now stand up! For I have appeared to you to appoint you as my servant and my witness. You are to tell the world about this experience and about other times I will appear to you. And I will protect you from both your own people and the Gentiles. Yes, I am going to send you to the Gentiles, to open their eyes so they may turn from darkness to light, and from the power of Satan to God. Then they will receive forgiveness for their sins and be given a place among God's people, who are set apart by faith in me." (Acts 26:12–17)

This was obviously the defining moment in Saul/Paul's life. Considering the circumstances of Saul being on his way to capture and imprison Christians, this event was more than extraordinary. The message was that he would be used by God to open the eyes of many. But open the eyes to what? For what purpose?

MB: We have been taught by our scientists to only trust the things that we can see, feel, hear, touch, and taste—the things that our senses respond to. Yet there is a whole world out there that is accessible only through our spirit. Our God deeply desires us to be aware of this other dimension of life and that we enter in to relate to Him and impact the world for His purposes. The reality is that many in the world live their lives as if the spiritual world does not even exist, either through ignorance or choice. They are blinded to the realities of life. And they are perishing.

RS: This study is titled *Living in the Spiritual World*, yet I think most of us spend our time thinking about the physical world: "What will my job net me this month?" "Is the month bigger than the money?" I have always been interested in the subject of spiritual warfare from the standpoint of solving problems in my life. I think there are a lot of things written that help explain the theory of what is out there and who we are wrestling with, but I am more interested in actually attaining *the-bearing-fruit-in-my-life* stage that God intends for me.

MB: That bearing-fruit process begins by having an understanding of what is out there in the spiritual world and the dynamics of this unseen realm. It is like flying in an airplane at night when you can't see what is ahead. Without a chart to navigate or radar, you don't have a clue to what is out there in front of you. On the A-6 Intruder jet I flew in the Navy, we had a very sophisticated ground-mapping radar that allowed us to fly low-level through a mountainous area safely. I think that this is what God gives us in His Word and through His Holy Spirit—an accurate map of the spiritual topography and very sensitive radar to pick up what is out in front.

Michael and Randy
Rio Coco, Nicaragua

RS: So in essence, through this study, we are creating a spiritual radar and awareness of the spiritual map that the Lord has given us.

MB: Let me give you one example of what having the map can mean. We had a Youth With A Mission (YWAM) team with us at our ministry base in Auka, Honduras in 1989. The team was there as part of their discipleship training school outreach. Auka is a Honduran Miskito village that had many refugees from Nicaragua. Since we were only seven miles from the border, many families of the Nicaragua Resistance forces lived in this village.

During the weeks before the team's arrival, we had noticed a sharp increase of drunkenness in the refugee village. Merchants from the coast were bringing merchandise into Auka to sell to the refugee families (whose husbands had US dollars [pay from their military service]). There were two "stores" that had suddenly appeared selling clothes, beer, and rum. The cargo was coming in trucks over a very rough "road" from Puerto Lempira and in small airplanes. Now with this availability of alcohol, we noticed drunken men lying in the roads and on porches, along with the associated problems.

When the team arrived, we began to pray about this situation. One morning, after our morning worship time, one of the team members mentioned the story in Joshua about how the Israelites marched around the walls of Jericho for seven days and the Lord brought down the walls of the city. Although we didn't understand fully what the significance of walking around the walls was, we decided to take similar action and devote specific prayer for the situation "on location" as we walked. If it worked for the Israelites, it may bring these walls of alcoholism down in Auka.

We divided into two teams. One group hiked into the village and walked around the houses where the stores were many times, praying that God would stop the flow of liquor into these families. I led a group to the airstrip, and we walked the length (about 2300 feet) several times, praying that God would not allow alcohol to come into the village via this airstrip. Both groups finished by 9:00 A.M., and we all met back at our house. About 10:30 A.M., we heard the sound of an airplane approaching Auka. A few minutes later, a small Cessna from the local air service landed and began unloading boxes. I looked through my binoculars and saw that the cargo was cases of Flor De Cana, the local Honduran rum.

After unloading the boxes of rum, the pilot got back into his airplane to start the engine. But for some reason, the engine would not fire! The pilot continued cranking the engine, and the speed of the propeller blades became slower and slower as the battery drained. Soon, the battery was dead.

I was watching all this with interest and knew that the pilot would soon be walking up to our house to use our radio. He did a few moments later and called his base in Puerto Lempira. During lunch, another airplane arrived with a portable generator to charge his battery. I walked down to the airstrip and saw that the pilot of the other plane was a good friend, Barry.

Barry is a Miskito who had lived in the US where he had gotten his pilot's license. I first met him when I began flying around Miskitia in our 1953 Piper Pacer (which we affectionately called the *Flying Banana*). Barry's father was a missionary pastor from the Moravian church who was responsible for bringing Christianity to many places on the Coco River. However, for many reasons, Barry had rejected Christianity or at least the "religion" that he saw growing up. I am always happy to see Barry, and we have had many good conversations.

I told Barry that I wanted to apologize to him for the situation. He looked puzzled. While the generator was charging up the other airplane's battery, I explained what we had done that morning by marching up and down the airstrip seven times. He looked even more confused. Barry disconnected the generator and told the pilot to crank the engine. He did, and after a few turns of the propeller, the engine fired. The pilot closed his door, gave a wave to us, and took off. Suddenly, it was silent, and Barry loaded the generator into his airplane. We said goodbye, and he cranked his engine—then, *guess what?*

His engine would not start. He continued cranking, but the engine refused to fire. I looked inside the cockpit to the instrument panel, and it appeared that the fuel pressure was too low on the start cycle to fire the engine. He tried again but to no avail. An hour of recharging and cranking followed. As the hour was approaching sunset, I told Barry to relax, that we had plenty of food and an extra bunk for him to sleep in. By this time, many of the YWAM team had gathered at the airstrip. I know Barry was thinking hard. I don't think he relished the idea of spending the night in Auka with twenty-three young missionaries.

Barry looked at the setting sun, then to me, and said, "Those must have been some powerful prayers." With that acknowledgement, he cranked the engine one more time—and it fired! With a look of surprise, he quickly loaded the generator into the airplane, said goodbye, and took off.

That night, a few team members went to one of the stores and began a conversation with the daughter of the owner. She became convinced that Jesus was an important part of her life and accepted Him as her Lord.

After our prayers on the airstrip, the rum flights abruptly stopped. The following week, one of the stores was robbed of all its merchandise. The merchants soon left the village. Were our "prayer marches" responsible for this? Was this a spiritual principle from the "map" (book of Joshua) that guided our situation in Auka?

Along with the "map," having a "spiritual radar" can make all the difference. Here's one example: A few years ago, I visited my former home in Coupeville, Washington. I lived there during my years in the Navy when I was not serving the Lord. In fact, during those years, I was actually playing on the *other team*, and my house was the site of many parties and activities. I had returned to visit friends in the area and stopped by to show the house to my wife and children and to visit with Mary, the lady who had purchased the house from me. Mary was retired schoolteacher with whom I had kept in touch.

When we entered the house, Laura had a real "oggy" feeling and immediately took the kids out into the backyard. I stayed and talked with Mary and began to remember all the "stuff" that happened in the house. Mary was having severe health problems that required her to be on an oxygen machine with a long cord and nasal tube. As I spoke with her, I began to feel difficulty in my breathing. I felt mounting pressure in my chest, and breathing was getting more difficult. I knew that this was unusual. My spiritual radar told me that I was under attack and that there were spiritual forces trying to affect my health. I excused myself and went out to find Laura. I told her what was happening and we prayed. We pointed our offensive weapons toward specific areas, and I began feeling better. We collected the kids and left. By the time we were out of Coupeville, I was back to normal.

RS: I think that spiritual warfare and all of the issues that come out of understanding the spiritual world in general are well exemplified when we face problems. One of the things that people often struggle with in their theological development is the big question in their heart: "If God loves me, why am I going through difficult and painful times?"

In 2 Kings, chapter 6, there is a relevant passage about such a problem. This story is about Elisha and the children of Israel. There is a serious problem: There is a war going on, and a young servant, Gehazi, is looking at the situation saying, "What shall we do?"

The king commanded, "Go and find out where Elisha is, and we will send troops to seize him."

And the report came back: "Elisha is at Dothan." So one night the king of Aram sent a great army with many chariots and horses to surround the city. When the servant of the man of God got up early the next morning and went outside, there were troops, horses, and chariots everywhere.

"Ah, my lord, what will we do now?" he cried out to Elisha.

"Don't be afraid!" Elisha told him. "For there are more on our side than on theirs!" Then Elisha prayed, "O LORD, open his eyes and let him see!" The LORD opened his servant's eyes, and when he looked up, he saw that the hillside around Elisha was filled with horses and chariots of fire. (2 Kings 6:13–17)

In reality, when we look at the physical things in our hand, the amount of money in our bank accounts, the size of our congregations, and we see all the evils of society that are pressing in on us, it is easy to feel overwhelmed. All you have to do is watch the news and you are overwhelmed—it often seems the whole world is going crazy!

Here's a young man ready to follow the man of God and to do the right thing, but he can only see the crisis and not the salvation. The problem wasn't that help was unavailable. The problem was not that the help was too small. The problem is in our lives. *Like this young servant, Gehazi, we don't see where the help is.*

The phrase, "There are more on our side than on theirs," is an echo of the passage: "Greater is He that is in you than he who is in the world" (1 John 4:4).

Perhaps this perspective from Laura will help.

ALIVE IN THE SPIRITUAL WORLD

We live for and are influenced by innumerable forces—seen and unseen. However, we live most of our lives primarily by what we can see, hear, taste, touch, and feel.

We find ourselves influenced by the weather, our health, the time, the economy, the system, and all that is tangible to our senses. We live our lives here and now mainly for the urgent needs of the moment. Yet there is an entire host of heaven, including a Creator Being, longing for our attention and affection.

A Creator that is totally engrossed in us and our activities on this planet, so much so that He made visible to us His Son, so that we would have the opportunity to look into the unseen world all around us. By the death of Jesus Christ, we have access to an eternal world far greater than our minds could conceive.

We are made alive in His Spirit and have been given the right to know the mysteries of our God—the unseen mysteries that move our universe and influence our daily existence. Things hidden from plain view and only disclosed to those with the faith to believe. The unseen forces that influence are more powerful than the forces that can be seen.

Whether we believe these forces exist or not does not change the fact

Laura riding down the Rio Coco Nicaragua

that they are there and that they do influence. Indeed, it is with an influence so great that lives are devastated and destroyed because of them. Just as lives are changed, empowered, and renewed by them. Satan attempts to steal, kill, and destroy all that belongs to God.

God, the Victor through Jesus Christ, empowers us to overcome all the influences of Satan and his demonic hosts. He uses the power of His angelic creations to wage this battle in the heavenly realm. We are a part of this war whether we know it or not. It is far better to know it than to be ignorant of it and bashed back and forth by the forces that be.

In understanding the Lord's creation—the seen and the unseen—, we are able to deal with life with the greatest insight. Our level of discernment into the spiritual realm will heighten, and we will experience an effectiveness that will impact not only what is seen but also all that is unseen.

Our lives will enter the realm of the eternal—a realm far more profound and lasting. A realm that rises above the circumstances and influences of this life.

Personal Reflections

1. Why is it difficult to shift from natural thinking to a spiritual mindset?
2. How can we increase our level of spiritual discernment?
3. How can we bear more spiritual fruit?
4. What are some of the practical aspects of spiritual living?
5. How would you introduce someone to life in the spiritual world?

Who lives in the spiritual world? Obviously, God is the most important resident, but there are others as well. Historically, one of the main quests of mankind has been to find an entrance into this world through a physical portal, a religious act, or an encounter with a spiritual entity. These citizens of the other world have often made their appearance in the lives of men and women, affecting lives and human history. Since the beginning of time, they have been labeled with many names and titles. We know them simply as angelic beings.

Angelic Beings

Paul of Tarsus, one of the great missionaries of the first century, wrote a letter to the church in Ephesus in an attempt to explain our place in the spiritual world. In chapters 1 through 5, he describes our position, our purpose, and how we function as the body of Christ. In chapter 6, he describes our interaction with another of God's creations—the angels.

> For we are not fighting against people made of flesh and blood, but against the evil rulers and authorities of the unseen world, against those mighty powers of darkness who rule this world, and against wicked spirits in the heavenly realms. (Ephesians 6:12)

As we look at the Scriptures, we see that these angelic beings fall into two categories: First, evil spirits (also called demons):

> For Jesus had already said to the spirit, "Come out of the man, you evil spirit." Then Jesus asked, "What is your name?" And the spirit replied, "Legion, because there are many of us here inside this man." (Mark 5:8–9)

And there are God's angels:

> For I, the Son of Man, will come in the glory of my Father with His angels and will judge all people according to their deeds. (Matthew 16:27)

Understanding angels and demons help us live victorious lives in the spiritual world.

Arielle: Angels? Demons? Are you kidding? We have never seen one except in the movies and on television. How can they exist if we can't see, hear, smell, or touch them?

MB: There are many things that exist that are not detectable through our five senses. Have you ever watched an airliner accelerate down the runway and take off? Every time I see an airplane lift off, especially a jumbo jet like the 747, I am reminded that there is much more going on than I can see with my own eyes. When you look at the wing of a jet in flight, can you see the lift dynamics happening? No, but obviously something is making that 500,000-pound aircraft fly! Have you listened to a radio? Do you watch television? Can you see the radio and TV waves pass through the air?

Arielle: Well, not exactly. . . .

MB: It's the same with spiritual things. Much is going on around us that we cannot sense with our eyes, ears, nose, etc. Once we are spiritually connected to God, we are able to discern these things.

RS: Developed within Judaic theology was a place for angels. By the time of Jesus, the Sadducees rejected the notion of angels, while the Pharisees believed in angels. The reality of angels is confirmed in thirty-four different books of the Bible. Paul had a great spiritual sense from his own walk; he talked about visiting the third heaven where he saw things that he couldn't relate in his writings. Later, he advised the early believers in Jesus to be careful about the way that we are behaving in the church because of the angels (1 Cor 4:9). To the church in Corinth, he said that a woman there should have her head covered "because of the angels" who were obviously watching (1 Cor. 11:11).

The Bible relates that there are several different kinds of angels. There are *cherubim* that guard the holiness of God and *seraphim* that are always before the throne crying "Holy, Holy, Holy" (Is. 6:3). Then there are *archangels*. We have at least the naming of Michael in Jude 9 and Daniel 10 as an archangel. There are also *angelos*, the messenger angels. This is the infantry-troop-type of angel doing work: sometimes bearing messages, sometimes creating disturbances, or maneuvering behind the scenes. I think we have a mirror image of that on both sides. I can't prove that because Scripture is fortunately vague—it is not designed to give us the ranks of evil. In reality we need to know our enemy. However, we need to be cautious in our study, as some spend an inordinate amount of time studying the ranks of the enemy. The most important thing to know is what he does. I think we as spiritual beings have felt that warfare. I don't think there is any doubt in any of our minds that these guys exist and that they affect our lives.

For us, the impact is what happens in our lives. We understand that difficult things are happening, tough times are there, and even as a Christian, I have noticed thorns grow just as quickly on my roses as they do on my neighbor's roses. Some of the difficult issues and circumstances we face are related to what angelic beings are doing, some relate to the influence of the world, and others are simply the flesh—our human nature. The Scriptures make it clear that there is a lot more than meets the eye and that there is involved in my life both angels who are there to help me and those who are there to hinder me.

MB: It is very important to understand the nature of these very important players in the spiritual world. Whether you realize it or not, you are interacting with them (the good angels and the "fallen" ones) on a regular basis.

Angels are not gods, because the Lord created them:

Praise him, all his angels! Praise him, all the armies of heaven! Let every created thing give praise to the LORD, for he issued his command, and they came into being. (Psalm 148:2–5)

They cannot die because they have eternal life:

And they will never die again. In these respects they are like angels. They are children of God raised up to new life. (Luke 20:36)

They are invisible to man until they want to be seen. Recall Elisha's servant in 2 Kings 2? Also:

Then the LORD opened Balaam's eyes, and he saw the angel of the LORD standing in the roadway with a drawn sword in his hand. Balaam fell face down on the ground before him. (Numbers 22:31)

Angels are not robotic, computer-like creatures but rather have emotions:

"In the same way, there is joy in the presence of God's angels when even one sinner repents." (Luke 15:10)

They are not all knowing and rather curious about mankind:

It was revealed to them that they were not serving themselves, but you, in these things which now have been announced to you through those who preached the gospel to you by the Holy Spirit sent from heaven—things into which angels long to look. (1 Peter 1:12 NAS)

John the Baptist's father, Zacharias, had an interesting encounter with and angel while he was serving in the temple. Gabriel came to deliver the message that he and his wife, Elizabeth, would have a son, despite their old age. Even though he had prayed for years for a child, he still could not believe his ears! The entire account is in Luke 1:5–25.

The angel answered and said to him, "I am Gabriel, who stands in the presence of God, and I have been sent to speak to you and to bring you this good news. And behold, you shall be silent and unable to speak until the day when these things take place, because you did not believe my words, which will be fulfilled in their proper time." (Luke 1:19–20 NAS)

From this we can see that angels can move freely through space and time and can alter human physiology.

Lukas: OK. You got my curiosity up. How did some of the angels become demons, or evil spirits?

MB: There are three angels mentioned by name in the Bible (KJV): Gabriel, Michael, and Lucifer. It seems that one of these chief angels, Lucifer, decided that he was worthy of the praise and worship that God received. That's when the problems began. Ezekiel describes what happened:

> "You were the perfection of wisdom and beauty. You were in Eden, the garden of God. Your clothing was adorned with every precious stone. . . . I ordained and anointed you as the mighty angelic guardian. You had access to the holy mountain of God and walked among the stones of fire. You were blameless in all you did from the day you were created until the day evil was found in you." (Ezekiel 28:12–15)

There is not a lot in the Bible that elaborates on this subject; however, if you piece three biblical passages together, you get a pretty good idea of how it all happened. These three are worth reading: Revelation 12, Isaiah 14, and Ezekiel 28. Lucifer became known as the adversary, or in Hebrew, *Satan*. At one time in his existence, Satan was the worship leader of the heavenly host of angels. Some believe that he was the chief worship leader of heaven. This is why we really need to pray for our worship leaders.

What was Satan's specific sin? Isaiah tells us that it was pride. The entire account is in Isaiah 14:12–17.

> For you said to yourself, "I will ascend to heaven and set my throne above God's stars. I will preside on the mountain of the gods far away in the north." (Isaiah 14:13)

RS: I always found it interesting that we begin time with God creating these beings that are in a perfect environment (God had obviously made them in an unflawed way—they're perfect), there is perfection all around, and out of this comes the rise of an evil heart. Where did that come from? That is a question that only the Lord Himself can answer.

God's call in my life is a call similar to that of the angels—to be willing to serve Him with all of my heart and not to be concerned about receiving the credit for that. The basic sin that occurred was "I want the glory that belongs to Him." Essentially, that is the first sin that man would later take part in.

It seems to me that there is an underlying theme. There was a small plaque that set on President Reagan's desk that said, "There is no limit to what a man can do if there is no concern who gets the credit." Within the servant heart of the believer, there is an angelic pattern that must be followed; a basic process of dying to self has to happen.

MB: Once Satan felt that he was as worthy as the Lord was for honor and praise, he led a rebellion against God, and a third of the angels joined him.

Suddenly, I witnessed in heaven another significant event. I saw a large red dragon with seven heads and ten horns, with seven crowns on his heads. His tail dragged down one-third of the stars, which he threw to the earth. (Revelation 12:3–4)

Michael and the other angels fought against the rebels and forced them out of heaven and onto the earth.

Then there was war in heaven. Michael and the angels under his command fought the dragon and his angels. And the dragon lost the battle and was forced out of heaven. This great dragon—the ancient serpent called the Devil, or Satan, the one deceiving the whole world—was thrown down to the earth with all his angels. (Revelation 7–9)

Many years ago, Apollo astronaut, Jim Irvin, came to Maui. During one meeting, he told us that while he was on the moon, for the first time in his life, he felt the "absence of evil." What an interesting comment! Very few people have had to opportunity to travel away from planet Earth; fewer were spirit-filled believers when they traveled there. Are the demons indeed confined only to this planet? Here's an extraordinary witness!

Now, Satan and his fallen angels have a plan to wage war against the human race, especially the members of the body of Christ.

He stood before the woman as she was about to give birth to her child, ready to devour the baby as soon as it was born. . . .

Then the dragon became angry at the woman, and he declared war against the rest of her children—all who keep God's commandments and confess that they belong to Jesus. (Revelation 12:4,17)

This war is very real. A few years ago, we were at our home in La Ceiba, Honduras, meeting with our ministry co-workers. There was a lot of spiritual activity; many of us were having dreams where demonic images were speaking to us. One evening, I half awoke, feeling a presence hovering over our bed. A bony finger reached out from a dark form and touched me on my right shoulder near the collarbone. I knew that when I awoke, I would have pain there. Sure enough, the next morning, I did. The pain persisted for three weeks, during which time we traveled to Florida. One night I had my family pray for this pain. As they prayed, I had the sensation of a needle being withdrawn from my shoulder. I knew the pain would now disappear. The next morning I awoke with the pain gone.

Satan was so bold that he even tried to convince Jesus to join his rebellion. Today, he is trying to convince and deceive all of us into joining the rebellion too.

> Next the Devil took him to the peak of a very high mountain and showed him the nations of the world and all their glory.
>
> "I will give it all to you," he said, "if you will only kneel down and worship me."
>
> "Get out of here, Satan," Jesus told him. "For the Scriptures say, 'You must worship the Lord your God; serve only him.'" (Matthew 4:8–10)

Jesus gave us a great description of these fallen angels and how they operate in Matthew 12:43–45. It is worth taking a few minutes to study and draw tactical information out of this passage:

> "When an evil spirit leaves a person, it goes into the desert, seeking rest but finding none. Then it says, 'I will return to the person I came from.' So it returns and finds its former home empty, swept, and clean. Then the spirit finds seven other spirits more evil than itself, and they all enter the person and live there. And so that person is worse off than before." (Matthew 12:43–45)

Neil Anderson points out in his excellent devotional, *Daily in Christ*, that from this passage we can see that demons (evil spirits):

- exist inside and outside of humans;
- travel;
- make decisions;
- have individual identities;
- remember and make plans;
- can unite in battle with others; and
- vary in degrees of wickedness.

Mikaela: OK! I'm beginning to understand. What do "good" angels do anyway?

MB: Think about any situations where you may have encountered angelic or demonic activity. Let's look at some biblical examples of what angels and demons do. Angels are powerful and serve God:

> Praise the LORD, you angels of his, you mighty creatures who carry out his plans, listening for each of his commands. (Psalm 103:20)

They serve us as "lifeguards":

> For the angel of the LORD guards all who fear him, and he rescues them. (Psalm 34:7)

RS: There is an interesting story in Acts 12 where an angel comes to Peter while he is in prison, wakes him up, releases the chains, opens the gate, and leads him outside into the street.

> The night before Peter was to be placed on trial, he was asleep, chained between two soldiers, with others standing guard at the prison gate. Suddenly, there was a bright light in the cell, and an angel of the Lord stood before Peter. The angel tapped him on the side to awaken him and said, "Quick! Get up!" And the chains fell off his wrists. Then the angel told him, "Get dressed and put on your sandals." And he did. "Now put on your coat and follow me," the angel ordered. (Acts 12:6–8)

Peter thinks that he is dreaming, and only after (as the text reads) "Peter came to himself" did he realize that it was a rescuing angel. The encouragement for me as a believer is even those who were the movers and shakers of the Book of Acts who "shook the world" were taken by surprise when these heavenly messengers broke into their life. Suddenly, Peter finds himself outside saying, "I must be dreaming." The reality is that, even for those of us who walk with God, He never runs out of an arsenal of new things to present in your life that take you by surprise.

MB: The interesting end to this story is when Peter arrives at the home of Mary, the mother of John Mark.

He knocked at the door in the gate, and a servant girl named Rhoda came to open it. When she recognized Peter's voice, she was so overjoyed that, instead of opening the door, she ran back inside and told everyone, "Peter is standing at the door!" "You're out of your mind," they said. When she insisted, they decided, *"It must be his angel."* Meanwhile, Peter continued knocking. When they finally went out and opened the door, they were amazed. (Acts 12:13–16)

I find it amazing that everybody thought it was "Peter's angel" at the gate and nobody went out and see this "angel."

Angels are used to provide for God's people. We see a great example of this in the life of Elijah:

Then he (Elijah) lay down and slept under the broom tree. But as he was sleeping, an angel touched him and told him, "Get up and eat!" He looked around and saw some bread baked on hot stones and a jar of water! So he ate and drank and lay down again. (1 Kings 19:5–6)

Angels also act as guides:

As for Philip, an angel of the Lord said to him, "Go south down the desert road that runs from Jerusalem to Gaza." (Acts 8:26)

There was a Marine Corps AV-8B Harrier (Jump Jet) pilot who was flying with seven other Harriers from Hawaii to California. It was an overcast evening when they took off from Honolulu and climbed to 29,000 feet to join with the Air Force tanker for in-flight refueling. This pilot was number eight in the flight, and during the climbing rendezvous, he began to fall behind the rest of the flight. As he pressed the throttles as far forward as they would go, he also focused on the tail lights of the airplanes in front, knowing that if he lost sight, there could be more problems. He still could not close the gap and was falling farther behind.

I have been in this exact situation many times during my flying years in the Navy. In night "running rendezvous," it is imperative that you not lose sight of the formation that you are joining on. Often, in your concentration on the visuals in front of you, you neglect to scan your instruments and slight inputs to the flight controls go unnoticed. I totally understand what was happening to this Marine pilot.

Suddenly he sensed a presence nearby and looked over his left shoulder. What he saw shocked him. It was another Harrier flying perfect "parade" (very close) formation. But this jet was upside down! He focused for a moment on the visor of the pilot of this inverted jet and then looked into his own cockpit and scanned his instruments. Suddenly, he realized that he was inverted and not climbing but in a descent. In his concentration on the formation, he had inadvertently begun a slow roll of the Harrier, which resulted in an inverted nose-down attitude!

He immediately rolled right side up and brought the nose up to reestablish the climb. He looked back for his "wingman," but he had disappeared. He was nowhere to be seen.

Eventually, he joined the tanker and saw the seven other Harriers. After six hours, they all landed in California, and he asked each one of the other pilots if they had been the one who had dropped back to help him. None had—each one in the flight had all been in front of him when the incident took place. This pilot later gave his testimony to the Full Gospel Businessmen's Association, convinced that an angel had saved him that night.

Daniel gives us some good descriptions of the function of angels. From this passage in chapter 10, we see that angels are messengers and warriors. They can give strength to humans and can take on human appearance.

Then he said, "Don't be afraid, Daniel. Since the first day you began to pray for understanding and to humble yourself before your God, your request has been heard in heaven. I have come in answer to your prayer. But for twenty-one days the spirit prince of the kingdom of Persia blocked my way. Then Michael, one of the archangels, came to help me, and I left him there with the spirit prince of the kingdom of Persia. Then the one who looked like a man touched me again, and I felt my strength returning." (Daniel 10:12–13, 18)

RS: Look at the incredible number of ministries that angels have been involved with in Scripture, such as predicting the birth of Jesus in Luke 1 or announcing the birth of Jesus, which is probably the number one place that people around the earth acknowledge the heavenly host. Suddenly there appeared this great angelic host. We know the shepherds were awestruck. I have always wondered what the sheep and goats reactions were.

There was a whole process whereby the angels were protecting Jesus as a baby and later in the strengthening of Jesus in the Garden of Gethsemane. I think there is a good illustration in the life of Jesus for what angels can be and can do for us. The important thing is that there is never a focus on them. They are always messengers, pointing to someone else. They are never about what they were. What an example for us!

MB: How many angels are there? According to Jesus, there are at least twelve legions (there are 4,500 to 6,000 troops in a Roman legion!).

"Or do you think that I cannot appeal to My Father, and He will at once put at My disposal more than twelve legions of angels?" (Matthew 26:53 NAS)

Jesus made an interesting comment regarding angels and children:

"Beware that you don't despise a single of these little ones. For I tell you that in heaven their angels are always in the presence of my heavenly Father." (Matthew 18:10)

Arielle: OK. So I've got some angels watching over me. Why do I need them? What about those bad ones? What can they do to me?

MB: First of all, Satan has used them to keep you from seeing the truth.

Satan, the god of this evil world, has blinded the minds of those who don't believe, so they are unable to see the glorious light of the Good News that is shining upon them. (2 Corinthians 4:4)

Demons are also experts at deception. They take a little truth and mix it with a big lie. It's a deadly recipe! Paul told his friends in Corinth:

But I fear that somehow you will be led away from your pure and simple devotion to Christ, just as Eve was deceived by the serpent. You seem to believe whatever anyone tells you, even if they preach about a different Jesus than the one we preach, or a different Spirit than the one you received, or a different kind of gospel than the one you believed. But I am not surprised! Even Satan can disguise himself as an angel of light. (2 Corinthians 11:3–4, 14)

They also set traps for us, so that we will be held captive through spiritual bondage to them.

Then they will come to their senses and escape from the Devil's trap. For they have been held captive by him to do whatever he wants. (2 Timothy 2:26)

Satan and his horde are murders and liars. Jesus himself said:

"For you are the children of your father the Devil, and you love to do the evil things he does. He was a murderer from the beginning and has always hated the truth. There is no truth in him. When he lies, it is consistent with his character; for he is a liar and the father of lies." (John 8:44.)

Lukas: It seems overwhelming. I feel powerless when the bad guys attack.

MB: It's true that Satan has a plan for your life! It is to steal from you, destroy your life, and kill you (spiritually and physically)!

"The thief's purpose is to steal and kill and destroy. My purpose is to give life in all its fullness." (Jesus speaking in John 10:10)

However, the good news is that Jesus' plan for you is quite the opposite. That's why being a member of the family of God is so important. When you have the power of the Holy Spirit inside, you can resist and be victorious in this spiritual battle!
Here are a few encouraging reminders from the Word:

And don't sin by letting anger gain control over you. Don't let the sun go down while you are still angry, for anger gives a mighty foothold to the Devil. (Ephesians 4:26–27)

We have the option of allowing Satan into our life by opening a "spiritual door" and literally inviting him in. How do we do this? By allowing our thoughts and emotions to be influenced by him. The Bible says to:

Watch over your heart with all diligence, for from it flow the springs of life. (Proverbs 4:23 NAS)

If we take all of our emotions and filter them through the Word of God, we will not allow the enemy to have a foothold in our lives. Invading armies need to establish a "beachhead" or "foothold" on enemy territory, so that they can build up their forces for the main attack. Likewise, Satan attempts to cause us to hold on to certain emotions (bitterness, lust, frustration, etc.) that naturally occur but are contrary to the character of God. As we hold on to them, we literally give Satan a "legal right" to have influence in our lives. That's why the Bible says to "Watch over our hearts (emotions) with all diligence." The emotion itself is not often the sin, its what you do with it. Holding on to emotions that don't fall into the category of "love" and "others-centeredness" are usually beachheads for Satan to later mount a major attack.

Two of my favorite movies are about invasions. As a child, I enjoyed the epic *The Longest Day*—the story of the Normandy invasion in World War II. Almost every major star of the '60s appeared in that documentary filmed in black and white so it could include actual combat film from the invasion. A few years ago, *The Saving of Private Ryan* gave us the realistic account of this same invasion, focusing on a squad of soldiers invading Omaha Beach.

One of the reasons why these films are a personal favorite is that my father, Forrest, was one of the invading soldiers at Omaha Beach. He, along with others from the Second Armored Division, rolled their tanks ashore, right into intense fighting. They fought for weeks to secure the beachhead, and eventually the Germans were outflanked, outfought, and overcome. Paris fell, and Forrest and his buddies began a high-speed advance eastward toward the Rhine that was only temporarily slowed by the Battle of the Bulge. Within a year, Forrest and the rest of the Second Armored were the first Americans to enter Berlin.

How did the Americans and the British get to Berlin? By first taking the beaches in Normandy. Without that critical beachhead in France, there would have been no surrender by the Germans in Berlin.

Our thoughts are another potential foothold. We are constantly bombarded by thoughts from ourselves, from the world, from Satan and his demonic cohorts, and from the Lord.

RS: In 2 Corinthians, chapter 10, there is a fabulous image of the battle to take a human heart and to conquer our own thoughts and beliefs. We have a very interesting second-century Roman document about the collapse of a city fortress wall. It is not an interesting document until you look with the eyes of trying to figure out the strategy of what is happening.

There are four steps in which you take an ancient city. These mounted, walled garrison cities have a glacis, or an angled wall, at the base of the vertical wall. This is about a thirty-degree angled slope that prevents a battering ram of doing its job effectively by deflecting the force—it will glance off. The glacis also prevents attackers from having a firm level ground to try to climb up and over the wall—usually this slope is slippery (from oil), and it makes ground attack more difficult.

The only way to take a city like this was to bring in shielded men called *sappers* who would crawl into the sewer pits, the drains at the base of the wall, and take out a section of the wall from below. The problem is that if you are a sapper and are good at your job, you only get to do this once, because the wall usually collapses on top of you.

Old City Jerusalem
Southern Wall

When the wall collapses, the second team comes in. They are called the *casters*. They cast away the bodies of the sappers, and, of course, the stones of the fallen section of the wall, allowing the third group, the infantry, to pour through the breach in the wall. They will begin to take each section of the city, block by block, in a sustained attacked.

Finally, just in time to take credit for the battle, you have the fourth element, the captains, who come in and put up two poles. There is a pole—a gallows—set up for the execution of everyone who will not get with the program, and then a flagpole allows the captives to pledge their allegiance to the new regime.

Paul picks up on this illustration and uses it with the people of Corinth who are familiar with warfare because they have been soldiers and naval officers. He says in 2 Corinthians 10:3–6:

> For though we walk in the flesh, we do not war according to the flesh. For the weapons of our warfare are not carnal but mighty in God for pulling down strongholds. . . .

We are the sappers at the bottom of the wall, pulling down these weighty things that have imprisoned us for so long. It seems that, like the sappers, we will die in the process. The reality is you won't die doing this—you may feel like you are dying, and there is a spiritual sense that you are dying to yourself, but your physical body will live.

> casting down arguments and every high thing that exalts itself against the knowledge of God . . .

Now we are like the casters, removing all the plans and strategies that exalt ourselves.

> bringing every thought into captivity to the obedience of Christ . . .

As the infantry moves in and takes control of each part of the city, we allow God to move into each room of our lives and take control. Finally,

> and being ready to punish all disobedience . . .

The captains bring in the gallows, and everything is placed in order.

You have a great warfare analogy for a simple conclusion. It is a big grandiose picture to produce one point, which is: How is the life of the believer lived? *One thought at a time . . .*

Go into the base of yourself and remove all the garbage and thoughts of self-importance. The heart of God is an *"other-persons centeredness,"* which is what He called on the angelic being to be and is exactly what He calls on the believer to be. *As long as I am interested in getting the credit, I'm not interested in God's work.*

MB: It is often said that the battleground is the mind. We must analyze every thought to determine its origin and how it lines up with the thoughts and character of God. Things that fall outside the category of "from or like God" are red flags and need to be handled with extreme caution. Thoughts that fall into the category of "from the devil" or overly "self-oriented" should be flushed out. In this way, we will keep the enemy from establishing those footholds that he needs to attack us.

Next:

Submit therefore to God. Resist the devil and he will flee from you. (James 4:7 NAS)

There are three specific steps that James gives us in our spiritual battles. First, he says to *submit*, or bring everything in our life under the authority of God. If we don't, then we have an open "spiritual door" that invites the enemy into our lives. We must bring all those secret sins and areas of disobedience under the authority of our Lord. After all, if He is Lord, then that is our appropriate response.

Once all the doors are closed, *then we must resist*, or fight against, the thoughts and temptations that the enemy is trying to snare us with. One good technique when you have a thought that is out of line with God's thinking or a temptation to do something that you know that He knows is not good for you is to quote a Scripture verse that tells the devil who you are (in the spiritual realm) and remind him that he doesn't have any right to attack you. Keep it up. Jesus had to do that three times in His temptation in the wilderness.

Another technique is to begin praying for someone or something when you are being attacked or tempted. Satan doesn't like to do things to us that cause us to pray.

Singing praise and worship songs is another effective tactic in your spiritual battles. Not only is your faith affirmed but also there was a reason why God told Joshua to send seven priests blowing ram's horns to lead Israel's army as they marched around Jericho.

As we resist the devil in these and other methods, the Bible says that he will flee from us. Many quote this verse as "Resist the devil and he will flee." *That won't happen without submitting all areas of our life to the Lord and closing all the spiritual doors.*

It's interesting that the Bible doesn't say that Satan will simply back off and stop attacking but rather uses the word *flee*. Why would he suddenly flee from the attack? Probably because someone more powerful shows up!

Peter, who experienced many attacks from Satan, gives us a similar strategy:

So humble yourselves under the mighty power of God, and in his good time he will honor you. Give all your worries and cares to God, for he cares about what happens to you. Be careful! Watch out for attacks from the Devil, your great enemy. He prowls around like a roaring lion, looking for some victim to devour. Take a firm stand against him, and be strong in your faith. Remember that Christians all over the world are going through the same kind of suffering you are. (1 Peter 5:6–9)

Dean Sherman, a noted spiritual warfare teacher with Youth With A Mission, points out that Peter addresses two potential "handles" that Satan could use to pull you away from God in this passage.

First there is the big sin—pride. Pride is not needing God in your life, not submitting all areas to Him. As Samuel spoke to Saul:

"Rebellion is as the sin of divination, and insubordination is as iniquity and idolatry." (1 Samuel 15:23)

Pride is indeed a bright, bold neon sign inviting the enemy to come into your life!

Fear is another "handle." Are you believing God and His promises to you, or are you ignoring them and buying into lies the enemy is telling you? *Fear is disbelief.* Not believing God is calling Him a liar. That's sin and a big handle to turn you away from God! That's why Peter says to *give all your worries and cares to God.*

Eliminate pride and fear from your life, and you become an effective spiritual warrior. Here's something important to remember:

Jesus called his twelve disciples to him and gave them authority to cast out evil spirits and to heal every kind of disease and illness. (Matthew 10:1)

Jesus has given His disciples authority over the rebellious angels. Authority is defined as "the power or right to give commands, enforce obedience, take actions, or make final decisions" (*Webster's New World College Dictionary,* 4th ed. s.v. "*authority*"). When Jesus' disciples exercised this authority in their ministry, Luke reports that:

The seventy returned with joy, saying, "Lord, even the demons are subject to us in Your name." And He said to them, "I was watching Satan fall from heaven like lightning. "Behold, I have given you authority to tread on serpents and scorpions, and over all the power of the enemy, and nothing will injure you. "Nevertheless do not rejoice in this, that the spirits are subject to you, but rejoice that your names are recorded in heaven." (Luke 10:17–20)

As a pilot in the United States Navy, I was given authority by President Gerald Ford and later President Jimmy Carter (via the chain of command) to enforce the laws and policies of the United States in my role as a carrier attack pilot flying an A-6 Intruder, defending the Pacific and Indian Oceans. This meant I could use any of a variety of missiles, rockets, bombs, and even nuclear weapons to carry out United States laws and policies when ordered by my squadron commander.

Using the authority was a different matter. Even though I may have the orders from above to use it, I always had the ultimate choice whether I would use that authority. It took a conscious decision and action on our part to press the bomb release button on the stick or pull the trigger. We often joked that in the event of a nuclear war, we pilots would suddenly have stuffed sinuses and runny noses and be medically unfit for flight rather than go flying to drop "the big one."

In spiritual matters, it is the same. When you realize you are in a spiritual battle, showing your "badge of authority" is the first step

Lieutenant Bagby with A-6 Intruder

in seeing the enemy back off. Sometimes, for whatever reason, we don't do that and deal with the situation through our own strength and resources. This is a formula for protracted struggle and ultimate defeat.

The disciples Jesus sent out saw results, and Jesus cautioned them to remember the reality—it all comes from Him. Without His authority, we are nothing. With it, and Him, we are formidable in spiritual battles.

Just as this authority is *relationship-oriented*, so is the "armor of God," which Paul describes in Ephesians 6:

> Be strong with the Lord's mighty power. Put on all of God's armor so that you will be able to stand firm against all strategies and tricks of the Devil. For we are not fighting against people made of flesh and blood, but against the evil rulers and authorities of the unseen world, against those mighty powers of darkness who rule this world, and against wicked spirits in the heavenly realms.

Use every piece of God's armor to resist the enemy in the time of evil, so that after the battle you will still be standing firm. Stand your ground, putting on the sturdy belt of truth and the body armor (or breastplate) of God's righteousness. For shoes, put on the peace that comes from the Good News, so that you will be fully prepared. In every battle you will need faith as your shield to stop the fiery arrows aimed at you by Satan. Put on salvation as your helmet, and take the sword of the Spirit, which is the word of God. Pray at all times and on every occasion in the power of the Holy Spirit. Stay alert and be persistent in your prayers for all Christians everywhere. (Ephesians 6:10–18)

When you read Paul's description in Ephesians 6 of the armor of God, notice that all the pieces—the belt of God's truth, the breastplate of His righteousness, the helmet of salvation bought by Him, the shoes of God's peace, a shield of faith in God's promises, and the sword of God's Word—all rely on our relationship with Him. It has nothing to do with ourselves; it all comes down from Him.

This spiritual armor is the defense that a close and obedient relationship with God gives you.

- Believing His truth vs. Satan's lies;
- knowing your relationship as an adopted son or daughter of God Himself, right standing before Him, and the legal rights that go along with that relationship;
- your willingness to share the good news of this relationship;
- your faith in God to protect you; and
- your knowledge that you have eternal life with Him no matter what may happen here in this life;

This is the defensive armor that God offers us.

But there are offensive weapons as well. The "sword" in the spiritual realm is God's Word—truth to apply to every situation where you feel yourself under spiritual attack; truth about your identity; truth about God's promises to you; truth about the limited power of the evil one over you.

The other weapon He gives us is prayer—communion with Him. Prayer to align ourselves with God and His will and move with Him to accomplish His plan for our lives and for this world. Truth and prayer are powerful dynamics in the spiritual realm.

A final reminder:

Don't forget to show hospitality to strangers, for some who have done this have entertained angels without realizing it! (Hebrews 13:2)

We sense activity of the fallen angels in our lives more than the good ones because we tend to notice when bad things start to happen. Most North American and European Christians believe that they deserve "good" things in this life. Yet there is an angelic host constantly guarding over us and protecting us without being too intrusive in our lives. It seems like if God's angels are doing their jobs that they often go unnoticed.

Consider those times when your car skidded on the wet road and didn't hit that telephone pole or the car in front. "Good reflexes" are sometimes just "good angelic protection."

Flying in remote places in the world can present many challenges not experienced in the civilized world. Many times as we are approaching an airstrip in Central America with thunderclouds and showers around we pray for a clear landing area. With no weather reporting, it is impossible to predict weather conditions at remote destinations. We have come to rely on prayer and angelic activity. Often, as we have flown through heavy rain showers to get to the airstrip, we break out to discover that it is indeed clear over the landing area. That's happened too many times to be just coincidence.

Years ago, a Bible teacher and author was driving alone across Texas one night on his way back to Dallas. He was planning to drive through the night, so he began asking the Lord to provide him with a traveling companion, so that he could stay awake. Soon he saw a young man hitchhiking and stopped to pick him up. They began to talk, and it was soon apparent that this young man was a believer and knew a lot about the Bible and God. They talked for hours as they drove the flat, straight roads across Texas. The teacher was amazed at some of the insights the young man expressed.

The red rays of the rising sun began to peek over the horizon, and the young man asked to be let off at the next exit, for his destination was a town a short distance off the main road. They pulled off and stopped at an all-night café. They entered and sat down in a booth. The professor ordered two cups of coffee, and they continued their discussion about God until the cups were empty and it was time to go. After saying goodbye, the professor got into his car and drove off. After a few minutes of driving, he decided that he had the time to drive that nice young man to his destination after all and turned around. He arrived at the café expecting to see his friend standing outside by the road waiting for a ride, but he saw no one. The place was deserted. He parked, went inside, and asked the waitress if she had seen the young man he had come in with. The waitress gave him a puzzled look.

"You didn't come in here with anybody. I thought it was strange that you ordered two cups of coffee. It was even stranger to see you talking to yourself in the booth."

The professor didn't say anything. He just got into his car and drove on to Dallas, thanking God for this angelic visitation.

Personal Reflections

1. If Satan was to set a trap for you, what would he use as bait?
2. Have you had any sudden and unexplained physical problems lately?
3. How can you recognize demonic activity in your life?
4. What is the difference between a spiritual attack and the natural consequences of sin?
5. What is the best way to prevent a spiritual attack?
6. How do we use the authority that Jesus has given us in spiritual warfare?

Deeper Water

A. Read the account of Balaam in Numbers 22, 23, and 24. Here we see many incredible things happening that can only be explained in terms of living in the spiritual world. Here are some questions to consider:

1. Why could Balaam not curse the children of Israel?
2. How did the donkey speak (22:28)?
3. What is the meaning of sorcery (24:1)?

B. We see the appearance of an infamous character named Jezebel in 1 Kings 16: 31. She appears again in 1 Kings 19:2, causing Elijah to run for his life. Read the account of the encounter between Jezebel and Jehu in 2 Kings 9. What can we learn from these passages about this manipulating spirit and how to combat it?

C. In 2 Kings 18, we read about Hezekiah and the Assyrian invasion of Judah. In verse 19, the representatives of Sennacherib begin a campaign of fear and intimidation against God's people. What can we learn from this account that may apply to our own spiritual attacks?

D. The Book of Nehemiah presents one of the best descriptions of spiritual warfare recorded in the Bible. Closely read chapter 4.

1. What are the tactics that Sanballat and Tobiah use to discourage those rebuilding the walls of Jerusalem?
2. What does Nehemiah do in response to these attacks?
3. How was Nehemiah successful in accomplishing his mission?

E. What is the significance of Proverbs 26:2?

Go to any bookstore or library. There you will find books on history, relationships, wisdom, business, biographies, and drama. There will be books filled with facts and books filled with theories. All these are tomes made of paper and bound with fabric or leather. Men and women wrote them all. One book written in human history stands above all the rest. Although it contains law, drama, history, poetry, biographies, wisdom, and predictions of the future, the one aspect that makes it special is the unique claim that it is the Living Book.

The Living Book

Lukas: What do you mean "Living Book?" Is the Bible as alive as Pancho the monkey?

MB: Exactly! God, through His Holy Spirit, wrote the Bible through the means of many individuals. Through the Bible, God sends us truth, descriptions of Himself (so that we may know Him and His ways), and directions on how we should live. When we read the Bible, we are not just reading any book but rather one that is alive with God's Spirit.

Lukas and Pancho

The Bible declares itself a "living, breathing document":

> For the word of God is living and active and sharper than any two-edged sword, and piercing as far as the division of soul and spirit, of both joints and marrow, and able to judge the thoughts and intentions of the heart. (Hebrews 4:12 NAS)

RS: Look at the influence of the Bible in our world. If you stuck a syringe into human history and sucked out the influence of the Bible, I think Western history as we know it would completely collapse. Just look at the influence of the Bible on our Declaration of Independence. The Bible has had a direct impact even on the lives of those who have tried to prove it is wrong.

Every believer knows there is a direct actual involvement of the Bible in his or her life. They read passages this year that they read last year; and because of the circumstances in their life now, changes that have occurred, or greater yielded-ness to God, they see things they didn't see before. The life of the Book is very obvious to them.

MB: That life is the Spirit of the Lord speaking to them through the words of His book at that moment. I had an incredible experience a few years ago that demonstrated this. It was December 26, 1986. I was on a flight to Honduras, and there was an incredible view out my window. We were above a cloud deck at 33,000 feet; it was in the early afternoon. The white light of the sun was making a starburst pattern on the window of the Boeing 737 with white clouds below, deep blue sky and ocean all around. I sat there for an hour totally captivated by this incredible sight, having moments of conversation with the Artist of this masterpiece.

Finally, I said, "Lord, if there was any time that You would want to speak to me, I am listening right now."

I took out my Bible and randomly opened the pages; it happened to be in the Book of Psalms. My eyes fell on the page, and the first line that I read was "How lovely are Thy dwelling places, Oh Lord of hosts!" It was Psalm 84 that I "happened" to turn to. God was speaking directly to me, sitting in seat 19F, on a flight to Honduras.

I read on, totally enthralled at this encounter with the Living God through His Living Book, finally coming to verse 10 and 11: "For a day in Thy courts is better than a thousand outside." Looking out the window, I had to agree. There was more—a very personal message for me, a single man who was at the time wondering about career and family issues: "For the Lord is a sun and a shield. The Lord gives grace and Glory. No good thing does He withhold from those who walk uprightly. Oh Lord of Hosts, How blessed is the man who trusts in Thee!"

Looking back many years later, I realize what a specific word this was to me. He has not held back many good things from me. I have the best wife, good children, and a great job. All good things in life He has given me, just as He said He would on this day, as I sat in seat 19F on the Boeing 737!

RS: I had a similar experience recently when I was in front of a group in a question and answer session. In our work, we often are in situations explaining Judaism to Christians and vice versa. Often, these sessions are very uncomfortable due to the nature of the questions being asked, as I find myself on the firing line of their theological debates.

They say the definition of a pioneer is the guy who gets all the first arrows, and I found myself in this particular situation, pioneering a new trail, talking to a group of people about some of the practices they were involved in. That morning, I awoke and knew I was in trouble because I was facing a question and answer session, and my morning reading in Galatians 2 read: "I withstood Peter to his face because he was to be blamed." I said, "Oh no Lord, what am I getting into?"

I got in front of these people, who were very nice people trying to do the right thing, and they began asking some tough questions. I remember standing behind the lectern saying, "Lord, You need to give me the verses because it needs to be something so powerful and to come directly from your Word."

I kid you not, three times I opened my Bible, three times it dropped open to the exact verse to answer the question. Now, this is not the recommended kind of preparation. I am a believer in preparing and studying, but I didn't know what they were going to ask. So it happened on the first question, then the second, and finally, by the third, the group thought I knew all the answers, and I stood there chuckling to myself because I knew none of them. It was a wonderful opportunity, not only to see God at work, but also to see God at work through His Word to His people. The great legacy He has given us is this living love letter from Him.

MB: This letter is the table on which we lay all extra-biblical "revelation" that we receive from God to see if it matches what He has already said in principle in His Word. This is so important; we have this standard to measure our "spiritual experiences" by. Recently, we were in Berea together; this is where a crowd listened to Paul's message about the Messiah. They went home and "searched the Scriptures" to see if what Paul said washed with God's Word. It did, and they became believers.

RS: Technically speaking, a theologian would use the term "revelation" for that which God reveals that is otherwise not known ahead of time. If I buy you a new car and I have a covering over it, and you have never seen it, and no one else has seen it, when I take the cover off, it becomes a revelation. The word for God revealing in my heart is biblical *illumination*. That is the "light going on" for me. God revealed His Word inside His text. God is in the business of revealing Himself to mankind and then through a second process of revealing Himself to you specifically by taking little cloaks off your eyes and hearts, allowing the light to go on where there was before darkness. Before there was me; now there is Him.

MB: There is nothing more special to the believer than when that light comes on; when you feel yourself flooded with God's presence and an understanding of something you know is just for you. I have piloted some of the fastest jets, eaten in some of the finest restaurants, skied down the best mountains in the world, but there is nothing more special than this personal experience with God through His Word.

RS: I can hear in the background that there will be skeptics. The skeptics will say, "This Mike and this Randy; they are just fanatics." By the way, a definition of a fanatic is one that cannot change their mind or the subject. The whole process of illumination is not that I am so rooted in fanaticism but that I can change my mind, as God shows me in His Word. The characteristic of a person who is filled with God's Spirit, walking with God and is spiritually mature, is a person who has flexibility.

Flexibility is what Jesus was highlighting in Luke 15 when He told about the lost sheep, the lost coin, and, finally, the prodigal son. In the latter story, the older brother refused to come to the banquet because he did not forgive his younger brother. The whole purpose of Luke 15 is to say, "You who are mature should be the most willing to embrace that new person or new thing I am doing in the life of another person." It seems to me, in my Christian experience, that more often than not, the more "mature" an individual is, the less flexible he or she is. But that is not at all a scriptural way of being. The Bible characterizes maturity as "flexible and able to change."

MB: In fact, it was Jesus Himself who said:

"Every teacher of religious law who has become a disciple in the Kingdom of Heaven is like a person who brings out of the storehouse the new teachings as well as the old." (Matthew 13:52)

There is a dynamic here to be recognized. We should always be ready to be touched by God's Spirit, to be continually changed and to realize things that He told us today He may tell us in a different way tomorrow. It is like when I talk to my eleven-year-old son today. I talk to him in one way, and then when he is sixteen, I will talk to him in a different way, telling him different things. It is the same way with God. That's why the Bible to us is such a living document. It's our heavenly Father speaking to us personally on a daily basis if we let Him. It is our choice.

For many years, it was my choice not to read the Bible. After my years at university studying history, I considered the Bible nothing more than Jewish mythology and men's opinions. That changed in 1981 when God began to show me this book was an important input into my life. I then began rereading the Bible through the eye of an historian, and I discovered the Bible is good history.

RS: In the time in which we were growing up, we were in an "enlightened age of rationalism." Ultimately, what people were saying was fundamentally, "There is no God. Therefore, all this is nonsense."

We have the more modern rationalizer who says, "I think there is a God. I think the Force is with us. But to actually pin down what God is saying is difficult. Man has to be the final judge of revelation." The problem with all of that is the Bible is self-authenticating. It begins with "In the beginning . . ." God takes no time to express, "By the way, let Me prove I exist." He says instead, "And now a word from your Creator—*I exist.*"

You can believe or not believe it. In the same way an ostrich sticks his head in the sand when a rhino is charging at him, you can say there is no God, and that's not going to change the end result. Ultimately, the rationalistic kind of age we live in tries to find a way to say, "Look, there is no God."

But the Bible says, "*I am God. I AM and I spoke.*" Those are the two fundamentals of my faith. If I am going to come to God, I must understand that He is and that He is a rewarder of those who diligently seek Him. Both of those presuppose that I know He exists and there is a way to find Him. We need in our society to articulate a standard of truth. If God does indeed exist, then there is a standard of truth.

Randy and Michael discussing truth in Athens with
Jason, Hal, and Craig

MB: It's not the situational ethics type of truth we are taught in school but solid truth we can plant our feet on. To me the definition of truth is simple: It is God's opinion on the matter. How does God feel about this? What does He think? That is truth.

However, today we have *relative* truth. Truth that is good for me may not be good for you. Some dictionaries are now defining truth as "values shared by a group of people." There is no indication of the right or wrong of the value, just the sharing by a group. We see the natural extension of this in terror groups who justify their killing by their "truth," organized crime members taking from others because their belief system has become their truth, and child pornographers who demand the right to an open Internet web site because their morality is just as correct as anybody's.

RS: Some years ago, there was a change in the logical standard in which education was done. It happened to be 1961, when there was a shift in the educational policy in the US, in particular. Up until that time, they had used a standard called Aristotelian Logic. This Aristotelian Logic is very simple. If A is true, and B is opposite of A, then B is false. It is the standard we use in business, economics, and mathematics. But in ethics, we changed to what is called Enlightened Logic. A is true. B is true, and A can't tell what is true for B. It has become "my truth or your truth."

The funny thing is, when you lay that down against the simple business community practices, it doesn't work. Aren't you glad it is not "my math" and "your math" when you go to the store? I feel like some banks already have my math and your math. I want to be able to pick up the ledger and read the math. I want to know that if I have $100, and you take $80, I will have $20 left. I need to know that is always going to be true and is not relative.

When it comes to things like ethical standards in life and things rooted in Scripture, people react against any biblically based ethics and suddenly throw out the logic that has been part of Western civilization for ages. They go back to Pilate's famous question to Jesus, "What is truth?"

MB: If you just observed things in life, there cannot be my truth and your truth. There is a standard of truth that fits all situations. In the simple tasks of flying an airplane or driving a car, there is truth of using the physical laws of aerodynamics and staying in your lane. Crashes happen when pilots ignore these aerodynamic truths and do what they "feel" is right. In some places in the world, driving truth is relative. In the third world, traffic lanes are often meaningless ("It's only paint on the road," says a friend from Nigeria), and traffic signals only "advisory." You see the resulting chaos on the roads: It's "my traffic rules and your traffic rules." We may all have values that are shared by our groups, but God also has His values. He is the definer of truth, and He gives it to us in the Bible—His Living Book. This is why the Bible is so important.

Mikaela: I'm getting interested. Tell me about this Living Book.

MB: You might expect that a "living book" would be unique in many ways. It is. Here are a few things that make the Bible unique:

In the market at Firenze Italy

- It's the all time best seller. Since the invention of the Guttenberg press, over 2.6 billion Bibles have been printed. If all the Bibles printed were stacked on top of each other, the pile would reach one-third the way to the moon!
- How the Bible was written is unique. Written by more than forty authors, who come from all walks of life (kings to peasants), over a 1500 year time span (1400 B.C. to 90 A.D.), on three continents (Europe, Africa, and Asia), and in three languages (Hebrew, Greek, and Aramaic). Amazingly, all the authors agree on the basic message!
- A most unique feature of the Bible is fulfilled prophecy. A famous "prophet" of the Middles Ages, Nostradamas, has been about fifty percent correct in the things that he predicted. Jeanne Dixon, a modern day "prophetess," is less than fifty percent. So far, the Bible has been one hundred percent correct in its prophetic messages.

Here are just three (of many) fulfilled prophetic messages:

1. That the Persian king Cyrus would allow the rebuilding of the temple in Jerusalem after it was destroyed by the Babylonians.

> "It is I who says of Jerusalem, 'She shall be inhabited!' And of the cities of Judah, 'They shall be built.' And I will raise up her ruins again. It is I who says to the depth of the sea, 'Be dried up!' And I will make your rivers dry. It is I who says of Cyrus, 'He is My shepherd! And he will perform all My desire.' And he declares of Jerusalem, 'She will be built,' And of the temple, 'Your foundation will be laid.'" (Isaiah 44:26–28 NAS)

This was a prophecy given by Isaiah about 690 B.C. before the Persian Empire existed and was fulfilled in 539 B.C. by the Persian king who happened to be named Cyrus.

2.   That the powerful Phoenician city Tyre, one of the most important and powerful cities in the Mediterranean world, would be destroyed and become a fishing village.

> Therefore, thus says the Lord GOD, "Behold, I am against you, O Tyre, and I will bring up many nations against you, as the sea brings up its waves. And they will destroy the walls of Tyre and break down her towers; and I will scrape her debris from her and make her a bare rock. She will be a place for the spreading of nets in the midst of the sea, for I have spoken," declares the Lord GOD, "and she will become spoil for the nations." (Ezekiel 26:3–5 NAS)

This prophecy was given about 575 B.C., and it was fulfilled a few centuries later when Alexander the Great surrounded Tyre, and after a long siege, destroyed the city. Years ago, I saw a photo of the site of ancient Tyre in a magazine (probably *National Geographic*), and it showed a few buildings of a fishing village with nets spread out over the bare rocks along the shore!

3.   That Jesus would be crucified. This prophecy was given over 500 years before crucifixion was invented as a form of capital punishment.

> My God, my God, why hast Thou forsaken me? Far from my deliverance are the words of my groaning. . . . For dogs have surrounded me; A band of evildoers has encompassed me; They pierced my hands and my feet. I can count all my bones. They look, they stare at me; They divide my garments among them, And for my clothing they cast lots. (Psalm 22:1, 16–18; A Psalm of David NAS)

Does this first line of Psalm 22 sound familiar? It should. It is what Jesus said while hanging on the cross. This prophecy was given about 1000 B.C. and fulfilled about 33 A.D. Read Matthew 27:33–50 for the chilling almost word for word fulfillment of this prophecy.

Lukas: Just a minute! How do we know for sure that what David, Matthew, Peter, and those other guys wrote is what we are reading today?

MB: That's a good question! There are certain tests historians make on an ancient document that give us a reasonable level of certainty that what was written then is what we are reading today.

Lukas: Historians?! Is the Bible really a good history book?

MB: Well that's the basic issue. *Is the Bible historically reliable?* A book that claims to be the truth and written by God *must* be a good history book, right? That's the conclusion I came to, and I addressed this issue during my first years on Maui. I used to think the Bible was *nothing more than Jewish mythology and some men's opinions.* But once I got turned on to the Lord, I began making serious inquiries into the validity of the book. I was a history major at university in Luxembourg, and we had

At Masada Israel

a class called Historiography (the study of the techniques of historical research and historical writing) in which Dr. Herbert Oerter taught us how to evaluate of works of ancient literature. The three tests we historians use to judge the accuracy of ancient works of literature are: *manuscripts, internal evidence,* and *external evidence.* Can you stand a slight digression into some technical but very valuable information?

Lukas: As long as you keep it simple!

MB: Then let's look at the first.

Test # 1—Manuscripts

Specific questions to ask when you evaluate a piece of ancient literature are:

- How many manuscripts of the document do we have, and what is the length of time between the oldest one we have and the original writing?
- How does this book compare to other works of ancient literature?

Remember, before the Guttenberg press, all copies were done by hand, which means the more time between the original and the copy we hold in our hand, the more margin there is for error.

As far as the New Testament, we have over 25,000 manuscripts, and the closest one is the Ryland manuscript of the Book of John that dates from about 125 A.D., which is about thirty-five years after John died. That's very close to the original date of writing—a very small margin of error.

On the other hand, Homer's *Iliad* was written about 900 B.C., and the earliest copy dates from about 500 B.C. That's about 400 years between when it was written and the earliest existing copy. We only have 643 "ancient" copies of the *Iliad*. Compared to the New Testament, the *Iliad* has a greater margin of copying errors, yet scholars accept the modern version of the *Iliad* as what Homer wrote.

By accepted historical standards, the Bible stands out as having enough manuscripts close to the actual dates of writing to verify what we hold in our hands is almost without a doubt what was written.

Arielle: So, what you are saying is that we are probably reading what the guys wrote, right?

MB: Yes! This was confirmed a few years ago by a discovery down by the Dead Sea. Isaiah is a book in the Old Testament written by the prophet Isaiah in the seventh century B.C. The earliest manuscript we have is the Massoretic text, which dates from about 916 A.D. If you look in your Bible, your Old Testament is probably an English translation of this 1,000-year-old-plus document. There is a gap of about 1500–2200 years between the time these books were written and the copy we use for our English translations. This gap has caused critics to speculate that our modern translation does not accurately follow the original text and has been changed over the centuries.

In 1947, a shepherd boy named Mohammed Dib was down by the Dead Sea in a place called Qumran, looking for some lost sheep. There are many caves in this desert region, and the sheep sometimes wander into these caves or fall into holes in the ground. Mohammed threw a rock down into one hole, hoping to hear movement of his sheep but instead heard the sound of something breaking. He crawled down inside the hole and

A cave at Qumran where one of the scrolls was discovered.

discovered his rock had hit and broken a clay jar. There were other clay jars; many containing leather scrolls with writing and immersed in oil.

He took these to a friend, and eventually they ended up in Jerusalem where they were identified as books of the Old Testament, dating from about 125 B.C. Suddenly, we had a text of the Bible that dated almost 1,000 years earlier than the Massoretic text, much closer to the time they were written. All this was happening while the Israeli War of Independence was being fought!

Lukas: Are the Dead Sea scrolls the same as our Bible?

MB: There are cases where the scrolls don't match up exactly word for word with other manuscripts (like to the Masoretic Text, commonly used for the Old Testament), but in terms of theological differences, there are none. Let me give you one example: Of the 166 words in Isaiah chapter 53, there is only one word (of three letters—*light*—in verse 11) in question, along with some punctuation marks, none of which changes the meaning of the passage. Now that the Dead Sea scrolls are available to the general public, it is fun to read some of the translations. You will notice some differences in wording and obvious spelling errors, but they are remarkable in their confirmation of the biblical record.

RS: Remember that in a scriptorium where the Essene community at Qumran copied the scrolls, one person is reading, and all the other people are writing and copying. Now, I defy any audience anywhere to take a document like Isaiah that has the specifics it has in it and the kinds of funny words and names, even in the Hebrew language, and copy it and not have any spelling mistakes. And every scroll is going to yield that. But what is essential to us is, *"Does that mean that what I am holding in my hands is an accurate reflection of the original writing?"* Not in terms in spelling. I'm not concerned if the word *archaeology* has a second "a" (as in Old English) in it or not. What I am concerned about is: Does it say, *archeologist;* is it the same word?

When I see there was such a precise way these texts were transmitted, I am amazed. To understand that the Essene community, whom we believe lived in Qumran and devoted themselves to the copying of the Word, took such attention to detail that they were washing themselves seven times every time they wrote the name of God. Which is fine, until you get to Exodus 34 when you have twelve names of God right in a row. These had to be the cleanest guys who were ever writing anything.

It's important for us to understand that the Bible is not a "whisper down the lane." This is a very important transmission of something that, in the Hebrew mind, was highly, highly kept track of.

One of the Dead Sea Scrolls

MB: The bottom line is the Dead Sea scrolls confirm the biblical text with great accuracy. They show that the Bible we hold in our hands today passes the test of manuscripts with flying colors! This is the first test historians use to judge the accuracy of an ancient work of literature. Are you ready for the second test?

Lukas: Sure!

MB: Here's test number two.

Test #2—Internal Evidence

- Is the record from eyewitnesses (primary source)?
- Does the book describe how people of that time reacted to the events?
- Are all the facts and themes consistent with the work?

Peter and John, who together wrote seven (really eight, as Mark's gospel is probably Peter's gospel narrated to Mark) of the twenty-seven books of the New Testament, leave no doubt they were eyewitnesses.

Listen to Peter:

For we were not making up clever stories when we told you about the power of our Lord Jesus Christ and his coming again. We have seen his majestic splendor with our own eyes. (2 Peter 1:16)

John testifies in a very personal manner:

The one who existed from the beginning is the one we have heard and seen. We saw him with our own eyes and touched him with our own hands. He is Jesus Christ, the Word of life. (1 John 1:1)

How did contemporary witnesses react to the words of the apostles?
Here's Peter speaking before a large crowd at the temple in Jerusalem:

"People of Israel, listen! God publicly endorsed Jesus of Nazareth by doing wonderful miracles, wonders, and signs through him, as you well know."

Peter's words convicted them deeply, and they said to him and to the other apostles, "Brothers, what should we do?" Peter replied, "Each of you must turn from your sins and turn to God, and be baptized in the name of Jesus Christ for the forgiveness of your sins. Then you will receive the gift of the Holy Spirit.

Those who believed what Peter said were baptized and added to the church—about three thousand in all. (Acts 2:22, 37–38, 41)

Peter appealed to them about an event that all of Jerusalem had witnessed—the crucifixion of Jesus—and explained its meaning. Did the people shout "No Peter, you are lying!"?

Mikaela: Well, no, not according to the Bible.

MB: You're right! Instead, they were convinced in their hearts and over 3,000 accepted Jesus as their Lord that day! Another example was Paul testifying before Festus and King Agrippa. Read the record of that conversation in Acts 26:1–29. What was Agrippa's reaction to Paul's testimony? He asked if Paul thought it would be that easy to convert him!

"King Agrippa, do you believe the prophets? I know you do—" Agrippa interrupted him. "Do you think you can make me a Christian so quickly?" (Acts 26:27–28)

The reactions of these contemporary witnesses leave no doubt that the events that were described were acknowledged and accepted as having happened. This is very strong historical evidence!

Lukas: Aren't there some contradictions in the Bible?

MB: One common problem is that two statements in the Bible can differ from one another, but this does not mean that they are contradictory. To be contradictory would be to say that Jesus was born in Bethlehem and in another place say that he was born in Nazareth. For example, Matthew 20:29 tells of two blind men that were healed by Jesus at Jericho, but the same story in Luke 18:35 mentions only one blind man. Luke only mentions one man, but he does not say there was not more than one. If you saw your aunt and uncle at the mall today, and later your mother asked you if you saw her sister (your aunt) while you were at the mall, you would reply "Yes." Later, your dad asked you if you saw his fishing buddy (your uncle) while you were at the mall and you would reply "Yes." Are you giving contradictory information? No. *Only partial information.*

Another problem comes from *translation of Greek and Hebrew* words into English. An example of this happen in the differing stories of Paul's conversion:

And the men who journeyed with him stood speechless, hearing a voice but seeing no one. (Acts 9:7 NKJV)

And those who were with me indeed saw the light and were afraid, but they did not hear the voice of Him who spoke to me. (Acts 22:9 NKJV)

These two descriptions of the same event appear to be contradictory until you discover the Greek verbs for "to hear" used in these passages are different. In Acts 9, the verb means that they heard a sound but did not understand what it meant. In Acts 22, the verb doesn't mean they didn't hear but just that they didn't understand or comprehend the voice. Compare the New King James translation of Acts 22:9 to the New American Standard, which reads:

And those who were with me beheld the light, to be sure, but did not understand the voice of the One who was speaking to me. (Acts 22:9 NAS)

Sometimes a translation that is more word for word (as the NAS is) eliminates these problems. Another problem occurs when the Bible records what a person says, but *this does not mean the person was telling the truth*. A good example of this is when Saul fell on his sword and died to escape torture.

Then Saul said to his armor bearer, "Draw your sword and pierce me through with it, lest these uncircumcised come and pierce me through and make sport of me." But his armor bearer would not, for he was greatly afraid. So Saul took his sword and fell on it. (1 Samuel 31:4 NAS)

Later, an Amalekite came to David and reported:

"So I stood beside him and killed him, because I knew that he could not live after he had fallen. And I took the crown which was on his head and the bracelet which was on his arm, and I have brought them here to my lord." (2 Samuel 1:10 NAS)

The Amalekite was a battlefield scavenger. He lied to David, hoping to gain favor. David had him killed.

RS: Maybe I can explain it this way. There are three things that Scripture contains: *facts, truth,* and *myth.*

Fact is most of what happens. But remember, when you tell a story, you summarize it. You don't give every detail, just the facts that make your point. The result in a biblical narrative is often only partial information.

For example, Matthew gives us fourteen generations between one person and another, but clearly there are more if you look at other records in the Bible. The point is there are fourteen that he is mentioning—the ones that he wants you to know about. John says at the end of his Gospel:

There are also many other things which Jesus did, which if they were written in detail, I suppose that even the world itself would not contain the books that would be written. (John 21:25)

But these are written so that you may believe that Jesus is the Messiah, the Son of God, and that by believing in him you will have life. (John 20:31)

Discussing some myths in the ancient Philippian amphitheater

Truth is a little harder to grasp. Often when Jesus teaches, He uses a parable such as: "There was a man traveling from Jericho to Jerusalem," and you can imagine the crowd yelling out, "What was his name?" What did he do for a living?" It doesn't matter. The parable, or illustration, gives us a true biblical principle, an everlasting truth that is applicable to all of mankind in all cultures. The point of the parable is just a truism. Details don't necessarily matter. Hopefully, the illustrations that we use are like windows, opening our eyes to a *principle of truth*.

The third category is much more difficult to lay your hands on. This is *myth*. These are often capitalized on and misused by various groups trying to use the Bible to prove a particular point. Myth is when the Bible records accurately something that is not true. There is Satan saying to Eve, "You surely shall not die!" Now you can read that in the Bible, but it doesn't mean it's true. It is true to say there are untrue things written in the Bible, but you have to read it understanding that the writer is saying *this is not true, but this is what was said*.

There is a major difference in the Bible between a narrative of what happened or what was said and instructions for the believer. In the text, we have to ask ourselves, "Is this an instruction or a report of what was said?"

MB: Paul understood the difference between narrative scripture and instructional scripture and wrote the following to his friends in Corinth:

Now these things, brethren, I have figuratively applied to myself and Apollos for your sakes, so that in us you may learn not to exceed what is written, so that no one of you will become arrogant in behalf of one against the other. (1 Corinthians 4:6 NAS)

62

Sometimes we place more meaning into a passage of Scripture than the writer intended. Paul cautioned the Corinthian church not to do that.

Here is an example of narrative scripture:

Late one afternoon David got out of bed after taking a nap and went for a stroll on the roof of the palace. As he looked out over the city, he noticed a woman of unusual beauty taking a bath. He sent someone to find out who she was, and he was told, "She is Bathsheba, the daughter of Eliam and the wife of Uriah the Hittite." Then David sent for her; and when she came to the palace, he slept with her. (2 Samuel 11:2)

This is obviously a narration of something David did that was not a good thing for him or his country. Can you use this scripture as a justification for adultery? Of course not! Instructional scripture is different:

Don't use foul or abusive language. Let everything you say be good and helpful, so your words will be an encouragement to those who hear them. (Ephesians 5:29)

This is a clear instruction of how to speak to others. The differences may seem obvious, but through the centuries, groups and individuals have taken portions of Scripture that are meant to be narratives and turned them into instruction and built their churches around them. Even in our modern culture this issue has been confused. One example of this was a group of well-meaning believers in California in the '60s who taught that you couldn't own private property because the church in the Acts chapter two "held all things in common."

What about Gideon? He was a man who received a specific command from an angel and responded by the famous "fleece test."

Then Gideon said to God, "If You will deliver Israel through me, as You have spoken, behold, I will put a fleece of wool on the threshing floor. If there is dew on the fleece only, and it is dry on all the ground, then I will know that You will deliver Israel through me, as You have spoken."

And it was so. When he arose early the next morning and squeezed the fleece, he drained the dew from the fleece, a bowl full of water.

Then Gideon said to God, "Do not let Your anger burn against me that I may speak once more; please let me make a test once more with the fleece, let it now be dry only on the fleece, and let there be dew on all the ground."

God did so that night; for it was dry only on the fleece, and dew was on all the ground. (Judges 6:36–40 NAS)

Are we to lay out fleeces when God commands us to do something? This seems to be a common practice in our present Christian culture.

RS: Just because Gideon put his fleece out doesn't mean we must teach our churches that we must all go out and buy fleeces, put them out, and that is how we make decisions. That is a report, a narrative of what Gideon did. Actually, the fleece test is the result of a man of God not believing a message from God given through an angel.

The instruction is to study the Scriptures, to know the Word, and then to walk with God through His Word—not through fleeces.

MB: This is the principle in this passage, and God showed Gideon a lot of grace by responding to his fleece test. God met this man of little faith right where he was. I think God also gave Gideon a great faith-building lesson in a rather humorous manner by whittling his army down from 32,000 to 10,000, and finally down to 300 soldiers carrying ram's horns and clay jars. (Judges 7:7). It was almost a fleece test in reverse!

Does the Bible pass the test of internal evidence? The Bible was written by at least thirty-nine different guys, and the correlation between their thought is amazing. Even secular writers acknowledge this fact. The historical facts presented are consistent. Apparent contradictions disappear when you understand the historical and cultural context and the literary styles of the time.

The internal evidence is *exceptionally* good. Are you ready for the last test?

Mikaela: OK, Pops, we are still with you.

Moselle: Can we move on please!

MB: Here is test number three.

Test #3—External Evidence

- Is what was written consistent with other records from that same period?

Archeology in the past seventy years has discovered many artifacts of ancient civilizations. Pottery, clay writing tablets, leather scrolls, paintings, tombs, statues, staella (columns of carved stone with writing and pictures), palaces, homes, temples, and even entire cities have been discovered, uncovered, and recovered. I've been to some of the sites in Central America, Europe, and the Middle East.

It is safe to say there has not been one archeological discovery contradicting anything in the Bible. Instead, the artifacts discovered support the lifestyles and cultures described in the Bible. Often, exact names and dates discovered on the artifacts match the information given to us by biblical accounts!

There are many writings existing from early Christian writers (Justin, Eusebius, and Polycarp, among others) that contain large portions of Scripture, which match our modern records. The information in these second—, third—, and fourth-century documents supports the information given to us by the writers of the Bible. The writings of contemporary historical figures, such as Josephus, support the biblical account of history.

RS: Archeology is a baby science. We have had "archeologists" around for over a hundred years, but the early ones were "plunderers"—a' la *Raiders of the Lost Ark*. We are really in the infant stages of understanding and interpreting what we find on a site. I worked in Old Testament Jerusalem, the city of David, on a dig where we found a series of small rooms attached to the side of the homes, and these rooms were stacked against each other like steps as they descended the Kidron Valley. Each of these rooms was about a meter square, and found inside one of the rooms was a round, donut-shaped stone with a hole in the top. Yigal Shilo, the head excavator, with years of study under Dame Kathleen Kenyon and others and with an excellent academic background, studied this and declared these small rooms to be "cultic rooms"—rooms for worship.

The following year we dug down a little further and discovered connecting pipes and realized that these were bathrooms—more exactly, toilets. (Isaiah had flush toilets.) They were on a slope so that you could use the facility, dump a bowl of water, and everything would flow downhill. Here were some of the best minds that we have, and they totally missed it for one season. What I state emphatically this year may be overridden by the evidence found on the dig next year.

It is true to say that there are problems between archeology and the Bible. Just getting from Joshua chapter 2 to 10 and dealing with Jericho and dealing with Bethel and Ai and succeeding events brings up unresolved archeological problems.

Randy teaching in the ancient synagogue at Masada

Every academic person is going to come to the dig with a base. It's like when you are an artist painting and you have to decide which medium you are going to use. You start with canvas and decide the base is going to be blue since the painting will be a naval theme.

I come to archeology with the Bible as the truth I am going to hang the illustrations of archeology on. Many archeologists do not have that base. Theirs is that the archeology is going to determine whether or not the historical record of the Bible is accurate. Our predisposition will determine what we find on the site. I know we will find a lot of rocks, pottery, and other implements, but how we interpret them will depend on our base we are working from.

I find it startling that an archeologist will go to a dig at Masada near the Dead Sea and start reading from Josephus, the Jewish Roman historian who wrote a history of the revolt against the Romans, and be so willing for Masada to validate Josephus as an historical record. But when that same archeologist works on a site from Bible, he is critical of the Scripture and is trying to find a way to show "Well, you really can't trust the Bible." I think it has to do with his predisposition and not his finds.

When I go to Jericho and I look at what is at the ancient site of Jericho, I am confident that I cannot show a single wall from the time period of Joshua. Yet I, as an archeologist and historian, believe the wall fell as recorded in the book of Joshua, just as it was written. How do I do that? First, I go to the site and investigate as many have.

In 1920, John Garstang went with an expedition financed to find the wall of Jericho. He dug, and with his predisposition of believing the wall existed (*and pressure to produce from the expedition sponsors)*, he found a wall he declared to be "the Wall of Jericho." In the '60s, Kathleen Kenyon went to Jericho and dug in the site and discovered the *stratigraphy* (or layers) used by Garstang was wrong and that this was not the wall. Immediately, everyone in the Church accused her of being a skeptic. It posed an interesting problem. She was predisposed to disbelieve the Scripture, and Garstang was predisposed to believe it. Neither was right. Neither examined what was there without a predisposition to prove something.

If I go to Jericho and don't find the wall, maybe I am at the wrong site. Yet, we have found pottery on the site with the word *Jericho* written on it. So we have the right site. Maybe I misread the verses. So I go back and read, and it seems very clear that they marched around the city seven times and the walls fell down. So what happened?

The only thing I can figure is that the verses go on to say, "When you come into Jericho, leave this site as a *corban*—as a sacrificial site. Don't rebuild the site."

Now as we travel around the land visiting archeological sites that have been abandoned and left alone, what is the state of the site? What do you see? Has the site grown or diminished in size? Actually, it diminished, as it appeared the stones were taken away and used to build at another site. It is what we call human erosion. It is easier to build with stones already cut and shaped. The fact that Jericho was sitting and not rebuilt in my view was the result of obedience of the people. If the people had disobeyed and tried to rebuild, as others later tried to do, they would have preserved a layer. But the upper layer is gone simply because they obeyed.

Archeology is often misused, even by evangelical, Bible-believing people. They are rushing off to look for the chariots in the Red Sea or other things with any wind of scientific basis. Always look to see who is doing the exploration. Is this person trained to do this? If someone tells me I am healed of a terrible disease that I have, I want to see his credentials and know if they have any background to interpret the laboratory tests, not just someone who had a dream and an opinion of how they think it might be.

There are a lot of books both written and bought by people who really love the Lord, but we are wasting our punches on ridiculousness. We have guys who have "discovered" this or that, and if you send $29.95, they will be glad to send you the video. I even got one of these tapes. A guy showed a picture of the Ark and ended with "If you send an additional $19.95, you will get the actual footage of the location."

MB: Major archeologists have set out to prove the Bible is inaccurate, only to find it is indeed an excellent history book and a source book for their digs. Sir William Ramsey, head of the British Museum, was one who doubted the historical validity of the Bible. After exhaustive research, he found the Bible to be a valuable asset in his projects. He was especially impressed with Luke, who reported things such as prevailing winds, tides, geographical features and locations, and details of travel with great accuracy.

Randy and Michael at the site of ancient Bethsaida with the three Miskitos and Kathy

We visited the dig at the recently discovered ancient site of Bethsaida (the home of Peter, James, and John on the north side of the Sea of Galilee) and saw many examples of biblical accounts being verified through the buildings, walls, wine cellars, fishermen's homes, and other artifacts they discovered. We also saw the recently uncovered ruins of Roman temple that was built to honor Julia, the mother of Caesar. Coins were found verifying that this temple was built in 30 A.D.

There has always been a question of why the Zebedee Fishing Company and Peter left their hometown and economic center and moved around the lake to Capernaum. With this discovery of a pagan temple, we finally have a reason why the boys left town— it was because of that temple built by the Romans. Religious Jews could not live in the same town where a pagan temple existed. They would be continually "defiled." The head Israeli excavator who discovered the coins did not come to the same conclusion— probably due to his predisposition! For us, it was a profound experience to walk the streets of a recently discovered village that Jesus visited and performed miracles in and to know that all that was uncovered supported the biblical account. Indeed, the external evidence is extremely good. I think it is safe to say the Bible is a very good history book.

Lukas: How does it compare to a religious book like the Book of Mormon?

MB: Ever read *Alice in Wonderland? The Adventures of Winnie the Pooh?* The Book of Mormon is a nice story, but there is no historical evidence for the events described in the book. None. That's the difference. The amazing thing about the Bible is that it is a book, not only historically accurate, but for those who read its pages with faith it has dynamic power. As you read it, words jump off the page and speak directly to you. I believe it is indeed "God-breathed" as the original Greek text (2 Timothy 3:16) says, and it is indeed a "living book."

> All Scripture is inspired by God and is useful to teach us what is true and to make us realize what is wrong in our lives. It straightens us out and teaches us to do what is right. (2 Timothy 3:16)

Lukas: So, it seems like there are more than a few reasons why I should be reading the Bible.

MB: You are absolutely right! Here are at least *seven reasons* why you should be studying the Bible.

1. *So that you can personally know God.* God tells us of Himself and His ways through His Word. Reading the Bible is a great way we can really get to know God. Paul believed knowing God was the best thing that he could do in this life.

   > Yes, everything else is worthless when compared with the priceless gain of knowing Christ Jesus my Lord. (Philippians 3:8)

2. *Because you need to know the truth.* Truth is not relative. It is absolute. Truth is simply God's opinion on the matter. Over the door of my junior high school in Ohio were the words *"You Shall The Truth And The Truth Shall Set You Free."* I later discovered that this was an incomplete statement. Jesus said if we first become His disciples by obeying His teachings, then we will know the truth and then we will be set free. It's a three-step process. We cannot know the truth unless we are truly disciples of His.

   > Jesus said to the people who believed in him, "You are truly my disciples if you keep obeying my teachings. And you will know the truth, and the truth will set you free." (John 8:31–32)

3. *To receive guidance in your daily life.* With all the conflicting advice offered in this world, we need to know God's will when it comes to making decisions in our lives.

Your word is a lamp for my feet and a light for my path. (Psalm 119:105)

4. *The Bible is the ultimate source of wisdom.* Other books have their value, but it is the Bible that sets the standard for wisdom in our culture.

    All Scripture is inspired by God and is useful to teach us what is true and to make us realize what is wrong in our lives. It straightens us out and teaches us to do what is right. (2 Timothy 3:16)

5. *We are commanded to study and know the Bible.*

    Work hard so God can approve you. Be a good worker, one who does not need to be ashamed and who correctly explains the word of truth. (2 Timothy 2:15)

The kids we work with in Miskitia all know how to handle a machete. At age four, they begin using this versatile tool. They can clean a field, plant crops, harvest food, clean a fish, and build a house. No Miskito child could survive without knowing how to use this tool. It's the same for God's children and the Bible. We must be familiar with it so we can use it as a source of wisdom as well as a spiritual weapon in this life.

6. *Knowing the Bible will keep you from falling into error.* With so many different teaching going on in Christian circles, it's very important to check everything you hear from a teacher (including things in this book!) against the Word of God. God wants us to walk in truth, not in doctrines that just "tickle our ears."

    And the people of Berea were more open-minded than those in Thessalonica, and they listened eagerly to Paul's message. They searched the Scriptures day after day to check up on Paul and Silas, to see if they were really teaching the truth. (Acts 17:11)

7. *So that you will be blessed!* There is great blessing that comes from reading and meditating on God's Word! As we incorporate this discipline into our lives, we will see many things come forth. The psalmist describes a process of watering, bearing fruit, not getting worn out, and prospering in all that we do. Can we ask for more than that in this life?

How blessed is the man who does not walk in the counsel of the wicked, Nor stand in the path of sinners, Nor sit in the seat of scoffers! But his delight is in the law of the LORD, And in His law he meditates day and night. And he will be like a tree firmly planted by streams of water, Which yields its fruit in its season, And its leaf does not wither; And in whatever he does, he prospers. (Psalm 1:1–3)

Let's wrap up this session with this perspective from Laura.

THE SEARCH FOR TRUTH

Pilate therefore said to Him, "So You are a king?"

Jesus answered, "You say correctly that I am a king. For this I have been born, and for this I have come into the world, to bear witness to the truth. Everyone who is of the truth hears My voice."

Pilate said to Him, "What is truth?" (John 18:37–38)

We seek truth continually, often looking to books, to man, to universities. We continually seek it but seek it ever too frequently in the wrong places, using the wrong methods. We want to "know," yet we fall short in our search, for we do not go to the Source in our seeking. The Source of truth has it all, yet we grope, wonder, rationalize, deny, and go on in our busy lives, forgetting to look where we can find it all—all that pertains to life and true freedom living.

"If you abide in My word, then you are truly my disciples of mine; and you shall know the truth, and the truth shall set you free." (Spoken by Jesus in John 8:31–32)

There is a source of truth. It is one that many of us have read and studied over the years but yet often mechanically and without inspiration. Yet the Bible claims to be "God-breathed" (2 Timothy 3:16) and applicable to every area of our lives.

Where is the zeal? Where does it go? It seemingly evaporates as time passes. . . . Years go by and we think we are all the more wise because we know doctrine; we've read every Bible story at least ten times. Doctrine isn't an end in itself; it is the mere beginning. It has to work. It has to affect our lives and all the lives around us.

"Knowledge makes arrogant, but love edifies." (1 Corinthians 8:1)

We learn a lot about God from Scripture and do not know Him at all. The goal is to know Him and to keep our love alive and fresh for the Lord Jesus Christ. Without a growing, ever-dependent love, we simply will be "working" for our Master rather than serving Him in love and dedication. Eternity cannot be impacted in this manner. In our knowing Him, we become like Him. In becoming like Him, we will shine His character forth. He increases while we decrease.

We often encourage memorizing Scripture instead of thinking scripturally. We are to incarnate the Word of God, having our lives transformed by it and our minds renewed by it (Ephesians 4:23–24).

Laura atop Mt. Pilatus in Switzerland, named after the famous Roman procurator

"The Word became flesh, and dwelt among us." (John 1:14)

As Scripture becomes alive in us, we become alive to others and show forth His mind, His heart, and His ways.

It is a shame to admit that we often hear the Word and then don't do it. We are people who are educated beyond our obedience. The will of God cannot be played out unless our level of obedience is up to par with our level of knowledge. We "know" more than we practice. It is sin to know and not do.

"If you know these things, you are blessed if you do them." (John 13:17)

The Word of God has a special personality ingrained in it. These are not mere words written in a book. The Bible is indeed a unique book, filled with life itself. In reading it, we come to know the Creator better and experience His true love for us more deeply. We are then able to give His love out more sincerely; thus, impacting the world around us for eternity.

Personal Reflections

1. What sources do you go to search for truth?
2. How does knowing that the Bible is a good history book change the way you read it?
3. Have you made any personal doctrines out of narrative scripture?
4. Would people describe you as flexible in your walk with God?
5. In the parable of the prodigal son, with whom do you identify more: the prodigal, the older son, or the father?

Deeper Water

A. Read Psalm 22 and then Matthew 27. Do you notice any similarities? How can we reconcile these two passages of Scripture written 1,000 years apart?
B. What are some of the prophecies given in the Old Testament that Jesus fulfilled? What are the probabilities of one man fulfilling all of these?
C. Psalm 119 is the longest chapter in the Bible. Read through this song written by David, underlining each of the verses that describe some aspect of God's Word. Afterward, make a list of all these characteristics of the Living Book.

We view life through the lenses of our own experiences and culture. When it comes to God and life in the spiritual world, it is natural that we proceed in a similar manner. Over the past two millenniums, Christian traditions have developed that had significance for a group of believers with a cultural time frame. As a result, for the diverse language groups and cultures of our modern era, capturing the essence of the biblical message often requires a challenging expedition through centuries of doctrines and often conflicting interpretation of the Scriptures. We have discovered that to understand the simple message of the Bible, sometimes we must read it through first-century eyes.

First-Century Eyes

Lukas: I know I'm just a kid, but sometimes when I read my Bible, I don't understand what they are talking about.

MB: It happens to me, too, Lukas. What helps me in times when the meaning of the passage of Scripture is unclear is to try to read the Scripture through the eyes of those first-century believers.

Lukas: Why do you do that?

MB: Often we understand the meaning of Scripture

Lukas on the Sea of Galilee

the meaning of Scripture through our own culture in our own language, and sometimes this gives us a different message than what the writers of the Bible were trying to communicate. Let me give you one simple example. Mark records when Jesus went to His hometown, Nazareth, and began teaching His former neighbors, and extended family responded by saying:

"Is not this the carpenter, the son of Mary, and brother of James and Joses and Judas and Simon? Are not His sisters here with us?" And they took offense at Him. (Mark 6:3 NAS)

The Greek word translated here as *carpenter* is actually the word "Tekton", which in most dictionaries is given the meaning "builder; constructor." Most of the translations of the Bible in the Middle Ages were done by Europeans, many of whom lived in cities of wooden houses. It was very natural that they would take the word *tekton* and translate in English as carpenter. As a result, we get many images of the word *carpenter* in our minds. Thus we see paintings done by European artists that show Jesus working with carpenter tools, making chairs, tables, and handicrafts.

When you travel to the Middle East, one thing you notice right away is most of the buildings there are made out of stone. There are very few trees in Israel. The Bible records that when Solomon built the temple, the lumber came from King Hiram's country many miles to the north. For the Middle Easterner, *tekton* translates "stone mason" instead of the word *carpenter*.

Does this change the way we imagine Jesus to be? The stonemasons that I know in the third world are very broad-shouldered with muscular arms, backs, and necks. Their hands are rough and often cut from doing their work.

How does this image compare to many paintings of a frail, slender Jesus who often looks like He just stepped out of the beauty parlor? With this more realistic image of Jesus as a muscular, powerful man, I can understand what Luke describes happened at Nazareth when the crowd

got up and drove Him out of the city, and led Him to the brow of the hill on which their city had been built, in order to throw Him down the cliff. But passing through their midst, He went His way. (Luke 4:29–30)

Jesus, the stone mason, can power His way through the crowd better than the guy who just stepped out of the hair salon. This may seem like a minor point, but this modern cultural misinterpretation of the Scriptures can happen on a larger scale, resulting in doctrines and beliefs that would shock the writers of the Bible. The point is, when it comes to understanding the message the writers of the Bible were trying to communicate, often the best thing to do is to step back through centuries of our own cultural interpretations and try to understand the passage as the first-century believers read it.

It's important to realize that God spoke to the people of the Bible in a way they could understand. They were different people who thought in a different way and spoke in a different language than we do today. It is important to remember this when it comes to understanding and applying the Bible to our own lives.

A foundational principle of ministry is telling people the good news about relationship with God in a language they can understand, using cultural expressions that have meaning to them. When I am in Nicaragua working with the Miskito Indians in our primary education program, Project Ezra, I explain the Bible using words and concepts I know have meaning there. When I am at my home church in Maui on the beach with some of my local surfing friends, I use other words that have meaning to them that express what God is saying.

I know it may sound confusing, Lukas, but don't I talk differently to you than I do your three-year-old sister, Moselle? Have you noticed how Mommy changes the way she talks when we are in Hawaii? Once we arrive there, she falls back into the local pidgin language because she knows her family and friends will understand her best if she speaks to them in a language and through cultural expressions they all know.

This is an important principle of cross-cultural ministry. Anthropologists tell us the *message of the Bible must be communicated within the language and symbols of a culture.* This is the example God gives us in the pages of the Old and New Testaments. Why is this important?

The Bible is the Living Word of God. Through it we know God better and how to live our lives here on planet Earth. It is our guide to spiritual living. It is the book of ultimate wisdom and gives us practical steps in carrying out God's mission. The Bible prepares us for the life to come. This is the most important book we have!

Over the past two decades, we have worked in cross-cultural situations in the Middle East, Latin America, Pacifica, Europe, and North America. We have seen the amazing life-changing effects of believers discovering biblical truths and applying them to their personal lives and ministries. We have also seen the results of individuals and groups who read the Bible through their own "shaded lenses" and interpret the message in a convenient manner that supports their preconceived notions. One group experiences true relationship with God, spiritual growth, and abundant living, while the other dwells in religion, status quo, and the glory of yesterday.

The Bible was written many centuries ago to a different culture, in a different language, in another land. Our experience in reading the Bible through our "modern eyes" has often produced results that would have surprised the writers of the Bible. There are historical events, as well as events in our present spiritual environment, where biblical truth was skewed and misapplied, with sometimes comic and often tragic results.

When I first went to Central America in 1984 to work with Miskito Indian refugees, I immediately noticed many Miskito women wearing lace doilies on their heads when they were in a church. When I asked why, I was told simply that the Bible says a woman should not be in church without her head covered. After all, Paul told the church in

Apollo Temple in ancient Corinth with the Acropolis in the background

Corinth that their women should have their heads covered. It seems there was something going on in Corinth that caused Paul to order this practice.

Research reveals that there was a prominent temple to the goddess Aphrodite in ancient Corinth. Aphrodite was the goddess of love, and her temple was at the top of the acropolis where hundreds of priestesses joined the men in a *very* sexual form of worship. The head priestess became the richest and most influential person in town, along with other temple prostitutes. Eventually, the women of Corinth dominated the men of the city. When families began to come to Christ, many brought this same attitude into the Church, which was out of God's order. When Paul ordered the women to "cover their heads" (1 Corinthians 11), Paul was recommending a symbol of submission to God's order (verse 3), "because of the angels." When the missionaries brought the Gospel to the Coco River eighty years ago, women began wearing things on their head when they came to church even though there is not the same problem of female dominance in Miskito families that there was in Corinth.

When you apply a practice from the Bible apart from the principle behind the practice, there is a danger of becoming "religious." Doing things to gain favor from God has little meaning, especially if not having a headcovering excludes you from coming to the house of God.

During my high school years, a friend took me to her church, which was across the street from mine. As I looked around while waiting for the service to begin, I noticed the absence of an organ or piano. When the worship leader got up to begin the singing, he leaned over and blew into a small pitch pipe. The singing began without using any musical instruments. We sang acapella, and it was very nice. Afterward, I asked my friend why they did not use any instruments, and she replied (quite proudly!): "We are a New Testament church, and there is no mention in the New Testament of the use of any instruments. That's why we worship with our voices only."

I had to think about that one for a while. David used musical instruments, but I guess that was "Old Testament." Does it make a difference? I did notice an attitude of exclusivity among that congregation because of their "true" form of worship. There was very little interaction with other churches in the town.

In recent years, we have spent time at the School of Worship in Jerusalem and studied the culture of the early Church. The early Christians were worshiping God according to Jewish customs. One of the words in the Book of Psalms that is translated *praise* in English is the Hebrew word *zamar*, which means to praise the Lord by using a musical instrument (Psalm 108:1). Doesn't this command still apply? Here is another example of modern men and women who love the Lord interpreting and applying Scripture in a "modern" fashion, ignoring or ignorant of what was happening in the early Church, and in the process, building walls, separating them from the rest of the body of Christ.

RS: Our objective is to reach the world for Christ, but we place ourselves on the margins of society with our strange religious behavior. We speak our own special "Christianese" language, have our own dress codes, and have rules of behavior, which usually begin with *don't* and *can't*. Where Paul and the other first-century missionaries tried to blend in with the local culture (1 Corinthians 9), we seem to make an effort to stand apart in areas that are far from the heart of God. As a result, many of our evangelistic efforts are met with indifference, not because of the message, but because we have packaged the message in a container that looks strange and often irrelevant. In studying the Scriptures, this is clearly not the biblical model. We are to be holy (distinct, set apart), yet Paul continually tried to "fit in with them as much as I can" (1 Corinthians. 9:21). Holiness in morality and character and cultural revelance are not mutually exclusive.

MB: Historically, there are many examples of dubious applications of supposed biblical principles that are very hard to explain and make our job as foreign missionaries extremely difficult. A few years ago in Jerusalem, I met the family of Una and Leonardo, two of our Israeli friends who live in Maui and had become followers of Jesus there through some pretty extraordinary events. We had a very enjoyable evening at Una's family's home (I later found out that we were the first Christians her parents had allowed in their home!). That night we became good friends with her parents, Eli and Iris.

The following week, after Una and Leonardo returned to Maui, we were invited to have dinner with her family. As we sat down to eat with her mother, father, and sister-in-law, the first question came from Eli, her *abba.* He asked politely, "Why did Christian armies come here a thousand years ago and kill everyone in Jerusalem?"

How do you explain the Crusades using biblical principles? Where does it say we are to go and conquer lands and kill all the inhabitants? Did Pope Urban II possibly mistake a narrative of what happened in a portion of the Bible with a command to go out and do the same, by which he then ordered the first crusade in 1094? The advance of Islam through the Middle East, North Africa, and Spain in the eighth, ninth, and tenth centuries provoked a reaction on the part of Christian leaders in Europe that can be explained in geo-political terms but not on biblical grounds. The resulting crusades of Christian armies to the Middle East over the next 400 years were a series of wars where many Jews and Muslims died. This is still an extremely sensitive issue.

How could I explain it to a Jew who was wondering what belief system his daughter now held in light of history?

A few hundred years later, the Church in Spain began the Inquisition, which was infamous for torturing and killing "heretics." People with beliefs about Christianity that differed from official church dogma were questioned under torture, forced to "confess their sins," and recant their "heretical beliefs." If you look at the issues, it appears that many of us (including modern-day Catholics!) would have been on the torture rack!

Surprisingly, the major debate among the priests was not whether this torture was proper in accordance with God's Word but rather that when it came to killing one of these "heretics," could the priest actually do the killing or should the executioner be somebody else? After all, a priest has his role as a guide to life. Do you think these priests were missing major chapters and verses from their Bibles? How do we explain this torture and killing in light of the Scripture? *More importantly, how do we avoid these modern and ancient pitfalls of understanding biblical truth and applying it to our personal lives?*

As followers of Jesus Christ, we are continually given the opportunity to vocalize and live out our faith. In doing so, we are faced with a challenge of applying biblical truths to our lives and proclaiming the message of the Bible to those around us. How do we best do this?

Anthropologists tell us it is essential to understand the Bible within its own cultural and historical setting. This is the first step required if we are to draw truth from the Scriptures for our own lives and for the benefit of the people around us.

Dr. Paul Heibert, professor of anthropology at Fuller Seminary, is one of many experts who points out in his classic, *Anthropological Insights For Missionaries* (p. 14), the essential value of knowing the cultural-historical context of the Bible, as well as understanding the culture of the people we are trying to reach. Without these two essential elements, we are in danger of proclaiming a message to other cultures that has no meaning.

The Bible is meant to be a breathing, living document that God uses to speak to all mankind and cultures in the here and now, even though we read words written two millennium ago. Long ago, a Bible refugee named Ezra, faced a similar challenge. He had the assignment of returning to his homeland with a group of Israelite refugees and re-building a physically and spiritually devastated nation. He knew the proper application of the Word of God was critical to the success of his mission. It was the misapplication that had caused the problem in the first place!

For Ezra had set his heart to study the law of the LORD and to practice it, and to teach His statutes and ordinances in Israel. (Ezra 7:10)

For Ezra, it was a three-step process:

1.   study and understand the Word of God;
2.   put biblical truth in practice in his own life;
3.   teach it to the nation of Israel.

This process has not changed since the days of Ezra.
The challenge for us today is to:

1.   understand the Bible in its historical and cultural context;
2.   extract biblical truth that we can apply to our own lives;
3.   *then* we are qualified to proclaim this message and give this truth to those around us.

We have all been given the right to read and interpret the Scriptures and the re-sponsibility to put biblical truth into practical application in our lives. *How then are we to discern what the message of the Bible actually is? This is the challenge that continually faces us.*

As Peter declares (1 Peter 2:9), we are a nation of priests. We have all been given the right to read and personally interpret the Scriptures. Our interpretation must be accurate and faithful to the biblical text. It cannot be viewed only through our modern cultural perspective but must be understood within the context of when it was originally presented. After determining the message, we are then challenged to extract the applicable principles for our own lives. This may involve jumping between our modern cultural context and the historical biblical context. As we do this, it is important to remember that the Bible has a culture of its own: the values, moral, and truths of the Bible stand alone and above all other "cultures."

The authors with Rachel Smith in Kabala Greece, where Paul first came ashore in Europe

RS: Having stepped out of your North American culture into the Miskito culture of Central America, Mike, I know one of the startling things you learned right away was that these are not simply people who speak another language. They think differently.

MB: Yes, small gestures we think are totally innocent and harmless can cause major problems. I have to be very careful to ensure that I am communicating thoughts and concepts as well as words to the five men who manage our school project. We speak to each other in three languages: English, Spanish, and Miskito. A trilingual conversation across a huge cultural gap can result in profound misunderstandings. I know that you, Randy, during your first year in Jerusalem as an archeology student, created a serious situation when you innocently asked the daughter of your Arab cleaning lady if she wanted to go to a John Wayne movie playing at the theater. In her culture that was the same as proposing marriage! I know it took many gifts and social maneuvering for both of you to get out of that one unscathed.

RS: It did! What is important to understand is that because two people understand exactly what was said doesn't mean that two of them have the same concept of what was being communicated. That happens in marriage and especially in cross-cultural communication. As I come to the Scriptures and try to understand what is going on in the pages, I have to realize when I open my Bible, I step out of my twenty-first-century world and into another culture in another time. There is a little more involved than just reading it and believing it.

Mark Twain is the one who said "We know a lot of things that just ain't so."

You can read the Bible, see what they did, and you can ask yourself "What does that mean to me and my family sitting here in the twenty-first century as I face all the challenges in my life?"

I think it is worthwhile to point out that when God spoke, He spoke to a specific people, at a specific time, in a specific place to benefit me much later, but it was not written to me.

Can I say it this way: *There is not one word in the Bible that is written to me, but every word is written for me.* I know that may be shocking when you hear it for the first time, but let it sink in.

God said things 3,000 years ago to another culture in another land in another language in a way that they would understand it. *I've got to do something more than just read it and believe it.* It's like putting a teabag into hot water; I've got to allow the Scripture to permeate my "water" and change who I am by the principles involved in it. I've got to squeeze out of the story of God with Abraham, God with Moses, and God with David specific things: Who is God in this story? What does He want from David or Moses? *What everlasting truth can I draw from this story that is relevant and applicable to my life today?*

It is the principle behind the cultural practice that I am after. What truth was God communicating to those people then that I can apply to my life today in a way that makes sense? Leviticus 1 says:

Then the LORD called to Moses and spoke to him from the tent of meeting, saying,

"Speak to the sons of Israel and say to them, 'When any man of you brings an offering to the LORD, you shall bring your offering of animals from the herd or the flock.

If his offering is a burnt offering from the herd, he shall offer it, a male without defect; he shall offer it at the doorway of the tent of meeting, that he may be accepted before the LORD." (Leviticus 1:1–3)

Obviously, I cannot go today to the tabernacle in the wilderness to offer my sacrifice (*although I can go to the replica that we constructed near the Dead Sea a few years ago*), so what is in this passage of God's everlasting Word that He commands me to know and accurately handle (2 Timothy 2:15) that can apply to my life today?

The Wilderness Tabernacle Study Center near Jericho

In verse one, we see God calling out to Moses. From this I know God often takes the initiative in His fellowship with mankind. This is an important principle for me to remember when I am feeling far from God. In verse two, God orders the people to bring an offering from their own herd or flock. God wants me to return to Him some of the things that He has freely given me. This is a good principle of relationship between God and me and an important principle of God's economics. In verse three, God says to bring an animal without defect. From this I see that God wants my best; He will not be happy with a half-hearted response from me. If He asks me to give $100 to the missionaries, He will not be pleased if I give only $50. If I am to go paint the widow's house, He wants me to use the best paint I can afford.

I could throw out all of Leviticus by saying "*We are not under the Law!*," but I then would miss many of God's truths that apply very well to my life today. If we read the Scriptures and search for the principles and truths behind the specific cultural practices, then we begin to receive life from the Word of God, not just dusty out-of-date commandments.

MB: God wants to give us understanding. He wants us to have more than just "blind faith." He wants to give us *life*. That is why He is inviting us into an intimate relationship with Him. That is why He gives us example after example of who He is and how He interacts with mankind in the pages of the Bible. Understanding biblical culture, language, geography, and even politics gives us greater understanding of God and how He is relating to us.

Remember the challenge for us is to first understand the Bible in its historical and cultural context. It is only then that we can draw out principles and everlasting truths to apply to our own lives. Once we do that, we can take the message to any place, into any culture, with any people.

If we don't have understanding of what God is really communicating in the Scriptures, we can easily become "religious" and try to fulfill the letter of the Law without understanding the intent. You end up with Miskito women in Nicaragua wearing lace doilies on their heads because Paul told the ladies in Corinth to cover their hair when assembling together.

Paul was giving the women in Corinth a symbol to get their familial relationships in order—a symbol that was appropriate for their culture because of things going on in Greek society. This practice has no spiritual significance in Miskito culture as it did in Corinth, yet because a missionary told them to cover their heads without any cultural understanding, they do. It becomes a religious thing.

RS: Our experience working with indigenous people groups in Central America and the Middle East, along with our years of biblical and archeological studies in the Holy Land, has given us a more practical *"principle approach"* to understanding the Bible.

MB: This perspective and the following guidelines may be helpful as you approach the challenges of applying the principles of the Word of God to your own lives and ministry. *As we pursue intellectual understanding, we must never lose sight of the most helpful element of Bible study: an intimate relationship with the Holy Spirit.* He is the teacher and will teach to anyone, anywhere, in any culture. He is the one who makes the text come alive in your life.

RS: *When we open the Bible, we literally step out of the twenty-first century and back into time.* The writers of the Bible wrote to a particular audience in another land and in another culture. One of the important guidelines to remember is that God speaks to mankind in a way they can understand. He paints pictures of Himself and His ways through cultural expressions that have deep meaning to His audience, even if they have little meaning to us today.

MB: We see an example of this in Genesis 15 in one of the most important narratives in the Bible. God makes a promise to Abraham, and Abraham responds with faith. It is an act that Paul mentions in the Christian Scriptures and one that Martin Luther later used to change the course of Church history. Why did Abraham firmly believe God was going to do what He promised? It was through a very unusual (in our modern eyes) practice that "God sealed the deal."

> And He took him outside and said, "Now look toward the heavens, and count the stars, if you are able to count them." And He said to him, "So shall your descendants be." Then he believed in the LORD; and He reckoned it to him as righteousness. And He said to him, "I am the LORD who brought you out of Ur of the Chaldeans, to give you this land to possess it." [8]He said, "O LORD GOD, how may I know that I will possess it?" So He said to him, "Bring Me a three year old heifer, and a three year old female goat, and a three year old ram, and a turtledove, and a young pigeon." Then he brought all these to Him and cut them in two, and laid each half opposite the other; but he did not cut the birds. The birds of prey came down upon the carcasses, and Abram drove them away.

> Now when the sun was going down, a deep sleep fell upon Abram; and behold, terror and great darkness fell upon him. God said to Abram, "Know for certain that your descendants will be strangers in a land that is not theirs, where they will be enslaved and oppressed four hundred years. . . . Then in the fourth generation they will return here, for the iniquity of the Amorite is not yet complete." It came about when the sun had set, that it was very dark, and behold, there appeared a smoking oven and a flaming torch which passed between these pieces. (Genesis 15:5–17)

- What significance did the split carcasses have for politicians and businessmen of Abram's time?

  > Jeremiah 34:18–20 explains that in those days business men, politicians, and friends made pacts by cutting animals in half and walking together through the split carcass, pausing in the middle and looking at each other saying, "If I don't keep my end of this deal, may I become like this dead animal."

- What caused Abram to believe God?

  > When God passed through by Himself, Abraham knew that God's promises did not depend on whether Abraham kept his end of the deal.

This is a great example of how God spoke to a person in a way he would understand, even though it makes little sense in our world. This is an important guideline for our lives and for our study of the Word. I am glad to know that God will also speak to me in a way that I will understand and get the message.

People in ancient cultures thought differently than us. When God walked by Himself between the halved animals, this gesture had a major impact on Abraham. It changed his world. He suddenly got very excited about what God was doing. But it makes no sense to us. We say to ourselves "What is going on here?"

RS: My passion is to help people understand what the Scriptures are about and how they play out in the cultural and historical context of the time in which they are written. As I said earlier, when you open your Bible, you step out of your twenty-first-century world into first-century Jewish/Greco-Roman culture. There are major differences between their culture and ours when it comes to understanding the message of the Bible.

The first question to ask is "How do the Jews and Greeks think?"

Function vs. Form

Hold up a coffee cup and ask the first-century Greek and Jew to describe it. The Greek will tell you its color, the shape, how tall it is, how wide it is, and what the curve in the handle is like. The Jew will say simply: "With this I can drink coffee."

Greeks think in terms how it appears: the form. Jews think in terms of what it does: the function.

This is helpful when it comes to understanding a particularly confusing passage found in the Song of Songs. Here the writer describes his beloved by saying:

> Your belly is like a heap of wheat Fenced about with lilies. (Song of Songs 7:2)

Around my house, saying that would get me the cold shoulder or a quick slap. We are Greek thinkers. But the Jewish lover is saying his beloved will be very fruitful, bearing him many children from her belly, her

Classic forms in Athens
Laura at the Antiquities Museum

87

womb, the heap of harvested wheat. This will result in a secure "retirement" for both in their old age.

This functional thinking causes God to describe Himself as:

I, the LORD, am your God, who brought you out of Egypt to give you the land of Canaan and to be your God. (Leviticus 25:38)

He is saying simply: "This is what I did and what I am going to do."

When we read the Gospel of John, we hear Jesus describing Himself seven times as "*I Am* . . ."—the Bread of Life, the Light of the World, the Door, the Good Shepherd, the Way, the Truth, and the Life. These are images that John uses to appeal to the Greek-thinking person. Along with these seven "I Am's," John also gives us seven miracles: Turning water into wine, healing at a distance, raising the paralytic, feeding the five thousand, walking on water, healing the blind, and raising Lazarus from the dead. This would appeal to the functional Hebrew-thinking person. Since John's ministry was among both cultures, it is natural he would include functional and form descriptions of Jesus. This is what makes John's Gospel so successful in its universal appeal.

Another area of different thinking is:

Acceptance and Obedience vs. Speculation and Application

Jewish rabbis taught that it was the duty of God's people to accept the revelation God has given them and simply obey. They saw the pillar of fire and smoke at Mt. Sinai. This was God. As to what was above that pillar, they not only didn't know, but they felt they didn't have the right to even speculate about what God may or may not be. Their duty was to obey.

Greeks have a thing called logic, which is prominent in their culture, even today. They believe that if they know A is greater than B, and A is less than C, they can figure out the relationship between B and C. Remember they are the inventors of geometry! If they know some things about God, they can apply logic to figure out the rest. When the Greek-thinking people came into the Church in large numbers in the second century, theology was born, and speculation of who God is, what He is really saying, and how we are to respond began. Jews never really developed a theology of God. They didn't feel they had the right to.

MB: When we study Church history of the third through sixth centuries, we see councils, schisms, and excommunications. Applying logic to God often had divisive and disastrous results.

When Emperor Constantine called the first major church council (fourth century), many survivors of the persecutions of preceding emperors were present. It was a scene of amazement that those who, a few years earlier, were official enemies of the State were now dining with the emperor in his royal palace. At one of the banquets, it was reported that Constantine approached one bishop who had lost an eye to torture and kissed him where the eye had been.

When these church leaders (mostly Greek) later began meetings to establish official church doctrines, they couldn't agree, and many wanted to excommunicate each other. All agreed the Scriptures were inerrant, and many believed "inerrancy" applied to *their* logical interpretation of these Scriptures. That was a problem, and finally Constantine intervened, forcing the council to come to an agreement on some of the major issues. This was the result of "speculation and application." The Church has never been the same.

RS: The first-century Church was a Jewish church, but in the second century, thanks to the work of Paul, Barnabas, Luke, Silas, and others, there were more Greek-speaking and Greek-thinking Christians.

This was when the church went through the Greek "car wash."

The character of the Church changed, and issues that were not important to the first-century Church became paramount. There was an effort on the part of some of the Greek churches (in Alexandria, for example) to move away from their Jewish roots and turn to a philosophic approach. The Hebrew Scriptures were viewed as allegorical in nature, and there was an emphasis on including the teachings of Plato into Christian theology.

The end result was a guy like Marcion who eliminated all the Hebrew books of the Bible and any of the Christian portions of the Scripture that had any Jewish influences. He was left with a Bible containing the letters of Paul and portions of Luke's Gospel. He believed that there was a different god in the Hebrew Scriptures. For this he was eventually excommunicated.

A third area of importance is:

Tribal Mentality vs. Individualism

Most Jews were raised in an environment that emphasized the *collective* (the good of the many) over the *individual* (good of the one). They thought of themselves as first, family members; then extended family (clans); next, members of one of the twelve tribes;

89

and finally the nation of Israel. Their mentality dictated that what benefited the group was more important than individual gain and comfort. Thus the king could offer lifetime tax exemption to the families of the sappers (who crawled under the walls of the enemies' cities and dug out under the rocks until they finally collapsed on top of them!) and have volunteers for this important but often suicidal job.

Greeks were more "individual" thinkers. Their literature portrayed the "lone hero" who overcame great odds or fell prey to the schemes of the gods or his own failings. Painting and sculpture focused on the individual male and female forms. The importance of the individual gave rise to a unique form of government—democracy—where every man had a voice in society. Democratic concepts didn't really exist in Jewish society.

Greek influence was strong in Jewish society by the time of Jesus. In the first century, Jews began burying their dead in individual *kochim*-style tombs (where each body had its own separate chamber), instead of more traditional tombs where bodies were placed on a flat surface for decomposition; and, after about eighteen months, when the body decayed, the bones were place in a common ossuary (bone box) along with the bones of other family members.

MB: A major theme of Paul's letters to the churches deals with a concept of the body of Christ (gr: *soma*) and the importance of leaving behind a self-centered individualism and of adopting a "tribal mentality" of Christian community. He used the term at least thirty times in his letters.

> Under his direction, the whole body is fitted together perfectly. As each part does its own special work, it helps the other parts grow, so that the whole body is healthy and growing and full of love. (Ephesians 4:16)

He knew that this "collective" idea was a foreign concept to these Greek-thinking Christians, but he also realized the important value that God places on giving to and doing what's best for others, even when we have to sacrifice our own interests. After all, this value of self-sacrifice is at the very center of God's heart.

This is also a new concept to many modern "Western-thinking" individuals who come into the Church and become part of the body of Christ. We naturally model our lifestyles, our ministries, and our church government on democratic, individual-oriented principles, often without realizing that the biblical model points us in another direction. That's why the Holy Spirit included at least twenty-one commandments for loving "one another" in very practical and selfless manner in the Christian Scriptures (see session 6).

Another good question: *How did Jews learn?*

RS: Typically, Hebrew children grew up memorizing portions of the Torah, the first five books of the Bible. They used the Torah for all their academic classes. The Scriptures were divided up into portions, or *parshioth,* and students memorized these entire sections. The first book the rabbis taught children was Deuteronomy, because it was easy to read, understand, and memorize. Notice that Jesus quotes more from Deuteronomy than any other book in the Bible; it's because He knew His often poorly-educated audience would at least recognize scriptures from this book.

The rabbis used a technique called *remez* in teaching their students. *Remez* means "hint." They would speak a line or two of a portion of Scripture, knowing the students would be able to complete the rest. It would be like me saying, "Mike, it's because God so loved the world . . ." and very naturally you would complete the thought: "that He sent His only Son," etc.

In Matthew 11, Jesus uses this technique to answer the question John's disciples came to ask: "Jesus, are you really the Messiah, or are we to expect another?" Jesus responds by *remez.* He quotes a portion of Isaiah 35: "Tell John that the blind see, the lame walk," and so on, knowing that the rest of the passage says: "God is coming to destroy your enemies. He is coming to save you," a passage clearly referring to the Messiah, and one which John would be familiar with.

Next, Jesus asked the crowds: "Who was this man in the wilderness that you went out to see?" referring to John. He goes on to quote from Malachi 3:1: "Look, I am sending my messenger before you, and he will prepare your way." Jesus knows many in the crowd will remember the rest of the passage that says: "Then the Lord that you are seeking will suddenly come to His Temple." This is another passage that is certainly referring to the Messiah. Jesus is, in a cultural way, without inciting the religious and political authorities, declaring Himself to the crowd to be the Messiah. Understanding this style of learning can be helpful when it comes to passages that don't seem to make sense. (For example: Matthew 11:12, probably referring to Micah 2:13.)

MB: Remember that the writers of the Bible wrote to a particular audience. They never realized that 2,000 years later people would be reading their books and letters. However, the Holy Spirit did! The writers assumed you, the audience, would know certain things, many of which we have forgotten today. Understanding the background to the writings—the cultural, political, linguistic, and geographical contexts—will allow us to more accurately draw godly principles to apply to our lives and to the lives of those we are ministering to.

The challenge for us is to first understand the Bible in its historical and cultural context. It is only then that we can draw out principles and everlasting truths to apply to our own lives. Once we do that, we can take the message to any place, into any culture, with any people. If we don't have understanding of what God is really communicating in the Scriptures, we can easily become "religious" and try to fulfill the letter of the Law without understanding the intent.

Context is everything!

RS: Here are some examples of how knowing the background (or context) of the passage of Scripture might change the way you interpret it and apply it to your life.

Culture

How Bible-time people lived provides insight into the message of the Bible. Here are some relevant points:

- *The Greek culture was a "missionary" culture that sought to capture the hearts and minds of the world.* Alexander the Great had Aristotle as his tutor. He was as interested in spreading the superior Greek culture as he was in conquering nations! Gymnasiums, athletic competitions, drama, and worship of the Pantheon were the usual means of dispersing Greek culture, and it was successful in most of the places where Alexander and his armies went.
- *Jewish Culture clashed heavily with the Greeks.* Worship of many gods and morality were big issues. For a Jewish boy to go to a Greek "gymnasium" meant that he would have to discard much of the biblical morality, as athletic competitions were done in the nude.
- *Religious Jews lived apart from the Hellenistic (Greek-thinking and speaking) Jews and would not go into a town where there was a pagan temple.* This may explain why Peter, James, and John moved from their hometown, Bethsaida, where a temple to Julia, the mother of Caesar Augustus, was recently discovered, to Capernaum.

Understanding Greek culture helps our understanding of the Scriptures. Paul wrote to a church in Greece:

Randy teaching at the Bema Seat in Ancient Corinth

If I speak with the tongues of men and of angels, but do not have love, I have become a sounding brass (noisy gong) or a clanging cymbal. (1 Corinthians 13:1)

We have various understandings of this passage, but to Paul's audience, the message was perfectly clear: He was using terms familiar to Greek drama presentations.

- Sounding brass (gr: *echeô chalkos*): a metal drum that was used by Greek actors backstage to *simulate* the voice of a god.
- Clanging cymbal (gr: *alalazô kymbalon*): a piece of copper sheeting that was dropped to *simulate* the sound of thunder.

Paul says, "If I do all these things without love, I 'simulate' being a Christian," just as those *hypocrites* (Greek word for actors) simulated being gods. His audience in Corinth

93

understood the conventions of Greek drama. They received very clearly a message that often gets muddled in our modern interpretations of this famous passage.

MB: What is the number one reason why people don't come to church? It is because of the *hypocrites*, those who act like Christians in church but outside display a different morality and character. This was the issue Paul addressed in this portion of his letter to the Corinthian church. Obviously, they had a similar problem. His solution was to display genuine love toward others—all others.

There are significant Jewish cultural symbols that help our understanding of some important parts of the Scripture.

Jesus told His disciples:

"You are the salt of the earth. But what good is salt if it has lost its flavor? Can you make it useful again? It will be thrown out and trampled underfoot as worthless." (Matthew 5:12)

Salt had a special significance to Bible-time people. It was used for flavoring food and for "salting" fish and other meats to prolong their shelf life. If you go into a Bedouin tent today, you will find a bowl with salt (often clumped together with dirt) on the table. You reach with your hand, crumble the salt, and then sprinkle it over your food. When there becomes more dirt in the bowl than salt, the woman of the tent comes over, takes the bowl, and throws the contents out of the tent. Then she brings a fresh clump of salt to the table. Archeologists often identify the street of ancient cities by the salt content of the soil.

Salt has a deeper meaning to Middle Eastern people. In a modern Bedouin marriage ceremony, salt is placed between the hands of the bride and groom as they are pronounced husband and wife. To the

Mikaela collecting salt at the Dead Sea

Bible-time person, as well as the modern Middle Eastern, salt has the significance of loyalty and fidelity.

> "Salt is good for seasoning. But if it loses its flavor, how do you make it salty again? You must have the qualities of salt among yourselves and live in peace with each other." (Mark 9:50)

Jesus was instructing His disciples to be known by their loyalty to their friends and family. This is consistent to other biblical teaching about relationships, gossip, and disunity. Paul instructed the believers in Colossae to:

> Let your speech always be with grace, as though seasoned with salt, so that you will know how you should respond to each person. (Colossians 4:6)

Geography

RS: The form of the land, the climate, roads, trade routes, and vegetation play a big part in understanding the message of the Bible.

- Weather patterns are wet and green in the north and west, brown and dry in south and east. Elijah confronted the priests of Baal on Mt. Carmel, in the wet green corner of the country.
- The prominent geographical features in Israel are a flat coastal plain, a rolling piedmont, a high central ridge, and the deep Jordan Valley riff. Going "up" to Jerusalem means walking uphill. From Jericho to Jerusalem is less than fifteen miles with a 4,000-foot elevation gain.
- Trades routes and the location of tax stations help us understand why Jesus chose to locate His evangelistic headquarters in Capernaum.

Here is one example of an important geographical context:

Now when Jesus came into the district of Caesarea Philippi, He was asking His disciples, "Who do people say that the Son of Man is?" And they said, "Some say John the Baptist; and others, Elijah; but still others, Jeremiah, or one of the prophets." He said to them, "But who do you say that I am?" Simon Peter answered, "You are the Christ, the Son of the living God." And Jesus said to him, "Blessed are you, Simon Barjona, because flesh and blood did not reveal this to you, but My Father who is in heaven. I also say to you that you are Peter, and upon this rock I will build My church; and the gates of Hades will not overpower it." (Matthew 16:13–18)

This was the famous final exam of the disciples. Jesus took them to a Gentile region, away from the religious Jews. Caesarea was the site of temples dedicated to Pan and other gods. Behind the ancient city is a huge rock formation that has carved-out ledges where the statues of the idols stood. Inset in the rock is a huge cave from which flows one of the four tributaries of the Jordan River. This cave was so deep that the locals referred to it as the "gates of hell." Rabbinical writers also referred to Gentile cities as the gates of hell.

This famous statement: *"You are Peter, and upon this rock I will build my church, and the gates of hell will not overpower it,"* has led to many doctrinal controversies. The Roman Catholic Church claims this is where Jesus declared He would build His church on Peter as the head guy. Later, Reformation Protestants declared "the rock" was not Peter but rather the truth Peter had uttered that Jesus was the Messiah.

However, when you stand in the ruins of Caeserea and gaze at this huge rock formation where intense idol worship took place, the meaning seems obvious: *Jesus was going to build His church right on top of this culture of idol worship, and the Church would be such an offensive force that nothing could hold it back.*

What does that do to the often-held conception of the Church as a defensive fortress holding out the influences of the world—a place where we can retreat once a week to get healed and ready for the next onslaught of Satan and the world?

The message: God's Church is to be an awesome offensive force.

Political

The political environment is an important background in the biblical story.

- Herod the Great was a ruthless ruler who was paranoid of anyone who might try to usurp his throne. He slaughtered thousands of his own subjects during his long reign. Josephus records that as Herod neared his death, he ordered all the leading citizens and priests to be jailed at the hippodrome in Jericho and that on news of his death, his soldiers were to kill all these prominent members of Jewish society so that there would be "true mourning" at the time of his death, since he knew that no one would mourn his passing! Fortunately, his children did not carry out this final command.

Lion's Gate
Old City of Jerusalem

- *Pax Romana* (Roman peace) was often cruel and oppressive for the average person. Taxes were heavy, and Jews were always subject to forced labor and confiscation of personal property. In court, they had fewer rights than Roman citizens.

Understanding this political climate helps us discern the meaning of a very familiar event:

On the next day the large crowd who had come to the feast, when they heard that Jesus was coming to Jerusalem, took the branches of the palm trees and went out to meet Him, and began to shout, "Hosanna! BLESSED IS HE WHO COMES IN THE NAME OF THE LORD, even the King of Israel." Jesus, finding a young donkey, sat on it; as it is written, "FEAR NOT, DAUGHTER OF ZION; BEHOLD, YOUR KING IS COMING, SEATED ON A DONKEY'S COLT." (John 12:12–14)

MB: Palm branches? This always mystified me as a young boy trying to visualize what was happening on Palm Sunday in Jerusalem. Was this a sign of worship? Or was it a hot day and this was the first-century version of an umbrella?

The palm branch appears on coins minted during the Jewish revolt against Rome in 66–70 A.D. It appears that the palm was their national symbol—a national flag.

Hosanna? Was this an Aramaic word for "Praise the Lord"? *Hosanna* is a Hebrew phrase that means "save us now!"

What was happening this first Palm Sunday? It was a political demonstration! A crowd of Jews who were tired of the heavy yoke of Roman rule was welcoming their Messiah (who they thought was going to be a political leader) into His capital city, with encouragement to use His divine powers to destroy the Roman legions. They waved the national flag and shouted, "Give us our freedom now!" But Jesus didn't meet their expectations of a political messiah. This explains how a disappointed crowd could call for His execution only a few days later.

Actually, this day was the first day in the Passover week, the most holy Jewish holiday. It was the day pilgrims and locals alike streamed into the city to select their animals for sacrifice on the following Friday. It was the day the Lamb of God chose to present Himself to His people as the ultimate sacrificial offering. They didn't get it, as they expected instead for Jesus to be the conquering king.

Linguistics

Understanding the meaning of the original words of a passage of Scripture may change your application.

> Praise (*Hallal*) the LORD! Praise (*Hallal*) God in his heavenly dwelling; Praise (*Hallal*)
> him in his mighty heaven! (Psalm 150:1)

There are seven Hebrew words used in the Book of Psalms that are translated "praise" in English. In Psalm 150, the word *praise* is actually the word *hallal*, the word we get *hallelujah* from. *Hallal* means to praise the Lord by celebrating, by dancing, by shining forth, by acting clamorously foolish. It is a very robust, liberating kind of praise.

How does this translation affect the way you worship the Lord? For many of us brought up in churches where we were told "quietness is reverence to God" and to talk softly, not get excited, or move too quickly, this gives a new meaning to the word *praise*.

I have "*hallaled*" when my team scores at the football game. There is a lot of that going on at many sporting events and concerts. It seems God wants me to "*hallal*" when I worship Him as well.

Textual

The Scriptures are to be read as a whole, not as disjointed paragraphs or sentences. Here's an example: We could say, "According to Psalm 14, the Bible says there is no God", when the *entire* verse actually says:

"There is no God" (Psalm 14:1)

"The fool has said in his heart, 'There is no God'" (Psalm 14:1).

We often read a portion of the Bible apart from the surrounding chapters and verses and then attempt to make a doctrine out of the portion. This would be like taking one of the many letters that I wrote to Laura from Honduras before we were married, cutting out a paragraph from the middle of the letter, and then defining our relationship on that one paragraph. Letters are written as a whole, with introductory remarks and summary comments. It would be unrealistic to simply read a paragraph somewhere in the middle of our letter and use that to define the relationship.

It would be the same if we recorded a random five-minute conversation between us during the course of the day and used that out-of-context moment to define our relationship—"They are always discussing who is going to change the baby's diaper!" or "They are always hugging and kissing!" The truth is we do both and more!

Sometimes we read a verse or chapter of Scripture and come away with an incorrect impression of what the writer was communicating. We then incorporate this disjointed interpretation of Scripture into our thinking, which results in traditions and church practices that are inconsistent with the whole of Scripture. Denominations and cults are born out of this practice.

One common example of a disjointed interpretation:

"If your brother sins, go and show him his fault in private; if he listens to you, you have won your brother. "But if he does not listen to you, take one or two more with you, so that BY THE MOUTH OF TWO OR THREE WITNESSES EVERY FACT MAY BE CONFIRMED. "If he refuses to listen to them, tell it to the church; and if he refuses to listen even to the church, let him be to you as a Gentile and a tax collector. "Truly I say to you, whatever you bind on earth shall have been bound in heaven; and whatever you loose on earth shall have been loosed in heaven.

"Again I say to you, that if two of you agree on earth about anything that they may ask, it shall be done for them by My Father who is in heaven. "For where two or three have gathered together in My name, I am there in their midst." (Matthew 18:15–20 NAS)

Does verse 20 mean that Jesus is not present unless we are with another believer? This is the meaning often assigned to this passage; that it takes a small group of believers for Jesus to be present. That thought is not consistent with the rest of Scripture.

What is this passage of Scripture referring to? It is about discipline within the church.

RS: Reading this passage in its entirety often gives us a very different interpretation of its meaning. Paul's letters were meant to be read and understood in their entirety. Reading only a portion of one of his letters to a church may give you the wrong impression of the man and his message.

In Luke 15:1–2, the Pharisees complain that Jesus is associating with despicable people (even eating with them). In response to these complaints, Jesus tells them the story of the lost sheep and lost coin, both of which were found. This resulted in great joy by the shepherd and woman at the recovery of something that was lost. Then He tells the story of the lost son (prodigal son).

Reading this parable alone (out of its textual context) would lead one to believe that the point of the story of the prodigal is the great joy that the father has to see his lost son return. Yet verses 25–31 reveal the real message that Jesus was communicating to the complaining Pharisees:

"Meanwhile, the older son was in the fields working. When he returned home, he heard music and dancing in the house, and he asked one of the servants what was going on. 'Your brother is back,' he was told, 'and your father has killed the calf we were fattening and has prepared a great feast. We are celebrating because of his safe return.'

"The older brother was angry and wouldn't go in. His father came out and begged him, but he replied, 'All these years I've worked hard for you and never once refused to do a single thing you told me to. And in all that time you never gave me even one young goat for a feast with my friends. Yet when this son of yours comes back after squandering your money on prostitutes, you celebrate by killing the finest calf we have.'

"His father said to him, 'Look, dear son, you and I are very close, and everything I have is yours.

'We had to celebrate this happy day. For your brother was dead and has come back to life! He was lost, but now he is found!'" (Luke 15:25–31)

The parable of the prodigal son is really about the hard-hearted attitude of his older brother. Where he should have felt joy that his brother returned, he felt anger. In the same way, the Pharisees should rejoice that those who were far from God (prostitutes, drunks, tax collectors) were now coming back into relationship. This is the obvious message of Jesus that becomes apparent when we read the entire portion of Scripture.
Remember the challenge:

1. understand the Bible in its context;
2. incorporate biblical truth to my life;
3. teach biblical truth to others.

MB: Many modern Christians focus their reading and study on the New Testament, but it is hard for me to appreciate what God was doing then, unless I understand what He did in the pages of the Old Testament.

RS: Not only that, the writers assume you know the backdrop of the Old Testament to fully understand what they are describing in the pages of the New Testament.
When you read Acts 2:1–42, the birth of the Church, it says, "and when the day of Pentecost had fully come, they were all in one accord and in one place." The story is the sound of a mighty rushing wind, tongues of fire on their heads, and they begin to speak in known and unknown dialects, and people around them begin to accuse them of being drunk. Peter says that it's early in the day, and they are not drunk, but that this is what was spoken by the prophet Joel about an incredible move of God, and he begins to speak a message.
At the end of this message, 3,000 people are broken in their hearts and ask, "What shall we do?" And Peter replies "Repent, and be baptized for the remission of your sins." That day 3,000 people are baptized added to the Church.
The writer tells this wonderful story about what happened in Jerusalem that day, but he expects you to understand verse 1: "When the day of Pentecost had fully come . . ."

WHAT WAS PENTECOST?
The first Pentecost took place in the wilderness with Moses and the ex-slaves from Egypt at Mt. Sinai. Moses brought the people out of Egypt, and Exodus 19 tells us that

they arrived at the Mountain of the Law, fifty days after Passover. Moses goes up to the top of the mountain to meet with God, and he is there for forty days. There is incredibly strange weather, fire, and thunder. Moses comes down the mountain with the Law, and what does he see the people doing? Are they waiting patiently for him saying, "Oh, that we would hear from our God?" No! They are having a party—a wild sexual party. Moses tells the Levites to strap on their swords and go out to kill all who are involved in this party. That day 3,000 people died.

When Luke writes this in Acts 2, he assumes that you understand the common elements with the first Pentecost story—wind, weather, all in one accord, fire, 3,000 people—so that you will understand the second story. The point is very simple: *With the going up on Sinai and the coming of the Law came knowledge of my sinfulness and death.*

Michael and Mikaela with Fred the camel

But the coming of the Spirit brought a new revelation of God to write the Law within my heart and it brought life everlasting. And Luke thought the point was so obvious, assuming you understood the significance of Pentecost.

MB: Jesus' conversation with Nicodemus in John 3:1–18 has a similar quality. Here is this learned teacher of the Jews coming to speak to Jesus at night. Jesus tells him he must be *"born again."* Nicodemus is confused, and asks if he must crawl inside his mother's womb again. Jesus says, "No, I am talking about spiritual things—a spiritual birth."

Then Jesus, as all good teachers do, brings the student (Nicodemus) to a point of reference—of understanding. This point that Jesus refers to was, to me when I first read it, one of the most bizarre scenes in the Bible—Numbers, chapter 21.

It was the time when Moses was leading the people through the desert, and they were grumbling about their food, about water, about almost everything. Finally, they spoke out against Moses' leadership, saying "Why have you brought us into this desert to die?"

At this point, God has had it and sends venomous snakes into the camp. People get bitten and die. The people realize their sin and ask Moses for forgiveness and God for help. God says OK and tells Moses to make a snake out of bronze and attach it to a pole for all to see so that anyone who looks at the snakes will be healed of the snakebite. When I read that as a young Christian, I asked myself, "What is going on here?" It appeared as if some ritual cultic activity was happening that does not fit in with the rest of the Bible.

But Jesus brings it all together for me and Nicodemus when He says, "Just as Moses lifted up the serpent in the desert (John assumes we know Nicodemus knows that as those stricken people looked at the serpent the fatal poison injected by the snake into their body was removed)—I, the Son of Man, will be lifted up," implying that anybody who looks upon Jesus with faith will have that poison called sin removed from their body and they will have eternal life."

How can we appreciate Jesus on the cross unless we understand this picture that God gave His people over a thousand years before in the desert?

When I read the Gospels, I look back at what happened in the Old Testament to have a full appreciation and understanding of what is actually being communicated; *otherwise, I might get lost, I might not catch the full flavor or have the greatest appreciation God wants me to have, or I might even get off on some weird doctrine*, which happens all the time to those who don't understand the historical and cultural context of the Scripture passage.

Mikaela: What does it mean when you say "Old" and "New" Testament? Why even bother reading something old?

MB: The first reference to the Hebrew Scriptures as the "Old" Testament comes from an un-named Egyptian writer in a second-century document. Remember that in the church in Alexandria there was a movement to allegorize the stories in the Hebrew Scriptures and to marginalize the Hebrew cultural influences. Many Greek Christians tried to distance themselves from Hebrew culture, and like Marcion, minimize any Hebrew influence over Christianity.

RS: The name "Old Testament" is actually a misnomer. I usually refer them as the "Hebrew Scriptures," because when you say "old," you suggest that it is something out-of-date. The term "Old Testament" is misderived from that passage in Hebrews 8, which says:

When God speaks of a new covenant, it means he has made the first one obsolete. It is now out of date and ready to be put aside. (Hebrews 8:13)

If you look at the context of this passage, the author is talking about Levitical sacrifices versus the sacrifice that is Jesus. The Levitical sacrificial system was obsolete and out-of-date—the Romans even removed the place of sacrifice in 70 A.D.!

In my view, both testaments are new and alive, sharper than any two-edged sword, and are busy in my life. Whether Abraham is being directed to do something or Paul is writing to Timothy; to me, my understanding is that there is one Author of all this and that is the Spirit of God, a God who desires to draw me to Himself. And He does that in different ways in different places in the Scriptures. Understanding that helps pull it all together in a cohesive manner. So I don't use the term "old" and "new" in regard to the Scriptures. Instead I refer to the two major portions of Scripture as "Hebrew Scriptures" and "Christian Scriptures."

MB: Are there differences between the Hebrew Scriptures and the Christian Scriptures? What about the character of God? Did He really change? Some think that the God of the Hebrew Scriptures is a harsh, strict character, demanding obedience and ready to smash us when we step out of line. The God of the Christian Scriptures is seen as one of grace who says "call me Daddy" and invites us to jump in His lap. However, Psalm 103 (in the Hebrew Scriptures) declares:

He forgives all my sins and heals all my diseases. He ransoms me from death and surrounds me with love and tender mercies. He fills my life with good things. My youth is renewed like the eagle's. (Psalm 103:3–5)

It is obvious that many Old Testament people viewed God as merciful, loving, and the Giver of all good things.

For the LORD God is our light and protector. He gives us grace and glory. No good thing will the LORD withhold from those who do what is right. O LORD Almighty, happy are those who trust in you. (Psalm 84:11–12)

Regarding the perception that the God of the Old Testament is one that demands obedience, it is the "God of the Christian Scriptures" (Jesus) who declares:

"If you love Me, you will keep My commandments." (John 14:15)

Notice the order: "If you have a relationship of love with Me, where you trust Me for everything and know I have your best interests at the center of My heart and that I will do anything for you, even die for you, then obey the things I tell you to do." It's not: "Obey Me and I will love you more."

In regard to salvation, how was a person in the Hebrew Scriptures saved? Many thought it was strict observance of the Law. Yet David declares:

You take no delight in sacrifices or offerings. Now that you have made me listen, I finally understand—you don't require burnt offerings or sin offerings.

Then I said, "Look, I have come. And this has been written about me in your scroll: I take joy in doing your will, my God, for your law is written on my heart." (Psalm 40:6–8)

David knew it was all about a heart surrendered to God and not about sacrifices and offerings.

Some believe that "salvation by faith" is a Christian Scripture doctrine, yet the Hebrew Scriptures state plainly:

And Abram believed the Lord, and the Lord declared him righteous because of his faith. (Genesis 15:6)

A close examination of the Hebrew Scriptures and the Christian Scriptures reveals a consistency in important areas like worship, importance of the Word, the relationship between mankind and God, and between each other. That's because it is the living, unchanging God who is the Author of both. Paul told Timothy:

All Scripture is inspired by God and profitable for teaching, for reproof, for correction, for training in righteousness; so that the man of God may be adequate, equipped for every good work. (2 Timothy 3:16–17 NAS)

It's important to note at this point in history, only the Hebrew Scriptures (Old Testament) were the considered "Scripture." Of course, that was changing, but the point was well made to Timothy and to us: The Hebrew Scriptures "are" (not "were") important in defining and directing our spiritual lives.

RS: I think the beauty of the Scriptures is not only that they really show God's long track record of working with people but also that they reflect His heart for them, and the Scriptures show "real" people just like you and me. We always talk about Peter and give him a hard time because everything in Peter's life is in threes—he gets three calls: "Feed My sheep" (John 21); and three times, "Arise, kill, and eat" (Acts 10). Peter is the cranially-challenged disciple, but the thing is, this guy is so much like me, I can't believe it! Like the early apostles, I have to be moved by God's work. The models God gave us in Scripture are "real people" that have His heart. I am pleased God closed out the Scriptures with snapshots of leaders caring for their communities.

MB: I see a thorough revelation of God through these pages of the Bible—through the Hebrew and Christian Scriptures. I have descriptions, the Law, interactions, and prophetic messages in the Hebrew Scriptures, but I can still miss it. Suddenly, I have God Himself showing up in the flesh in the pages of the Christian Scriptures (just in case I did miss it). It is the ultimate contextualization. I don't have to wonder about God and what He said. He showed up in a specific location on my planet, dressed in the mind, body, and emotions of my own species; and He spoke very clearly and precisely in a way I can understand! It's not like in the "olden days" when one would have to go to the desert for forty days, fasting to hear from God. No! In the Gospels, He's standing on the steps of the temple speaking to everybody!

RS: It's like what the writer of Hebrews said:

Long ago God spoke many times and in many ways to our ancestors through the prophets. But now in these final days, he has spoken to us through his Son. (Hebrews 1:1)

In essence, He said: "I am going to put on skin and come down there Myself and tell exactly what it is I meant by what I said. You heard Me, but you didn't catch My heart. And I am not interested in the outward appearance of cutting the lamb's throat with the knife in a certain way and putting the blood in the proper place. I am interested in that, but to Me it is a means to an end. The end is that you understand My heart and walk with Me."

Many theologians, rabbis, and Bible scholars look at the technical details of the Law, the Gospels, Paul's letters, and the histories; and they get so focused on those details that they never step back to see God's heart. *The Bible is the presentation of God's heart.*

MB: God's heart is simple: "Hey, you guys, I want you to be members of My family. I want to have relationship with you. I want our relationship to be so tight. I am a loving heavenly Father that can give you all good things, and I want to do this! Please step forward and take My hand." You see this over and over again, and *it's only understanding this* that allows the minute details to have significance.

RS: I am always impressed with pastors, teachers, and fellowship leaders who are able to communicate past the details and into the heart of God. People don't come to our meetings to hear a great message—they come to meet the Living God. And short of meeting Him, they haven't done what they came for. People come looking for the hot coal that comes right out of the throne room of God to touch their lips, cleanse them, and give them a sense of direction.

I'm not advocating eliminating the detail, but I think we all have to get past just knowing where the furniture in the tabernacle sat. That is not whole issue. The issue is *"What is the heart of God for people?"*

In the end, one could read the Hebrew Scriptures and conclude that it's all about doing the right thing. But it's clear that it's not only about doing the right thing—*it's about doing the right thing with the right heart and walking with God.*

That is what is has always been about. Abraham knew that. So did Moses. So did Paul.

MB: The Bible is all about God going to work in your heart. He is doing a work in my heart, and everybody who picks up the Bible to read it gets at least sixty-six different points of view of God going to work in his or her heart. If you can't relate to one view, then there are sixty-five others.

We close this session with some thoughts from Laura.

To Know Him Is to Love Him

Reflect upon any relationship that you value. . . . think about the ways that you got close to that person.

We learn a lot about someone by knowing their history, the things that they like and dislike, and mainly just by spending time with them. Learning what they think—how they think or behave—makes a big difference in our knowledge of them and how we will respond.

The Hebrew Scriptures depict our God in such grandeur and detail. We cannot adequately understand His ways or His character until we understand Him via the Hebrew Scriptures. We cannot be altogether ready to receive His greatness or person until a full view is acquired.

The Jesus we know in the Christian Scriptures becomes One we can truly embrace with complete appreciation when we see Him in light of all that went before Him in history—a history that is revealed in the Hebrew Scriptures.

He has written words to touch the very core of our being and is inviting us to be a part of Him, His plans, and His purposes for our lives.

An incredible continuity exists within our inspired book, from the beginning to the end. To understand the Book of Hebrews, you must first know the Book of Leviticus. To receive from the Book of Revelation requires a knowledge of the words of Daniel. To truly catch the significance of Jesus on the cross, it is important to know why God commanded Moses to place a serpent on a pole. We must grasp the beginnings before we can comprehend and savor that which is to come.

God gave His people a portrait of Himself in the pages of the Hebrew Scriptures, in a cultural language that they could understand. He then made His appearance in the pages of the Christian Scriptures, giving visual and physical confirmation of what was previously said. God reveals Himself to us specifically and lovingly as we seek Him in Scriptures. His Holy Spirit brings revelation to us individually in ways that He knows we will understand, appreciate, and put into practice.

God desires relationship with His people. He has written to all of us and is inviting you to step into a special intimate place with Him.

Laura with octopus on the Greek isle of Paros

Let us strive to know our God and Father in His entirety.

Personal Reflections

1. What modern interpretations of passages of Scripture do you have that might seem strange to the first-century Church?
2. What traditions do you hold dear that might not have any significance in your culture?
3. How would you advise a new believer to study the Bible?
4. Which "heart issues" is God currently working on with you?
5. What principle in God's Word did you recently discover?

Deep Water

A. In Matthew 5:17, Jesus said that He came to "fulfill" the Law. In the original text, this word is *pleroo*. Often we translate this word as "to complete." According to the Dictionary of Biblical Languages with Semitic Domains, in this usage in Matthew 5, *pleroo* means "to give true meaning." This word was also used in ancient literature in a sense of a doctor putting a broken bone back in place. With this understanding of *pleroo*, now read the rest of chapter 5. The religious authorities had obviously taken God's Law out of the context that He demands. Jesus simply goes through an exercise of putting it back in its place and giving the Law its true meaning.

B. In 1 Corinthians 8, Paul addresses the question, "Should we eat meat sacrificed to idols?" In the next two chapters, Paul gives his answer and many principles of cross cultural ministry. How did Paul present the Gospel to different people groups and cultures? Read chapters 8, 9, and 10 for the answers. Remember, James, Paul, Peter and the other Jewish Christians believed that the Law was a good thing.

Ancient civilizations were known by their worship of many gods—polytheism. These "gods" were often personifications of natural forces (wind, fire, rain, fertility, etc.), as well as actual evil spirits. Out of the desert of the Fertile Crescent in the Second Millennium B.C. emerged the worship of the one true God of heaven through a group of "*Hapiru*"—the dusty ones. These descendents of Abraham changed human thinking and history through their monotheism. We know the one true God in the pages of the Bible as three divine personalities.

Divine Personalities

Mikaela: By the sound of the title, this session might include Mommy.

MB: You are close. Laura is divine in many senses, but now we will focus on the truly divine personalities—the Trinity: the Father, the Son, and the Holy Spirit.

> Hear O Israel, the Lord our God is one. (Deuteronomy 6:4)

In every synagogue around the world, these words are spoken on every Sabbath. Yet we as Christian believers see God not as *one* but as *three*. How can we resolve these two concepts? How can we proclaim that God is one, yet refer to God as the Father, Son, and Holy Spirit?

RS: Most Christians are not aware that both Muslims and Jews consider us polytheistic (believing in more than one

Lukas, Michael and Mikaela at the Western Wall Jerusalem

111

God). We are the only people who believe we are monotheistic. One of the reasons is that we cannot easily explain how "three is one." Scripture does give us background that is helpful and right within the words I just quoted for you, "Hear O Israel, the Lord our God is one," is a clue.

That term "one" is the Hebrew word *echad* (one) and is used in a number of scriptures to mean "one in essence" but not necessarily one in the cement or concrete character. For instance, when the Bible says the "two shall become one," *one* is *echad*. In the wedding and the bonding of the marriage, there is a sense in which we become one, but there is also a sense of still being two distinct individuals. My wife would not consider herself the Randy/Dottie person. She still has a mind of her own, and I still have a mind of my own, and occasionally, they need to be settled. We are one in essence, one in direction, one in spirit. We are one in purpose. In this sense, God is one. He has one purpose, one heart, one mind, one will, and one desire. There is no place in the Scripture you could argue that the Son would have a different desire than the Father or that the Spirit would have a different desire than the Father. There are, however, functions of each part of this "godhead," as we call it, that are different.

If you go all the way back to the beginning, you have a very ancient story of Adam walking in the Garden and standing behind him is God. Now at that time, somebody is running the universe. Somebody is making the planets do what they do. Somebody has got the whole thing under control. So you have a problem. Does God put on human skin in the text of Hebrew Scripture? Yes. Does He walk on the earth as a body? Yes! Is He a body? No. The Scripture clearly says He is a spirit. John 4:23 says, "Those who must worship Him must worship Him in spirit and in truth" because God is not a physical person. He is able to do many things. He is able to appear in many ways. Ultimately, we have to come back to the function of who He is.

MB: My understanding of the Trinity boils down to *function*. We see different manifestations depending on the function. Genesis 1:1 states: "In the beginning God created the heaven and the earth," and then in the next verse, we see the Spirit of God hovering over the earth. Was that somebody different? No, it was not, but it was a different manifestation of God—a different function. In Genesis 1:26, God said, "Let Us make man in Our image, according to Our likeness." It is very interesting that He used the plural (*us*)—"in our image."

RS: God uses that plural *us* in Genesis 11:7 at the tower of Babel: "Come, let Us go down there and confuse their language, so that they will not understand one another's speech." There are many who argue God used plurals of majesty. It's like the old Queen's English when she is constantly referring to "we" for "us" but really means "I" and "me."

The bottom line is that functions God performs in our lives and what He does in the universe are in some senses distinct.

You just quoted from Genesis 1 that "In the beginning God created." Yet Colossians 1 says the Son was actually the agent of creation. Now is that necessary for me to know—that it is this One and not that One? No, because in essence both are still God.

Many Christians make a mistake in the way they talk. They say the Spirit that hovered over the water is not God. God is the One that created. They are both God. It is one God we are talking about. We talk about Him in different forms according to the way He performs His acts with men. So, you see this model of a loving Father, an obedient Son, and a helpful Spirit. This model is to help you. I suspect it is not a diagram of God.

Let me explain it this way: When my daughter was about four, she asked "Dad, does turning the light switch on make the light go on?" I knew that electrons running across a resistor in a vacuum made the light come on. But I said, "Yes." I was not lying to her, and I was helping her understand in a language she could relate to. If there is a gap between a thirty-some-year-old man and a four-year-old daughter, what is the gap between the eternal God of ages and me?

MB: Exactly. I think when we look at God, using the word *Trinity*, we describe a concept in which we are like a four year old trying to understand the light switch and how that light comes on by the simple act of flipping the switch. We use the word Trinity to describe God in terms we can understand. Jesus spoke of the Father often, made many references to Himself as the Son, and told his disciples about the coming of the Holy Spirit. Finally, He commanded us to "Baptize them in the name of the Father, the Son, and the Holy Spirit." (Matthew 28:19)

We see that when Jesus began His ministry He was baptized by John, and the heavens opened. We see a dove—the Holy Spirit—descending upon Him and a voice from heaven speaking. Here we see the three functional personalities of God all at the same time.

RS: There was never a moment in that entire act that these three were not in harmony, one in essence or in desire and in purpose. I can't say for sure there are not four more things out there that are parts of the manifestation of God. I can only say He didn't express that to us. He expressed Himself in three persons. I am limited to the wonder of God as it is expressed in Scriptures to me. As the Holy Spirit guides me in understanding the Scriptures, I know this is what I am limited to. It is so big and so much information; I don't really feel a limitation here. It may seem hard to grasp, but I think it's in God's character—He is not somebody we can figure out!

Maybe it will be helpful to take a close look and dissect, so to speak, each of the personalities.

Arielle: I'm still a little confused.

MB: Let me see if I can help. Think of a cube. It has six sides. If you look at it from one side, it looks like a square. If you look at it from the front, it looks like a rectangle. If you look at it from the top, it looks like another, slightly different rectangle. Yet it is still a box, or cube. Your point of view determines what you see.

God presents Himself in three different forms—the Trinity. They are all three parts of the same, and each has His own distinct "personality."

Another way to understand the Trinity is to look at water. It is a liquid that flows from the tap; it is ice cubes in the freezer; and it is steam rising from a teapot. It is all H_2O, but one form is liquid, one is solid, and one the other is gas. These are "form" descriptions.

Peter gives us a functional view of the Trinity when he writes to those persecuted first-century believers:

God the Father chose you long ago, and the Spirit has made you holy. As a result, you have obeyed Jesus Christ and are cleansed by his blood. (1 Peter 1:2)

Peter understood it was the Father who chose you, the Son who saved you, and the Spirit who empowers you to live a life of obedience to God. Having heard the voice of the Father, walked with the Son, and been empowered by the Spirit, Peter naturally shared this unique experience and functional understanding of God with those who were challenged to understand God's role in their lives.

I think Laura has a perspective here that will really help.

114

PERFECT RELATIONSHIPS

And one of them, a lawyer, asked Him a question, testing Him, "Teacher, which is the great commandment in the Law?"

And He said to him,   "'YOU SHALL LOVE THE LORD YOUR GOD WITH ALL YOUR HEART, AND WITH ALL YOUR SOUL, AND WITH ALL YOUR MIND.'

"This is the great and foremost commandment.

"The second is like it, 'YOU SHALL LOVE YOUR NEIGHBOR AS YOURSELF.'

"On these two commandments depend the whole Law and the Prophets." (Matthew 22:35–40)

As big and complicated as life can be, there is only one thing that will last for eternity: *relationships*.

- *the relationship between God and man*
- *the relationships between God's people.*

It's amazing for us to realize that all Ten Commandments God gave in the Old Testament direct relationships: the first four deal with our relationship to God and the last six with our relationship to those around us. The value our God places on relationship was enough to die for. There is not enough emphasis we can place on the gift of relating. He gave us His most valued possession when He gave His only begotten Son for the redemption of our souls—the

Laura and Moselle at Capernaum

redemption of a relationship cut off from His heart. God went the whole length to gain that relationship back as He first intended it.

He longs to touch us. He longs for us to know Him in all of His vastness—not merely to know about Him, but to know Him intimately and significantly, so much that His life would be totally integrated within ours. He longs to be a living entity through us. That we would not only act like Him, but we would *be* and live out His divine personality. This is His eternal call. A call that will live on into forever.

Our relationship with the divine personalities so frequently exhibits itself in our lives with others. Thus, the second greatest commandment: "You shall love your neighbor as yourself."

"Beloved, let us love one another, for love is from God; and everyone who loves is born of God and knows God. The one who does not love does not know God, for God is love." (1 John 4:7–8)

"Beloved, if God so loved us, we also ought to love one another. No one has beheld God at any time; if we love one another, God abides in us, and His love is perfected in us." (1 John 4:12–13)

In our abiding in and submitting to God, we find ourselves more and more involved in His eternal purposes. We find ourselves in fuller relationship with Him and others. One cannot exist without the other—loving God and loving others.

In the three parts of the divine personality, we are given the models for all our relationships.

- A *Father* who loves you and wants to give every good thing to you and can;
- a *Friend* who will do anything, even to the point of dying for you;
- a *Helper* who will guide you through every step of life, giving you wisdom, love, joy, and peace along the way.

As we investigate the various aspects of the personalities of the Trinity, may you receive the guidance and the power to model all your relationships accordingly.

And may the Lord your God, by the relationship established through His Son and by the power of His Spirit, grant to you a renewed love for Him and for all those He brings into your path.

MB: Many years ago I was at a New Age spring retreat on Maui. I was invited there to speak about the crucifixion of Jesus. There was a table with pictures of gurus, Hindu gods, and Jesus, along with flowers, burning incense, and pakalolo. That weekend I heard many "speculations" about who God was and what He was really like. As I asked various people about the source of their information, most referred to a revelation that a guru received while in meditation or a book someone had written.

We all have our opinions of who God is and what He wants from us. On a subject this weighty, it is good that we actually have God's Word to turn to, which cuts through all the subjective "feelings."

Let's see what the Bible has to say about God the Father.

1.   God was there in the beginning. He is the only uncreated being.

     In the beginning, God created the Heavens and Earth. (Genesis 1:1 NAS)

2.   According to the Bible, God is
     *   unique:

         I am God, and there is no other; I am God, and there is no one like Me. (Isaiah 46:9 NAS)

     *   eternal:

         But the Lord abides forever. . . . (Psalm 9:7 NAS)

     *   trustworthy:

         God is not a man, that He should lie. (Numbers 23:19 NAS)

     *   righteous and just:

         Your throne is founded on two strong pillars—righteousness and justice. Unfailing love and truth walk before you as attendants. (Psalm 89:14)

- emotional:

> For the Lord your God is a consuming fire, a jealous God. (Deuteronomy 4:24 NAS)

3. If there is one characteristic that sums up God, it is love.

> The one who does not love does not know God, for God is love. (1 John 4:8 NAS)

4. God is all-powerful, or omnipotent.

> "Behold, I am the LORD, the God of all flesh; is anything too difficult for Me?" (Jeremiah 32:27)

5. He is also all-knowing, or omniscient.

> For God is greater than our heart, and knows all things. (1 John 3:20 NAS)·

6. And He is present everywhere, or omnipresent.

> "But will God indeed dwell on the earth? Behold, heaven and the highest heaven cannot contain Thee." (1 Kings 8:27 NAS)

God is all-knowing, all-powerful, and every where (but not "every thing"). Isn't it nice to know the most powerful individual in the universe is not off in some far corner of the galaxy ignoring us? Isn't it comforting to know that He is deeply concerned about us and His foremost characteristic is love?

We can look at this and ask ourselves, "What do I do with that? It's a good description, but what does it mean for me?" Let's look at a passage from Isaiah. The prophet says: "I've told you what God is like, but this is what He does for you." And in chapter 40, he says that "God gives strength to the weary." Is this important to me?

Have you never heard or understood? Don't you know that the LORD is the everlasting God, the Creator of all the earth? He never grows faint or weary. No one can measure the depths of his understanding. He gives power to those who are tired and worn out; he offers strength to the weak. Even youths will become exhausted, and young men will give up. But those who wait on the LORD will find new strength. They will fly high on wings like eagles. They will run and not grow weary. They will walk and not faint. (Isaiah 40:28–31)

Then I turned to a passage in Psalm 103, which is a great description of the things that God does for me. This has great significance!

Bless the Lord, O my soul, And forget none of His benefits; Who pardons all your iniquities; Who heals all your diseases; Who redeems your life from the pit; Who crowns you with lovingkindness and compassion; Who satisfies your years with good things, So that your youth is renewed like the eagle. . . . The Lord is compassionate and gracious, Slow to anger and abounding in lovingkindness. He will not always strive with us; Nor will He keep His anger forever. He has not dealt with us according to our sins, Nor rewarded us according to our iniquities. For as high as the heavens are above the earth, So great is His lovingkindness toward those who fear Him. As far as the east is from the west, So far has He removed our transgressions from us. (Psalm 103:2–5, 8–12 NAS)

I see in this passage that He pardons me. I need forgiveness in my life. He heals me. There are diseases and brokenness within that don't respond to anything except His touch.

He takes my life and redeems me. As a young boy living in North Carolina, I used to look for Coke bottles that had been tossed out of cars along the highway and take them down to the "filling station" and "redeem" them for a Moon Pie and RC Cola. Trash along the highway suddenly became something delicious and refreshing! He does that with the trash of my life, redeems me and turns my life into something of great value.

Psalm 103 goes on to say: "He crowns me with loving kindness and compassion." I like that phrase "crowns me." This is where God goes beyond the basics and actually lays some stuff on me far beyond the call. He crowns me; He renews my youth. I started having children when I was thirty-nine. I need my youthfulness to keep up with four young ones! He satisfies me with good things. If there is anything every man and woman wants in their lives, it is satisfaction in the things we do. In living our lives, we want to be able to sit back, draw in a deep breath, and say "Yes! Very nice, thank you."

RS: It is almost as if people have more now and are satisfied less in the world in which we live. When we apply the satisfaction of the Lord to our lives, we touch a

Laura and Lukas aboard Sharif with Mikaela leading in the Negev Desert

nerve—it's something everyone in our culture and everyone in our world is looking for today.

MB: We recently took the kids and spent a few days in the Negev Desert, learning about Bedouin culture. One of the stories our guide told us was about a young boy whose father died and left him an inheritance. His last words to his son were the hope that his son would always drink the sweetest water, eat the most delicious food, and sleep on the softest bed. Immediately, the son went to Cairo and spent his money, staying at the best hotels, eating the finest food, and drinking all the world had to offer. After months of riotous living, he ran out of money and returned home to the desert. He asked his uncle for a job working with his herds of sheep and goats. After a week of wandering with the flocks, he was tired, dusty, and worn out. He returned home, had cool water from the oasis spring, hot food from his aunt's kitchen, and slept on a mat inside his uncle's tent. It was then that he realized where the sweetest water, the most delicious food, and the softest bed were found—at the end of a demanding day's work.

The moral of this story for the Bedouin is that satisfaction is found living life at the "basics." For a believer, our satisfaction in life is very basic and has only one source:

God Himself and doing the things He has planned for you, even if it means having less creature comforts.

There is a photo in the book *Just Another Lump of Clay* that tells this story. It was in 1987 in Honduras when the war was cooling down. The photo was taken after a long walk on a very muddy trail from Turalaya to Utlamatha. This is the swamp between the Kruta River and the Coco River, and we often made this hike to get to this section of our school district. Sometimes the mud was at mid-thigh and the water at chest level. This particular day was very wet, and by the time I reached the bank of the Rio Coco, I was totally sopped, cold, and exhausted. It was then that my friend Trano's wife brought me a bowl of hot, steaming rice. When I felt the warmth of that bowl, I knew this was going to be one of, if not the most, delicious bowl of rice I would ever eat. Someone walked by and took a photo. It shows me sitting on the Honduran bank of the Rio Coco, with Nicaragua in the background, with a bowl of plain white rice in my hand, and feeling like I had never tasted anything more delicious!

The point is that God is a God who satisfies! We who live in the first world rarely get to the point of realizing that because we try to satisfy our lives by filling it with fast cars, nice restaurants, fashion, vacations to exotic places, skydiving, bungee jumping, and other adventures. When it comes down to it, it is only when we sit in the presence of the Lord and experience Him that we get a truly satisfied "breathe in and breathe out—Yes!" feeling. And that can happen anywhere God has called you to be, whether in a church in America or on a bank of the Rio Coco. I have had many years of primitive life there in Miskitia, a place devoid of creature comforts, yet because God has called me there, life has been immensely satisfying.

RS: I think the beginning of understanding the satisfaction that comes from God is time when you come to a critical point in your life and when you are really stuck. There is an interesting passage in Exodus 33 and 34 where Moses found himself so frustrated. He was just beside himself with the children of Israel. Now that was not an easy job. He was an older individual who was called to do this often-overwhelming job. All the time, God's encouragement to him when he said, "I can't do this" was always, "My presence will go with you. I know you by name." God was trying to encourage him, and finally you just see Moses pulling out his hair saying, "God show me who you are."

The satisfaction comes when we have a glimpse of who God is.

Moses was saying he could not do the task if God was not going to show Himself to him. Moses needed to know he and God were going to walk through this thing together and that God would give him the right equipment to deal with his situation. He felt he could not deal with it all in any other way. At the end of the passage in Exodus 33:21–23, God says:

"You cannot see My face, for no man can see Me and live!" Then the LORD said, "Behold, there is a place by Me, and you shall stand there on the rock; and it will come about, while My glory is passing by, that I will put you in the cleft of the rock and cover you with My hand until I have passed by. "Then I will take My hand away and you shall see My back, but My face shall not be seen."

This is a most interesting passage because God says, "I want to tell you who I am." Not only does He put His hand above the rock and walk by, but also He walks by with a loud recitation—the word in Hebrew is *koral*—meaning to shout with a loud recitation. *This is God shouting who God is. This is better than any theology book.*

The Lord passed by and said "I am the I am." God's name presents a question: I am what? That is what we find out in the rest of the book. You are supposed to read it and find out who He is. God goes on to say in chapter 34 verse 6–8:

"I am the LORD, the merciful and gracious God. I am slow to anger and rich in unfailing love and faithfulness. ⁷I show this unfailing love to many thousands by forgiving every kind of sin and rebellion."

In the literal Hebrew, God is essentially saying: "I am the strong and mighty one, I am the tender and compassionate one. I am the open giver who pities you. I am filled up with goodness. I am the absolute sure rock in your life. I am the one that guards my faithful loved ones. I am the one that lifts the guilt off of my children."

He passes all this information on to Moses, and Moses falls down and bites the dust. He gets into the dirt. The text says he bowed himself into the dust. What a fabulous passage!

Satisfaction can come to me when I understand who my God is, and I am struck with the presence of God. When I begin to see him, then I begin to understand why I don't need another thing in my life to be satisfied.

MB: I believe this is the whole point God wants to give to us: that entering into His presence is really all we need. The other stuff is just the "fluff," peripheral things. In the material world, we get so focused on other things to satisfy us that we forget the main point. It is good to retreat to a remote place where you get away from the phone, television, and many creature comforts. Spending a few days in the Negev Desert in Israel is one way to do this. The refugee village in Honduras where we lived for many years had no electricity, no running water, and was isolated from the outside world. No vehicles meant that you heard nature sounds in full volume—birds, bugs, monkeys, and people. In this environment, I learned that it was the simple things that bring satisfaction.

The portrait of God we see in the pages of Scripture is as our Father. Unfortunately, many have not had an earthly father who gave them the love and care they needed. Often it was quite the opposite! This "earthly experience" sometimes holds them back when it comes to having a relationship with our heavenly Father. If we could just understand how much our Creator loves us, we would run to have relationship with Him. The Hebrew word heard on the playgrounds here in Israel is *abba*—literally meaning, "daddy." God is a "daddy." He is not a theoretical theological person. He is a daddy who wants to give us every good thing and can. One of my favorite pictures of God is in Psalm 84:11 where the writer says, "No good things will He withhold from those who follow Him." If we can latch onto this concept, we will not go anywhere else.

RS: It is not only that He can, I think the big test in the life of a believer today is to not doubt the goodness of God. I can't underscore this strongly enough. Believers need to remind themselves daily that God not only *can*, but He also *desires* to do in my life that which will bring the most glory to Him. That should bring a deep sense of satisfaction. When something happens in my life that I interpret to be bad because it's either not what I want or it does not make things easier or less noisy and predictable, immediately I shake my fist at heaven and say, "God what are you doing? You've abandoned me."

Ultimately, God only does that which will bring most honor and glory to Him, and I can find rest in that. Whether I open my bank statement and am happy or stand at a funeral where I am obviously in

Randy making a point in Jerusalem

pain, in both of those moments I know what God's agenda is. If I can get myself there, I can remind myself that God is a good God who cares intimately about what matters to me. He's not sitting up there as a cosmic killjoy just looking for someone who is having fun so He can zap him. It's not about Him taking pleasure in my pain. It's about Him desiring me to be content. The Scriptures say, "If I delight myself in the Lord, He will give me the desires of my heart" (Psalm 37:4) I believe there is a problem with the way that many interpret this passage. I don't think it says, "If I love Him, I'll get what I want." Rather, I think it says, "If I love Him, I'll want what He wants, and then we will both get it together." It all has to do with just bringing myself in line with where He is. That's where I think you can actually capture the satisfaction that comes from getting the goodness of God in your life.

MB: If you can look back after a day or days, and realize that God's purposes were accomplished, this is what brings us satisfaction and a peace in our lives that surpasses all understanding. The world looks at us and asks, "Why are you so content? Why are you so joyous?" Joy is not an emotional expression of "ha-ha-ha" but rather knowing that God is there and He cares.

RS: I define joy in my own mind as the resolute assurance that God has neither lost interest nor power. He has the power to deal with my needs, and He has an intimate interest in every aspect of my life. He is not, as 1 Peter says, "slack concerning his promises, but is patient" (2 Peter 3:9). God knows how to wait. My problem is that I live in an instant world and don't know how to wait. I want everything now. If God is not coming to my defense in a situation, it is because He has a strategy. And it's only people who act in confidence toward God who can relax and rest in a Father who oversees them as a child and says: "I will not allow that bully to pick on you without recrimination. But I'm going to wait until he gets a long enough rope, and then he is going to tie himself up with it."

I think often of a story Pastor Joe Stowell of the Moody Bible Institute tells about the time that he took his son to swimming lessons at the YMCA. They had just moved to the Chicago area, and since there was so much water around, Joe felt it was essential his son learn to swim.

It was the first lesson, and, wisely, the YMCA required all the parents to stand behind a glass wall in a separate room as the session began. It was then that a burly instructor walked up to Joe's skinny eight-year-old son and promptly threw him into eight feet of water. Never having been in eight feet of water, the child began to sink, and Joe found himself terrified but unable to do anything as he watched this child he loved sink to the bottom of the pool. Lo and behold, he came back up, came over to the side of the pool, choking and spitting water, and Joe saw him mouthing the words, *"Dad! Why are you doing this to me?"*

Joe said in that moment, he captured the fatherhood of God. He found himself standing there thinking, "Son, I have a plan for you. I wouldn't put you through this pain without a purpose. I don't do that to you. But you must understand you will face real danger in your future, and this is the only way I can prepare you. If there was another way, I would do it, but there isn't."

Joe said standing there watching his son he understood so many things that had happened in his life.

The strength of my life is joy, as Nehemiah said, because joy is the assurance that He loves me, and He cares about me, and He won't give up on me; and when I'm going through tough times, He is working a plan.

MB: Looking at God, you realize He is not dealing with these human situations from a theoretical perspective. The fact that He inhabited the form of a human body and lived a rather harsh life here gives me great appreciation that He knows where I am at. God could have done it in a different way, but He chose to become a man.

One of my favorite authors, Gene Edwards, tells the story of how God grew up in Nazareth with two of His friends. When they reached age twelve, one of them went to Jerusalem to become a scribe. Another went to a rabbinical school to study the Law. Both spent the next eighteen years in study before finally entering into their profession. God chose to remain in Nazareth and live the life of a *tekton*, literally a "constructor," working with His hands cutting stone, sweating, breathing dust, dealing with aching muscles and sores on His hands and feet while often receiving low wages from ungrateful clients. He endured a life similar to ours. He had bills to pay! The fact that God chose to do this makes my understanding of His understanding of me so much greater! I can relax, and as the writer of Hebrews says, "Boldly approach the throne of grace" (Hebrews 4:16), because God has experienced much of what I have.

RS: I have been thinking about the minute before the birth of Jesus. I don't claim to know how this whole thing worked with God putting on human skin—I don't have the background to know—but I can tell you this: There was a conscious choice of the One who was sitting on the highest place on the throne of the eternal heavens to put on the skin of a baby and not even be able to change His own mess. That choice fascinates me. Because, here is God who had everything, who decides to put on the limitation of human skin and being in one place all of the time (when He was used to popping into history anywhere, anytime). Then add to that, not only the skin of a man, but the skin of a baby, and to place Himself entirely in His creations' hands.

We have two hamsters for pets. We just got them. And I want to tell you, I don't want them to get big and take over caring for me. This is not something I can envision—to allow them to decide when they are going to feed me, what they are going to feed me. This is the God of creation who knew every evil thought of man and yet He said, "I am going to put on skin, and let them handle Me."

We think of Calvary and the things that wenton during those last hours before His death as being so humiliating, but I think the real humiliation was being placed in that little feeding trough, surrounded with itchy hay, watching the chickens jump over His head. This is the eternal God of the universe. I find that striking. What I love about this picture is what Philippians tells us that we need to be. It says:

> Though he was God, he did not demand and cling to his rights as God. He made himself nothing; he took the humble position of a slave and appeared in human form. And in human form he obediently humbled himself even further by dying a criminal's death on a cross. Because of this, God raised him up to the heights of heaven and gave him a name that is above every other name, so that at the name of Jesus every knee will bow, in heaven and on earth and under the earth, and every tongue will confess that Jesus Christ is Lord, to the glory of God the Father. (Philippians 2:6–10)

I think it is interesting that we continually see pictures of the Son—pictures of obedience, of learning, of following after the heartbeat of His Father. That is one of the things that actually helps me when I go to prayer. I can't really think of a divine Father in heaven, rather I think of someone who has flesh—someone who is like me. Although I know that He is not like me in every sense, I know He knows what it means to be me. That is a comfort.

MB: And somebody you can very naturally talk to.

RS: Yes, somebody like me, who has paid bills, stood in line, somebody who has felt put down.

MB: This is an important point. It is necessary we have a view of God that becomes real and personal. Without it, we can become religious and worship something a few days a week that will not really affect the rest of our lives.

Apparently, God had long planned to reveal Himself fully to His creation. First, He did it with individual visits to Adam and Eve and a few others; then He revealed Himself through His Law to Moses; and the ultimate revelation was yet to come.

Anthropologists often use the term "contextualize," which means "placing something into a particular or appropriate context for the purpose of interpretation or analysis." It is an important principle of cross-cultural ministry. For us working with the Miskito Indians in Central America, it means to present the message of the Gospel in a cultural form that they can understand and receive and eventually call their own. Without such contextualization, we dress the Miskitos in our western clothes, teach them Western worship songs, and give them Christian rituals that have little meaning. But to truly reach them, we have to think like them, speak their language, experience their lifestyle, and understand their reality. Then we can present a message relevant to their lives that will make a difference.

Jesus was the ultimate "contextualization" of God to His creation. This is cross-cultural ministry "to the max." He became one of us, He lived like us, shared our life experiences, felt the emotions that we feel, including pain and sorrow. He is someone we can totally relate to, and who can relate totally to us.

Over five hundred years before Jesus arrived on the planet, God, through Isaiah, told us He was going to provide a miraculous sign—that a virgin would give birth to a son, and the baby would be called Immanuel, which means "God with us." In the historical context, this was a sign for King Ahaz, as well as a sign for future generations.

> Therefore the Lord Himself will give you a sign: Behold, a virgin will be with child and bear a son, and she will call His name Immanuel. (Isaiah 7:14 NAS)

John picked up on this prophecy and witnessed the fulfillment. Look at how he describes Jesus in the first chapter of his gospel. God manifested Himself through His Word, and the creation process was done through His Word. The Word took on human form and lived among us.

> In the beginning was the Word, and the Word was with God, and the Word was God. He was in the beginning with God. All things came into being by Him, and apart from Him nothing came into being that has come into being. . . . And the Word became flesh, and dwelt among us, and we beheld His glory, glory as of the only begotten from the Father, full of grace and truth. (John 1:1–3,14 NAS)

Paul gives us another discription of Jesus' role in the Creation in his letter to the church in Colossae:

Christ is the visible image of the invisible God. He existed before God made anything at all and is supreme over all creation.? Christ is the one through whom God created everything in heaven and earth. He made the things we can see and the things we can't see—kings, kingdoms, rulers, and authorities. Everything has been created through him and for him. He existed before everything else began, and he holds all creation together. (Colossians 1:15–17)

The prophet Micah told us that the Christ was to be born in Bethlehem. There are over sixty specific prophecies given concerning the Messiah that Jesus fulfilled. Calculate the probabilities for that!

"But as for you, Bethlehem Ephesiansrathah, Too little to be among the clans of Judah, From you One will go forth for Me to be ruler in Israel. His goings forth are from long ago, From the days of eternity." (Micah 5:2 NAS)

When Jesus was baptized by John in the Jordan River, all three divine personalities were present.

And after being baptized, Jesus went up immediately from the water; and behold, the heavens were opened, and he saw the Spirit of God descending as a dove, and coming upon Him, and behold, a voice out of the heavens, saying, "This is My beloved Son, in whom I am well-pleased." (Matthew 3:16–17 NAS)

The man Jesus was filled with God's Holy Spirit. The Father gave His approval. Jesus then began His ministry. John the Baptizer gives a very specific and personal description of Jesus just a few days later:

"He has come from above and is greater than anyone else. I am of the earth, and my understanding is limited to the things of earth, but he has come from heaven. He tells what he has seen and heard, but how few believe what he tells them! Those who believe him discover that God is true. For he is sent by God. He speaks God's words, for God's Spirit is upon him without measure or limit. The Father loves his Son, and he has given him authority over everything. And all who believe in God's Son have eternal life. Those who don't obey the Son will never experience eternal life, but the wrath of God remains upon them." (John 3:31–36)

Jesus came to His hometown, Nazareth, and proclaimed what the prophet Isaiah had described seven hundred years before. Can you imagine this scene in the synagogue where the toddler Jesus had taken small baby steps, where the boy Jesus had learned His first memory verses, where the young man Jesus had worked, serving members of His community? What was the reaction of His clan when He made this announcement? They didn't believe Him, which was pretty amazing, since the Netzor clan had always believed that the Messiah would come from their village.

When he came to the village of Nazareth, his boyhood home, he went as usual to the synagogue on the Sabbath and stood up to read the Scriptures. The scroll containing the messages of Isaiah the prophet was handed to him, and he unrolled the scroll to the place where it says: "The Spirit of the Lord is upon me, for he has appointed me to preach Good

News to the poor. He has sent me to proclaim that captives will be released, that the blind will see, that the downtrodden will be freed from their oppressors, and that the time of the Lord's favor has come." He rolled up the scroll, handed it back to the attendant, and sat down. Everyone in the synagogue stared at him intently. Then he said, "This Scripture has come true today before your very eyes!" (Luke 4:16–21)

Jesus openly declared His deity in cultural language that was impossible for a first-century Jew to misunderstand. In many ways He said, "I am God in the flesh."

"The Father and I are one." Once again the Jewish leaders picked up stones to kill him. Jesus said, "At my Father's di-

Lukas, Mikaela, and Michael at ancient Caeserea

rection I have done many things to help the people. For which one of these good deeds are you killing me?" They replied, "Not for any good work, but for blasphemy, because you, a mere man, have made yourself God." (John 10:30–33)

Lukas: OK. If Jesus was God in the body of a human, He would be very different. He would have been an amazing guy!

MB: You are absolutely correct. Jesus had an amazing ministry! Jesus was an amazing guy. You constantly see that word popping up in the Gospels, describing people's reaction to Him. It is a big word in a neon light. What else would you expect from God in the flesh?

People were *amazed:*

- at His teaching, because He taught with authority:

   And they went into Capernaum; and immediately on the Sabbath He entered the synagogue and began to teach. And they were amazed at His teaching; for He was teaching them as one having authority, and not as the scribes. (Mark 1:21–22 NAS)

- that He has the authority and power to cast out demons:

   And just then there was in their synagogue a man with an unclean spirit; and he cried out, saying, "What do we have to do with You, Jesus of Nazareth? Have You come to destroy us? I know who You are—the Holy One of God!" And Jesus rebuked him, saying, "Be quiet, and come out of him!" And throwing him into convulsions, the unclean spirit cried out with a loud voice, and came out of him. And they were all amazed, so that they debated among themselves, saying, "What is this? A new teaching with authority! He commands even the unclean spirits, and they obey Him." (Mark 1:23–27 NAS)

- that He has the power and authority to calm the wind and the waves:

   But as they were sailing along He fell asleep; and a fierce gale of wind descended upon the lake, and they began to be swamped and to be in danger. And they came to Him and woke Him up, saying, "Master, Master, we are perishing!" And being aroused, He rebuked the wind and the surging waves, and they stopped, and it became calm. And He said to them, "Where is your faith?" And they were fearful and amazed, saying to one another, "Who then is this, that He commands even the winds and the water, and they obey Him?" (Luke 8:23–25 NAS)

• that He has the authority to forgive sins and the power to heal:

And they came, bringing to Him a paralytic, carried by four men. And being unable to get to Him because of the crowd, they removed the roof above Him; and when they had dug an opening, they let down the pallet on which the paralytic was lying. And Jesus seeing their faith said to the paralytic, "My son, your sins are forgiven." But there were some of the scribes sitting there and reasoning in their hearts, "Why does this man speak that way? He is blaspheming; who can forgive sins but God alone?" And immediately Jesus, aware in His spirit that they were reasoning that way within themselves, said to them, "Why are you reasoning about these things in your hearts? Which is easier, to say to the paralytic, 'Your sins are forgiven'; or to say, 'Arise, and take up your pallet and walk'? "But in order that you may know that the Son of Man has authority on earth to forgive sins—" He said to the paralytic—"I say to you, rise, take up your pallet and go home." And he rose and immediately took up the pallet and went out in the sight of all; so that they were all amazed and were glorifying God, saying, "we've never seen anything like this." (Mark 2:13–17 NAS)

• that He has the authority and ability to raise the dead:

Now they were all weeping and lamenting for her; but He said, "Stop weeping, for she has not died, but is asleep." And they began laughing at Him, knowing that she had died. He, however, took her by the hand and called, saying, "Child, arise!" And her spirit returned, and she rose immediately and He gave orders for something to be given her to eat. And her parents were amazed; but He instructed them to tell no one what had happened. (Luke 8:52–56 NAS)

Yes, Jesus is quite amazing!

When you look at the life of Jesus, He comes across as such a hero. He is the ultimate action figure hero. I confess, as a child, I read Superman and Batman comics. We are in a culture now that looks to heroes, but have you noticed how in the past few years that term has been severely watered down? Now a survivor of an aircraft accident is described in the press as a "hero." He's really just a survivor. To me a hero is a person who bursts into the flaming airplane and rescues the trapped passengers at the risk of their own life.

In His life, Jesus portrayed Himself as the ultimate hero—a man who was willing to do anything and to give totally of Himself to accomplish His mission. He knew what His mission was. He knew that He would have to die one of the most horrible deaths imaginable. We are not talking lethal injection when you feel a little tingling and suddenly you black out; or a gas chamber experience when after a few breaths you pass out; or feeling a sudden jolt of electricity in the chair that immediately destroys your nervous system; or even hearing the sliding of the guillotine blade down the track as it approaches your neck when it immediately severs your spinal cord.

> "I am the good shepherd; and I know My own, and My own know Me, even as the Father knows Me and I know the Father; and I lay down My life for the sheep. . . . For this reason the Father loves Me, because I lay down My life that I may take it again. No one has taken it away from Me, but I lay it down on My own initiative. I have authority to lay it down, and I have authority to take it up again." (John 10:14–15, 17–18 NAS)

We are talking about a form of execution that sometimes lasted days. It was public torture, hanging on that cross with nails driven through major nerves in His wrists, unable to exhale unless He pushed up on the nail through His feet to release the stress in His chest muscles, and dying a very slow death of asphyxiation.

> But He was pierced through for our transgressions, He was crushed for our iniquities; The chastening for our well-being fell upon Him, And by His scourging we are healed. All of us like sheep have gone astray, Each of us has turned to his own way; But the Lord has caused the iniquity of us all To fall on Him. (Isaiah 53:5–6 NAS)

Jesus knew this was what was waiting for Him. This was going to be the price for us to become members of God's family. Yet He went forward with resolve and determination that this was going to happen. Oh yes, there were a few moments in the garden where He asked His Father if He could do it another way; now would be the time, but if not, He was ready to go.

> For God in all his fullness was pleased to live in Christ, and by him God reconciled everything to himself. He made peace with everything in heaven and on earth by means of his blood on the cross. This includes you who were once so far away from God. You were his

enemies, separated from him by your evil thoughts and actions, yet now he has brought you back as his friends. He has done this through his death on the cross in his own human body. As a result, he has brought you into the very presence of God, and you are holy and blameless as you stand before him without a single fault. (Colossians 1:19–22)

It was God's plan that He Himself would reconcile the relationship with mankind. Reconciliation is from both sides. The law is fulfilled, justice is done, and so God's just character is satisfied. Man is forgiven and, in God's eyes, we are declared "not guilty" and are now holy and blameless. A just God demanded punishment for sin. Jesus paid the penalty for our sins. How He paid it is a measure of His love!

Many years ago, in a California courtroom, a defendant was brought before the judge on a drunken driving charge. Evidence was heard, and the defendant was declared guilty and the sentence was a large fine. The judge stepped out from behind his bench, took off his robe, walked over to the bailiff, took out his wallet, and paid the fine. Then he turned to the defendant, who happened to be his daughter, and said, "Don't ever let me see you in my courtroom again."

God did a similar thing in His courtroom. Sin was condemned and the penalty paid. I now look at Jesus, analyze what He did, and decide, "This is somebody that I can respect."

Pilate therefore said to Him, "So You are a king?" Jesus answered, "You say correctly that I am a king. For this I have been born, and for this I have come into the world, to bear witness to the truth." (John 18:37 NAS)

The Bible says Jesus is my King. Now, I grew up in a democracy, and we Americans believe that democracy is the best form of government, and we try to export it to the rest of the world. But growing up in the '60s and '70s, I realized there were severe flaws in the democratic system. There were certain people in my government whom I could not trust, and many aspects of the political system were counterproductive for good things for all people. As a result, I became disillusioned with this form of government. Then I met Jesus. Now I am a "monarchist," and I am waiting for my King to come back and take His throne on this earth. This really excites me because this is a king I can respect. I know He has my best interest at His heart. He is a friend of mine. He will do anything for me. He has already proven that!

I can't wait for this King to come and take over the government of this world. Whatever happens, whatever is coming, I know I will spend eternity with Him, being part of whatever He is doing. There is nothing better.

RS: We've talked about God the Father, and now God the Son. There is a more illusive character, a personality who is very much in step with what is going on with the Church now because He was there at the inception, or birthday, of the Church as an organism of God's choosing, but He is a little harder to define. You can put on the Father the title of Great Overseer of all. The Son is much easier because He is concrete—you can touch Him. He's an actual person who walked on the earth and died, was raised, and will be back. But what about the Spirit? It seems that His life and His work in our lives are terribly important in the Church.

MB: When Jesus was with His disciples in the Upper Room in John 16, He talks about how He is going away so the Holy Spirit can come and attempts to explain some of the dynamics of that. It gets a little confusing.

> "But now I am going away to the one who sent me, and none of you has asked me where I am going. Instead, you are very sad. But it is actually best for you that I go away, because if I don't, the Counselor? won't come. If I do go away, he will come because I will send him to you. (John 16:5–7)

RS: He even said, "It is best for you that I go away" (John 16:7) . It seems every believer I know thinks, "Boy, if we could only have been there when Jesus was there in the room and listened to Him talk." And yet He told the disciples when He was in the room, "This is going to be even better than what you have with you now."

MB: It's like the heart of Jesus was distilled and placed within the heart of the believer in the form of God the Holy Spirit, and this is what is continually touching all of us.

RS: Now, this sounds mystical when you say this stuff and it sounds like people are going to be buying beads and doing some weird things here. But really, all we are saying is that the Spirit functions in a distinct way with a distinct personality, which is what defines the Spirit as different from the Son. He has intellect, emotion, and will. He wills, He desires, He moves. This Spirit of God is active, alive, and working in the Church today.

MB: Right, and it is in a manner every believer can partake of. Jesus Christ could only be in one physical place at one particular time. With the Holy Spirit we can all be "connected." A significant word for all Christians is *koinônia*, which literally means "sharing" or "partnership" with the Holy Spirit and thus each other. It is a concept that is very important to the lives of all members of God's family.

RS: Physically, Jesus was a limited item. The Holy Spirit on the other hand is someone who is able to permeate all forms. And He is not different in the respect that if He put on a body it would be like the Son. He is different in that it was never anticipated He would serve the function of the Son but do something totally different.

MB: The Holy Spirit is first mentioned in the second verse of the Bible.

And the earth was formless and void, and darkness was over the surface of the deep; and the Spirit of God was moving over the surface of the waters. (Genesis 1:2 NAS)

- During the Old Testament times, the Spirit was given to selected individuals and could be taken away (Psalm 51:11; Judges 6:34, 14:9).

  Now the LORD spoke to Moses, saying, "See, I have called by name Bezalel. . . . And I have filled him with the Spirit of God in wisdom, in understanding, in knowledge, and in all kinds of craftsmanship. . . ." (Exodus 31:1–3)

- The Holy Spirit is an emotional person:

  But they rebelled and grieved His Holy Spirit. . . . (Isaiah 63:10 NAS)

- It is *only though the Holy Spirit* that we accomplish the really important things in life:

  Then he answered and said to me, "This is the word of the Lord to Zerubbabel saying, 'Not by might nor by power, but by My Spirit,' says the Lord of hosts." (Zechariah 4:6 NAS)

- The work of the Holy Spirit is to convict the world of sin, righteousness, and judgement; He will guide us in to all truth and tell us what is to come:

  "And He, when He comes, will convict the world concerning sin, and righteousness, and judgment; But when He, the Spirit of truth, comes, He will guide you into all the truth; for He will not speak on His own initiative, but whatever He hears, He will speak; and He will disclose to you what is to come." (John 16:8,13 NAS)

- Joel prophesied that God would give the Holy Spirit to all mankind:

  "And it will come about after this That I will pour out My Spirit on all mankind; And your sons and daughters will prophesy, Your old men will dream dreams, Your young men will see visions." (Joel 2:28 NAS)

- The Holy Spirit was given during the feast of Pentecost, which was also called the Feast of First Fruits. This was when people brought the first harvest from their fields and offered it to the Lord.

  And they were all filled with the Holy Spirit and began to speak with other tongues, as the Spirit was giving them utterance. (Acts 2:4 NAS)

Arielle: What does the Holy Spirit have to do with my life?

MB: Jesus told us that when the Holy Spirit comes, He will convict you; He will display righteousness to you; He will lead you in the truth; He will teach you and remind you of the things that Jesus said. That's important for me in reading the Gospels, in that the Holy Spirit is helping these authors record what Jesus said.

"But the Helper, the Holy Spirit, whom the Father will send in My name, He will teach you all things, and bring to your remembrance all that I said to you." (John 14:26 NAS)

He will give us power to accomplish God's purposes in our lives.

"You shall receive power when the Holy Spirit has come upon you; and you shall be My witnesses both in Jerusalem, and in all Judea and Samaria, and even to the remotest part of the earth." (Acts 1:8 NAS)

When the Holy Spirit came in force on the day of Pentecost, He came in a form the Hebrew people would be able to receive Him. We see the Holy Spirit move and gift people in certain ways where they can perform the function God has created them for.

He will give all of us the spiritual gifts that we need to fulfill our purpose in the body of Christ. Some of the spiritual gifts are:

- word of wisdom
- word of knowledge
- faith
- healing
- miracles
- prophecy
- discernment
- tongues
- interpretation of tongues

> Now there are varieties of gifts, but the same Spirit. And there are varieties of ministries, and the same Lord. And there are varieties of effects, but the same God who works all things in all persons. But to each one is given the manifestation of the Spirit for the common good. For to one is given the word of wisdom through the Spirit, and to another the word of knowledge according to the same Spirit; to another faith by the same Spirit, and to another gifts of healing by the one Spirit, and to another the effecting of miracles, and to another prophecy, and to another the distinguishing of spirits, to another various kinds of tongues, and to another the interpretation of tongues. But one and the same Spirit works all these things, distributing to each one individually just as He wills. (1 Corinthians 12:4–11 NAS)

Other spiritual gifts given by the Holy Spirit are:

- service
- teaching
- exhortation and encouragement
- giving
- leadership
- mercy

137

> And since we have gifts that differ according to the grace given to us, let each exercise them accordingly: if prophecy, according to the proportion of his faith; if service, in his serving; or he who teaches, in his teaching; or he who exhorts, in his exhortation; he who gives, with liberality; he who leads, with diligence; he who shows mercy, with cheerfulness. (Romans 12:6–8 NAS)

There are other gifts mentioned in the Bible. One example is in Exodus 31:1.

We as believers need to ask God to show us what spiritual gifts He has given us. As we function in these special areas of ministry, we will see God's power manifested in our abilities to accomplish much for His kingdom.

We are involved in different types of ministry in Central America, the Middle East, and the US, doing things like relief, primary education, discipleship, and other things. God has given us specific gifting through His Holy Spirit, allowing us to accomplish what He wants. It's pretty amazing actually! For example, many who know us look at the education project on the Rio Coco in Nicaragua and can easily conclude that it wasn't Laura the haircutter and Michael the ice cream scooper doing it but God!

When Paul writes about spiritual gifts, he seems to begin his lists with those gifts that help others most. Indeed, this seems to be the focus of the giftings—to have special God-given abilities to help others in the body of Christ. Paul states it simply:

> And in any event, you should desire the most helpful gifts. (1 Corinthians 12:31)

The greatest spiritual gift is love.

> If I speak with the tongues of men and of angels, but do not have love, I have become a noisy gong or a clanging cymbal. And if I have the gift of prophecy, and know all mysteries and all knowledge; and if I have all faith, so as to remove mountains, but do not have love, I am nothing. And if I give all my possessions to feed the poor, and if I deliver my body to be burned, but do not have love, it profits me nothing. Love is patient, love is kind, and is not jealous; love does not brag and is not arrogant, does not act unbecomingly; it does not seek its own, is not provoked, does not take into account a wrong suffered, does not rejoice in unrighteousness, but rejoices with the truth; bears all things, believes all things, hopes all things, endures all things. Love never fails; but if there are gifts of prophecy, they will be done away; if there are tongues, they will cease; if there is knowledge, it will be done away. . . . But now abide faith, hope, love, these three; but the greatest of these is love. (1 Corinthians 13:1–8,13 NAS)

Nutie Melrose loving a Miskito baby

Doesn't this make sense? Obviously, love is the gift that will help every person in every situation.

Unfortunately, we often judge our level of spirituality through giftings that come to us really through nothing we have done. Paul is very clear in his letter to the church at Corinth that the Holy Spirit gives gifts of His choice to whom He chooses to. It is His choice. A real measure of true spirituality is "What fruit does the Holy Spirit have in our lives?" Is someone going to look at me and judge my spirituality by a particular gift I may have or not have? It happens all the time in Christianity. I think a better measure of my spiritual maturity is the fruit the Holy Spirit has cultivated in my own life, along with the intimacy of my relationship with my Heavenly Father, and these seem to go hand-in-hand.

I once heard Juan Carlos Ortiz, a very insightful pastor from Argentina, say, "Some people ask me if I am filled with the spirit according to Acts 2 ("and they spoke in tongues . . ."). I reply that I am filled with the Spirit according to Galatians 5:22."

> But the fruit of the Spirit is love, joy, peace, patience, kindness, goodness, faithfulness, gentleness, self-control; against such things there is no law. (Galatians 5:22–23 NAS)

The deeper work of the Holy Spirit is evidenced by spiritual fruit rather than a specific spiritual gift. If I am teaching, prophesying, serving, leading, giving, or speaking in tongues, and you don't see greater amounts of love, joy, patience, kindness, goodness, gentleness, and self-control, then it is obvious that something is curtailing my spiritual growth. Gifts are given. There is nothing you did to get them. Fruit is cultivated. This takes dedication, discipline, and effort.

May the Holy Spirit have His way with us and be allowed to cultivate His fruit in our lives so that it really may come forth, and people will look at us and say, "Yes, God is touching that person's life."

RS: It seems to me that we have two totally different things here. Like you said, the gifts of the Spirit are things God gave us. We really didn't have a hand in it. It was a gift. But when you talk about the fruits—and we are talking about love, joy, peace, and patience— these sound like things I am very much involved in, whether or not I reflect them. I can reflect that gift that I have been given. Fruit is something that I must work on.

MB: I believe the cultivation of the fruit is dependent on us. I am not going to allow the Holy Spirit to cultivate patience in me if I am continually "letting my emotions go." I think the first thing we believers must realize is that the Holy Spirit wants to cultivate it, and it is our responsibility to say, "Yes!" to Him, because He is not going to force anything on us. Once we say yes, the process begins. Paul told the church in Philippi:

Dearest friends, you were always so careful to follow my instructions when I was with you. And now that I am away you must be even more careful to put into action God's saving work in your lives, obeying God with deep reverence and fear. For God is work- ing in you, giving you the desire to obey him and the power to do what pleases him. . (Philippians 2:12–13)

The Greek verb, *katergazomai*, translated "put into action" or "work out" in other ver- sions, actually reads "accomplish with throughness or bring to completion."

It is a two-part process. We have our part of being willing and following through, and God's part is giving us the initial desire to change and grow. He is the one who gives us the power, enabling us to shift our thinking and change our actions. This is a powerful dynamic that is essential to every Christian's process of maturity.

RS: Isn't it amazing that God can even change my desires? I don't know about you, but a lot of times in my own life, I have to say, "Lord I want to do what is wrong right now. I want to hit this guy in the nose because he is wrong." But God has to flood the gates with His thoughts like: "The anger of man doesn't work the righteousness of God"

(James 1:20). That passage in Galatians 5:19–23 starts out with "The works of the flesh are very obvious; and they are these: adultery, sexual sin, uncleanness, contention, and others" and ends with "But the fruit of the Spirit is love, joy, peace, patience, kindness, goodness, faithfulness, gentleness, self-control."

These are things that you can visualize. You know what contention is and who is a contentious individual. I want in my own life for my children to see as clear a picture of the fruit of the Spirit as they would see of the works of the flesh in other's lives. I would like them to be able to look at me and say, for example, "My dad was a patient man," although at this point in their lives they couldn't say that. But that is my goal, and the story is not over. How do I address this need in my life, this need to bear that fruit?

MB: Paul says in Colossians 1:27, it is "Christ in you, the Hope of Glory." I have a particle of Christ inside me in the form of the Holy Spirit, and He is trapped inside this cage of intellect, emotions, and experience called Michael Bagby. It is a cage with very strong bars, built over years. Jesus says if I personally die to or set aside all my desires, thoughts, ambitions, and hurts, then He can come forth to touch those around me.

Therefore I have to say no to my own nature, my own feelings, and my own opinions. When I say no to it, then that is the open door God has to get out and display Himself to others around me through me.

This is the continual challenge I have as a member of the kingdom of God. I must die so He can escape and do His thing to the people and situations around me. The reality is that the cage is strong, and it is a continual process of giving Jesus the "keys" and letting Him out. It is a matter of being continually filled with His presence.

And do not get drunk with wine, for that is dissipation, but be filled with the Spirit . . . .
(Ephesians 5:18)

We are to be continually filled with the Holy Spirit. The verb form used here in the Greek is the progressive tense, denoting continuous action. Being filled is not a one-time experience! How are you filled? Through prayer, praise, worship, service, the Word, trials, along with other ways. Living without the Holy Spirit is like trying to live without breathing air. It is through Him that all of God's plans for our lives are accomplished.

There are two points that we want to close this session with:

- *The key to understanding the Bible is a close, intimate walk with the Holy Spirit.* Intellectual pursuits of biblical truth without the guidance of the Holy Spirit are in vain and often result in lifeless religion or *"doctrines of demons"* (as the Bible describes zealous error). We urge you to pursue a relationship with the Holy Spirit as you study His Word!

• *The Divine Personalities* make the difference in your life! The love of the *Father*, the sacrifice of the *Son*, and the power of the *Holy Spirit* make our relationship with God possible and our eternal destiny certain.

Personal Reflections

1. How do you understand the relationship between the personalities of the Trinity? Can we define it?
2. Where do you go for satisfaction?
3. When was the last time God "threw you in the pool"?
4. Do you relate to Jesus as your Savior or your King?
5. How does the Holy Spirit cultivate fruit in your life?
6. What are the strongest bars in your "cage" that keeps the Holy Spirit trapped inside you?

Deeper Water

A. The book of Job provides us with a rich description of God. Read chapters 38 through 42, and listen to God response to the questions and comments of Job and his friends.

B. In John 13 through 17, Jesus has a profound discussion with His disciples on His relationship with them, their relationships with God, and the relationship between the divine personalities. Read carefully these chapters, noting the different functions of the Father, Son, and Spirit. Remember, this is not meant to be a diagram! Use your Hebrew mind!

C. In Luke 1 and 2, there are four prophets who give words about Jesus. Read these words, noticing the attributes of this Savior and the meaning of His advent.

D. In the book of Acts, we see over and over again the appearance of the Holy Spirit. Read the first ten chapters of Acts, and note the role of the Holy Spirit in the lives of the disciples. Begin to underline each occurrence of an action or intervention of the Holy Spirit. As you read and underline, reflect on how the Holy Spirit is moving in your own life and ministry.

A Christian counselor was recently asked: "How many of your cases are based on identity issues?" She replied, "About 25%, but 90 % of the solutions to personal issues begin with knowing who you are in Christ." Evolutionists teach us the theory that we are a random collection of molecules that developed into single cell life and eventually evolved into more advanced creatures. However, science and the Bible give us a completely different picture. We are not the descendents of protozoa and monkeys. We are in fact God's favored creation.

God's Favored Creation

We begin with a word from Laura:

All my life I had the aspiration (even as a Buddhist) to be set apart—to be unique and special. I did not want to be one of the many but rather "picked out" in a sense. . . . I sought to have a special place in the eyes of my parents, teachers, and others.

When I became a Christian, I realized that it meant I was chosen, loved, and deeply cared for by an infinite, yet personal, Supreme Being. The changes and sense of security it wrought in me cannot be described in just a few pages. They are changes that go deep and amazingly keep going deeper and deeper.

To know that my Creator handpicked me from the beginning of time to be a part of His plan and kingdom has made me feel exceedingly special. This in itself has caused within me a sense of actually being "set apart"—uniquely made for His divine purposes and pleasure. It has provided inspiration for much change in my life. It provided a standard for living I never had previously in my Buddhism. I now have been set free to be and become who I was created to be, for in Him I found my identity—my true identity in Christ.

I have been crucified with Christ; and it is no longer I who live, but Christ lives in me; and the life which I now live in the flesh I live by faith in the Son of God, who loved me, and delivered Himself up for me. (Galatians 2:20)

Laura
Japanese dancer
Age 7

145

After becoming a parent, I have found myself continuously feeling a depth of love for my children that cannot be compared to anything else. The sense of pride and thanksgiving that wells up within me when we are together is hard to describe. The pleasure it is to hear them express themselves and their personalities is sometimes overwhelming. They are all unique in their own ways, and I cannot compare my love for any one of them.

Likewise I see our God looking upon us in this way—to love us all so completely yet separately and individually.

How He must look at us with a twinkle in His eyes or a shaking of His head when we act in our childish ways.

How He must look upon us with pride when we take our first steps in His ways and begin walking in them.

How He must feel so satisfied when we commit our ways to Him and dedicate our lives to serving Him and His purposes.

Yes, we are God's favored creation. It is only we who have been created in His image. It is only we who have been destined to be members of God's own family. It is only we who have been sealed with God's own Spirit. He went to great lengths to make this all happen. As a result, as the psalmist said, "There is no good thing that He will withhold from us."

> May the appreciation we have for Him,
> As well as our relationship with Him grow,
> As we grow in our knowledge of Him and His ways.

MB: Knowing where we came from and what happened in the beginning will help us to better understand our life here and how to get to where God wants us to be. Can there be any more important task for us in this life?

Let's begin with man living in perfect conditions in the Garden and think through what was actually happening. In the process, we may ask questions that have never been addressed before, yet are very important to fully understand and appreciate.

> Then God said, "Let Us make man in Our image, according to Our likeness; and let them rule over the fish of the sea and over the birds of the sky and over the cattle and over all the earth, and over every creeping thing that creeps on the earth." And God created man in His own image, in the image of God He created him; male and female He created them. (Genesis 1:26–27 NAS)

God created man out of dust of the earth to rule over Earth. One of the interesting aspects of the way God created man was that as He formed him from dust God didn't point His finger and send a lightning bolt into him, nor did He just snap His finger and cause Adam to jump up. Instead, the text reads that God breathed life into Adam. As I read it, something passed from God into this man to give him life and this made for a very close connection between the two.

> Then the Lord God formed man of dust from the ground, and breathed into his nostrils the breath of life; and man became a living being. (Genesis 2:7 NAS)

RS: If you look at the way God is, the way He thinks, and what He does, there is a certain element of who man is—a marred image, but nevertheless an image of who God is. There is the creative energy we have; there are the emotional desires and hungers and wants; all of these things make us different.

There have been many scientific attempts to prove a base similarity between humans and animals; but, ultimately, not only is our DNA different, there is another elemental difference, a fundamental difference in the way of being that distinguishes man as being in the image of God. Some like to refer to it as a soul. I see God's great plan for His greatest creation, which is man. I don't want to disappoint anyone, but I don't see a "doggie heaven" in Scripture. I see these animals as important but subject to God's greatest, highest creation. Man is the crown jewel of all His creations.

MB: It is such a creation that angels look at man with awe and wonder; and, ultimately, Paul declares we will judge angels. This is something special. I call it "God's favored creation." He has created many things; He probably will continue, but up to this point, we are His "most favored creation."

> And the Lord God planted a garden toward the east, in Eden; and there He placed the man whom He had formed. And out of the ground the Lord God caused to grow every tree that is pleasing to the sight and good for food; the tree of life also in the midst of the garden, and the tree of the knowledge of good and evil. And the Lord God commanded the man, saying, "From any tree of the garden you may eat freely; but from the tree of the knowledge of good and evil you shall not eat, for in the day that you eat from it you shall surely die." (Genesis 2:8–9, 16–17 NAS)

He put us in a perfect environment, in a garden complete with trees bearing fruit for physical nourishment: A tree called the "Tree of Life," which had something to do with

Randy teaching by the "Lydia Stream" near Philippi

man's spiritual nourishment, and the "Tree of the Knowledge of Good and Evil," which God said, "Don't eat from that one or else you will die." Now do you think God was kidding when He said that?

RS: No, and when you look at the creation of man, you see the image of something He had done before. There was another perfect creation, in another perfect setting—the angelic host. What followed the creation of those incredibly powerful and interesting beings we now call angels (which we talked about in our first session) is that some of them took on the desire to become like God. It is almost exactly like what you see in the early Garden scene. I think there is a reason.

If I understand Scripture correctly, it's the "Big Plan" of God—are you ready? This is it in a sentence: *God is showing all beings in the universe that He alone is God; His character may be seen in the events of history.* At the end of human history, those who are the redeemed will have God write on their forehead: "I Am." We are the trophies of His grace, and we become trophy pieces of an illustration that God is working out through human history. He alone is God, and we belong to Him. Paul wrote to the church at Ephesus:

So God can always point to us as examples of the incredible wealth of His favor and kindness toward us, as shown in all he has done for us through Christ Jesus. (Ephesians 2:7)

MB: Are we just a great illustration, an object lesson to the angels? Is that what you are saying?

RS: Actually, what I am saying is we have an over-inflated view of our own importance! Yes, God's heart is for man. God created us for very special and specific things, but why? *Why?* There was already a creation He was working with. He was already doing the angel-thing and that didn't seem to be working out very well—a third of them gone and further rebellion on the horizon. It seems in this illustration is God saying, "Let Me show you what I am like; let Me show you who the Lord is."

Paul later wrote in that same letter:

so that the manifold wisdom of God might now be made known through the church to the rulers and the authorities in the heavenly places. (Ephesians 3:10)

MB: It is almost like He is saying to those rebellious angels: "You guys didn't quite get it the first time, so watch me now and you are going to see by what I do who I really am."

RS: In the same way, we in the New Testament Church see God's work with Israel as a vindication of who He is; human history is a vindication of who He is to show to the angelic host. At the end, He can say, "By the way, this is who I am." We humans have become a very important part of His heart and a massive illustration at the same time.

MB: Everything was perfect in the Garden until Satan tempted Eve with a little truth mixed with a big lie. Where do you think Adam was when all this was going on? The text seems to indicate that Adam was nearby, passively watching his wife disobey God. Together, by disobeying God, they rebelled against His authority over their lives.

And the woman said to the serpent, "From the fruit of the trees of the garden we may eat; but from the fruit of the tree which is in the middle of the garden, God has said, 'You shall not eat from it or touch it, lest you die.'" And the serpent said to the woman, "You surely shall not die! For God knows that in the day you eat from it your eyes will be opened, and you will be like God, knowing good and evil." When the woman saw that the tree was good for food, and that it was a delight to the eyes, and that the tree was desirable to make one wise, she took from its fruit and ate; and she gave also to her husband with her, and he ate. (Genesis 3:2–6 NAS)

I have often wondered what was actually in that fruit of the Tree of the Knowledge of Good and Evil. Gene Edwards suggests in his book, *The Highest Life,* that there was some substance of the consciousness of Satan, since he was the one who experientially knew of good and evil. Something indeed was in that fruit. With it, they had a choice to obey God or to ignore Him.

RS: This is really a physical environment. I love the way the Hebrew language tells this story; it is all very earthy. If you haven't had exposure to the Hebrew language, it is hard to really appreciate what is being said. For example, Genesis 1:1 says "In the beginning . . ." The literal Hebrew translation of this word *beroshet* is "in the head." It is so earthy and physical. You are in a garden setting and you have Adam and Eve in perfection, but entering into the setting is the evil one.

In my view, the first sin is not the eating of the fruit, it is the *reaching* for it. At the moment I stop believing that God is looking out for my best interest and doubt the goodness of God and His agenda and believe that I have to take that on for myself (because, after all, if I don't do it, who's going to look out for Number One?), as soon as I reach out, whatever that fruit is (and it doesn't really matter), already in my heart I have changed. Where did I change? The agenda of my life changed from being a servant of the living God and trusting in Him to feeling I had to serve myself and trust only me.

MB: The text reads that when they ate the fruit, something changed because their eyes were opened. Suddenly, there was a major barrier between man and God. It was that three-letter word—*sin.*

Then the eyes of both of them were opened, and they knew that they were naked; and they sewed fig leaves together and made themselves loin coverings. (Genesis 3:7 NAS)

RS: Their eyes were opened. At that moment, as they began to eat, they realized they had gone through all the physical steps of turning away from God. Sin is an issue of the heart, but the physical steps show us the heart. That's why when the Pharisees came to Jesus and complained, "Why don't your disciples wash their hands the way we do?," there was a big rabbinic debate about if you should do it one time or seven times. Jesus said, "Look guys. You are not getting it. It is not what you eat or that your hands are dirty.

That is not the real problem you have. The much greater issue is what's already inside." (See Matthew 15, Luke 11)

When you squeeze a tube of toothpaste, what's inside is what comes out. When you squeeze a man, what comes out is what's already inside. People say all the time "Oh, I only said that because I was under pressure." When you are under pressure, the real *you* is what comes out. That's the one who is whiney and nasty who says, "I don't want to do this; I can't believe they put me in this position." That is the one who comes out because that's who is inside.

What I saw in that Garden scene was that Adam and Eve began to physically manifest what was already going on in their hearts. As they were biting and munching, they were acting out the rebellion of their heart. And that rebellion seemed so simple, but it comes down to this: God views obedience to Him as the greatest and highest thing that we can do. Mary told the people at the wedding in Cana: "Whatever He tells you to do, do it" (John 2:5). That's it in a nutshell.

MB: Jesus told His disciples in that Upper Room, "If you love me, then obey my commandments" (John 14:15).

RS: This obedience being breeched brought about two results: First, it brought about an eye-opening experience. And by the way, not all eye-opening experiences are good. There is a reason why romantic restaurants are dark! So you don't look across the table and see spinach between the love of your life's teeth! It is wonderful to be in a dark restaurant loving each other.

That eye becoming opened is a very academically stimulating thing. "Oh look, now they had a full knowledge!" What did they know? They knew that when they disobeyed God a tremendous sense of guilt would overcome them. There was a whole set of emotions they never knew of. There is innocence lost.

The second result was that they knew for the first time what it meant to be before God in disarray with something out of sync with God's harmony and their entire environment. When God comes down and explains what the consequences of their sin will be, all of a sudden, they were going to see introduced into the perfection of their lives all of these problems. Rust! Degeneration! Things were going to start to fall off, and it wasn't going to be nice anymore. They saw it all at one time.

I listen to people talk and they say, "We really need to show our kids what life is really like; we don't want them to be naïve." There is a wonderful thing about naivety. There is something wonderful about going through life and not seeing the underside of everything that is there. They lost that.

MB: It was here that sin indeed entered into the relationship of man and God. Man now had a "sin nature." And it seems like it became part of our genetic makeup. It inhabited the bodies of Adam and Eve and was passed on to all their descendents.

> Therefore, just as through one man sin entered into the world, and death through sin, and so death spread to all men, because all sinned. (Romans 5:12 NAS)

I didn't have to teach my children to grab toys from other children. I didn't have to teach my kids to disobey me. These things came naturally!

The consequences of Adam and Eve's sin were severe for them. They were forced to work hard for their food, there was going to be pain in bearing children, they were driven from the perfection of the Garden and not allowed to eat from the Tree of Life, and there would be physical death. Something physically changed in them as a result of eating this fruit. And we see the result of this sin and degeneration in the shortening life spans of the succeeding generations.

> To the woman He said, "I will greatly multiply Your pain in childbirth, In pain you shall bring forth children; Yet your desire shall be for your husband, And he shall rule over you." Then to Adam He said, "Because you have listened to the voice of your wife, and have eaten from the tree about which I commanded you, saying, 'You shall not eat from it'; Cursed is the ground because of you; In toil you shall eat of it All the days of your life. Both thorns and thistles it shall grow for you; And you shall eat the plants of the field; By the sweat of your face you shall eat bread, till you return to the ground, because from it you were taken; For you are dust, and to dust you shall return." (Genesis 3:16–19 NAS)

Jon Hamilton, a noted author and radio Bible teacher, pointed out recently that, according to the Genesis account, man was created for four purposes:

- to have fellowship with God;
- to cultivate God's garden;
- to be fruitful and multiply; and
- to rule over all the earth and all that is in it.

When man fell, Satan introduced several immediate strongholds designed to separate man from God's purposes:

1. *Their gaze turned inward.* They noticed for the first time that they were naked. People became self-aware and self-centered. Interestingly, the Tree of Knowledge of Good and Evil was in the center of the Garden. Man has been self-centered ever since.
2. *Man became fearful.* When God asked Adam where he was, Adam replied: "I heard the sound of You in the garden, and I was afraid because I was naked; so I hid myself" (Gen. 3:10). Fear is a major (if not *the*) motivating factor in any personality style. Our fears have become gods to us. If we fear rejection, acceptance becomes our god. If we fear criticism, praise becomes our god. If we fear failure, success becomes god to us. Fear is the opposite of faith. Faith is believing that you have received what you have hoped for, while fear is believing that you have or will receive that which you hope against. You are believing for the bad.
3. *Man began to accuse*: "It was the woman *You* gave me." (Gen. 3:12) "It was the serpent *You* placed in the Garden." (Gen. 3:13) Man found someone else to blame. As a result, we have become a society of victims. Everyone wants to blame everyone else. "My parents did this or that to me. That's why I have the problems I have." We don't call things sin anymore. Alcoholism is a disease—the only disease that becomes immediately cured by stranding the "alcoholic" on a deserted island.
4. *Man's eyes were opened.* Suddenly he became "wise." He had a concept of good and evil. He knew right from wrong, except these concepts were rooted in his fallen nature, so they were unprofitable to righteousness. Man could do "good works" all day long, but it could never buy him anything from God. That led to frustration, like with Cain, and it led to anger, to murder, and to religion.

As a result of these strongholds, man was separated from all four of his purposes for being created:

1. He could not have fellowship with God. He was separated by his sin.
2. He could not work in God's garden. He was cast out.
3. He could not "Be fruitful and multiply," because the fruit he bore was only wickedness. The children that came forth on the earth were sons of darkness.
4. By obeying Satan, he made Satan his lord and crowned him "the god of this world."

Man's purposes were derailed, and there was a huge offense against God. As Jon points out, the consequences are far reaching, affecting each of us even thousands of years later. Yet the story was not over. It was just a matter of dealing with this thing called sin. Paul wrote that mankind was spiritually dead in his sinful state, cut off from God and physically dying.

> And you were dead in your trespasses and sins. . . . (Ephesians 2:1 NAS)

Jesus stated that mankind was held in bondage to the power of sin. It was a part of his being that could not be overcome.

> Jesus answered them, "Truly, truly, I say to you, everyone who commits sin is the slave of sin." (John 8:34 NAS)

Mikaela: What does this word *sin* mean any way? What is sin?

MB: I always wondered what the word *sin* really meant, too. It's defined in my dictionary as an offense against God. That seems rather nebulous. Sin could be a lot of things, right? If you look at the Greek words used in the Bible that are translated "sin" or describe sinful behavior, then the concept becomes more precise and more personal.

Sin is defined in the Bible as:

Mikaela in Haleakala Crater, Maui

- *parabasis:* not lining up
- *harmartia:* missing the mark
- *parakoe:* disobedient to a voice
- *anomia:* ignoring the law that you do know
- *agnoemz:* ignorance of what you should know
- *paraptoma:* falling when one should have stood
- *hethema:* not giving a full measure when a full measure is required

154

I guess the important thing now is to know the "line," the "mark," the applicable "law"; what we should know; how much is a "full measure"; how far should we resist; and what does that voice of the Holy Spirit sound like.

God came up with a remedy for this issue of sin. For their nakedness, He provided them the skins for covering up. It is like God was saying, "I am going to work it out so that we can still relate, and in the meantime, I will be preparing the 'Big Solution.'"

And the LORD God made clothing from animal skins for Adam and his wife. (Genesis 3:21)

RS: What is interesting is that in the process, even *that* came at the expense of the animal. Look at it from the animal's perspective. This was not a good deal! There they were, walking along in the Garden, doing what they do, and suddenly they have to worry about the guy who named them, who was supposed to care for them, instead, killing them with the agenda of getting himself clothing.

MB: An amazing thing is that despite this rebellion, God continually refers to mankind in the books of the Bible as "My people" over one hundred times in the Hebrew Scriptures. Here was His favorite creation who had turned their backs on Him, who figuratively spit in His face, and yet He refers to them as "My people" over and over again.

And the LORD said, "I have surely seen the affliction of My people who are in Egypt, and have given heed to their cry because of their taskmasters, for I am aware of their sufferings." (Exodus 3:7 NAS)

In spite of man's rebellion against Him, God still loved mankind and had a plan to make man part of His family through the life of a man named Abraham. The Hebrew word *bless (barak)* used in Genesis 12 carries a con-

Michael in the Negev aboard Sharif

notation of "familial relationship." Already God was putting into action His plan to bring man back into intimate relationship with Him, if man wanted.

> Now the LORD said to Abram, "Go forth from your country, And from your relatives And from your father's house, To the land which I will show you; And I will make you a great nation, And I will bless you, And make your name great; And so you shall be a blessing; And I will bless those who bless you, And the one who curses you I will curse. And in you all the families of the earth shall be blessed." (Genesis 12:1–3 NAS)

The fact that He called these rebels "His people" and continued to relate to them was a great object lesson in itself. God is long-suffering and perseverant in this relationship.

RS: You must remember that love and justice run opposite to each other. There are people in your life who do the identical thing to you or to other people in your life, but in some cases you ignore it, while in other cases you are absolutely irritated by it. The difference is whether you love the person to begin with. With the people we love, we tend to overlook what is going on. And God's love is not like our love. The mystery of His love is that He goes looking for Adam and Eve when they have sinned in the Garden. Not just to get justice but rather to restore the relationship.

> And they heard the sound of the Lord God walking in the garden in the cool of the day, and the man and his wife hid themselves from the presence of the Lord God among the trees of the garden. (Genesis 3:8 NAS)

The heart of God is so unbelievable! If somebody bangs into your car in the parking lot, you don't go looking for that person so you can reestablish the relationship, you want to nail him to the wall and get justice. In essence, God set aside His need for justice for the moment in favor of His need to reestablish the relationship and created another way to deal with the justice issue.

MB: That way was revealed through His Law in the sacrificial system, which has caused a lot of confusion in Christian circles today. This system of "offerings" was described in detail by Moses in the Book of Leviticus and usually involved killing an animal and sprinkling its blood over an altar. In our culture today, this seems rather unusual, but for the time of Abraham, Jacob, and Moses, it was the norm when it came to relating to so-called gods.

Then the Lord said to Moses, "Give the Israelites the following instructions for dealing with those who sin unintentionally by doing anything forbidden by the Lord's commands. If the high priest sins, bringing guilt upon the entire community, he must bring to the Lord a young bull with no physical defects. He must present the bull to the Lord at the entrance of the Tabernacle, lay his hand on the bull's head, and slaughter it there in the Lord's presence. The priest on duty will then take some of the animal's blood into the Tabernacle, dip his finger into the blood, and sprinkle it seven times before the Lord in front of the inner curtain of the Most Holy Place. The priest will put some of the blood on the horns of the incense altar that stands in the Lord's presence in the Tabernacle. The rest of the bull's blood must be poured out at the base of the altar of burnt offerings at the entrance of the Tabernacle." (Leviticus 4:1–7)

RS: What pleases God? You look at the story of the Bible and see this God who says, "If you kill these animals and sprinkle their blood, I will turn away my wrath." To anyone in the modern world, that seems barbaric. And meanwhile, the ASPCA is going nuts! Kill the animal? For what? What did the animal do?

There are so many elements within those sacrifices that are helpful for us. Think about a young Hebrew child growing up in a family, raising a family pet, and watching that pet closely, giving it great care, more than we do our dogs and cats. No spot or blemish on this animal in any way.

Think about the same child holding your hand as you walk into the temple and watching the priests slice the throat of that animal the child loves and watching the blood be drained. Why? *"Because that is the price, Moshe, of our sin."* That is the price of what we have done. So we need to stand here and take the life of the one we love because that will show us sin has a price. From the beginning that is what the animals were saying: "Hey—wait a minute! This sin deal has a high price!"

There is a wonderful picture in this. It's not as if God was delighted with blood. It's not that He is sadistic. It's that He found a way with justifying—a way with dealing with this issue of the guilt of man—because the relationship with man was the greater heart.

MB: This was the issue: to maintain the relationship and yet have justice. God already had it planned out, because, quite frankly, I don't believe He was surprised by the happenings in the Garden. After all, He is God.

This idea of offering a sacrifice to God was not something new to Moses. When Abraham took Isaac up to offer a sacrifice, young Isaac asked, "Where is the lamb for the burnt offering?" (Genesis 22:7). The Bible records that Abraham was not justified in his "burnt offering" to God but rather because he believed what God told him about his coming family. It was a heart/faith issue. And this is in the pages of the first book of the Bible.

> And Abram believed the LORD, and the LORD declared him righteous because of his faith. (Genesis 15:6)

There is a bizarre scene in Numbers 21 of looking at the snake on the pole in the desert and believing God to heal you that would result in life. It's another lesson in the saving power of faith from the heart of mankind.

> So Moses made a snake out of bronze and attached it to the top of a pole. Whenever those who were bitten looked at the bronze snake, they recovered! (Numbers 21:9)

David said in Psalm 40 that he finally understood God didn't want sacrifices. He realized it was a *"heart issue."*

> You take no delight in sacrifices or offerings. Now that you have made me listen, I finally understand—You don't require burnt offerings or sin offerings. I take joy in doing your will, my God, for your law is written on my heart. (Psalm 40:6,8)

Jeremiah looked at the cause of the judgment and destruction that was falling on Jerusalem and declared there would be a new wrinkle in God's relationship with His people: God would not write His Law on stone tablets but rather on the believer's heart. *Again, a heart issue.*

> "The day will come," says the LORD, "when I will make a new covenant with the people of Israel and Judah. This covenant will not be like the one I made with their ancestors when I took them by the hand and brought them out of the land of Egypt. They broke that covenant, though I loved them as a husband loves his wife," says the LORD. "But this is the new covenant I will make with the people of Israel on that day," says the LORD. "I will put my laws in their minds, and I will write them on their hearts. I will be their God, and they will be my people." (Jeremiah 31:31–33)

RS: It's important to notice that God is not writing a new law but rather placing it in a different location—*the believer's heart.*

MB: Ezekiel reinforced this to the exiles in Babylon who saw the fruit of trying to please God with outward actions that did not reflect a heart committed to Him.

> And I will give you a new heart with new and right desires, and I will put a new spirit in you. I will take out your stony heart of sin and give you a new, obedient heart. And I will put my Spirit in you so you will obey my laws and do whatever I command. (Ezekiel 36:26)

These are almost "previews of coming attractions." I remember as a kid at the Saturday matinee seeing previews of what was coming next was almost as important as the movie. We see, for example, in the Star *Wars Trilogy* Han Solo getting "frozen" at the end of the second episode, and we know that there is a third movie already in production.

What was the coming attraction? It was God Himself in the flesh who would personally take care of the justice issue.

RS: I think that it is important for us to remember that in essence God was never satisfied with the blood of bulls, lambs, and goats.

> For the Law, since it has only a shadow of the good things to come and not the very form of things, can never, by the same sacrifices which they offer continually year by year, make perfect those who draw near. . . . For it is impossible for the blood of bulls and goats to take away sins. (Hebrews 10:1,4 NAS)

Even though the Bible refers to this as "covering" sin, it wasn't the covering that turned His wrath away. The Old Testament believer always came to God in the same way as the New Testament believer—by grace and through faith—because *what God was interested in was their hearts.*

> People may think they are doing what is right, but the LORD examines the heart. The LORD is more pleased when we do what is just and right than when we give him sacrifices. (Proverbs 21:2–3)

Now the outward actions that determined obedience in our hearts were different. So I don't have to sacrifice and stand in line at the altar because the Book of Hebrews is very clear that there has been one sacrifice and I don't need to do that anymore. I don't need to afflict my soul, bow into the ashes, and moan up into the sky. Whatever it is I have to do as a symbol of outward obedience is not what it is that saves me; *it's what is going on in my heart.*

So when blood was sprinkled on that mercy seat, it was not the blood that did it. It was the action of reaching out the hand. The same action that defiled man in the Garden (the reaching for the forbidden fruit) was the same action that later helped him, and both were a reflection of what was going on in the heart. The high priest reached out to pour blood; his heart was right, and because his heart was obedient and what was inside was right with God, the outward action came.

We have a lot of believers who run around saying: "Keeping the Law saves people." Keeping the Law never saved anybody. Walking with God saved people.

And how did that happen? When I submitted my heart and life to the God of the Ages and then demonstrated obedience in whatever way He told me. And if what He told me was to sacrifice a bull or goat, that is what I did. If it was to see the sacrifice of the Lamb on Calvary and to accept it, then I did that. Whatever truth was revealed, the important thing was always the heart response. We get caught up in the mechanics, and the mechanics are not the issue.

> He has told you, O man, what is good; And what does the LORD require of you But to do justice, to love kindness, And to walk humbly with your God? (Micah 6:8 NAS)

The Old Testament believer and the New Testament believer were always saved by grace through faith. You don't really believe unless you act on that. You can't tell me "I believe in my heart, but I don't feel I actually need to do anything about it." You mean to tell me that the God of the Ages gave His Son for you, and the most you can muster is mental assent?

Mental assent is not going to get you to heaven. That is just not going to do it. Ultimately, God is satisfied when my heart is submitted to Him. We can simplify this down to one sentence. God has only one objective in your life, only one: to get your attention on Him and keep it focused there. And everything else, as good as it may be, is not the number one objective. Everything in my life must be submitted to this.

> "And now, Israel, what does the Lord your God require from you, but to fear the Lord your God, to walk in all His ways and love Him, and to serve the Lord your God with all your heart and with all your soul, and to keep the Lord's commandments and His statutes which I am commanding you today for your good?" (Deuteronomy 10:12–13 NAS)

When you are part of a first-world culture, you are constantly faced with challenges to this objective of submitting everything to Him. Material things are a good example. There is nothing wrong with owning a nice car or a nice house. I am not suggesting you all sell all your material possessions and live in poverty. I am saying that you can only justify the things in your life if they are focused on the one thing. If I am going to buy this house or car, it is going to be because God is saying I can minister best in the lives of other people if I have this.

A few years ago there was a Billy Crystal movie called *City Slickers* where Billy was a guy approaching forty who was looking for the meaning of life. He had a significant conversation with the old, sage cowboy, Curly (played by Jack Palance), that went something like this:

Billy: "Your life makes sense to you."
Curly: Laughs
Billy: "What's so funny?"
Curly: "You city folk worry about a lot of stuff (expletive), don't you?"
Billy: "Hey, my wife told me that she didn't want me around."
Curly: Laughs "How old are you? Thirty-eight?"
Billy: "Thirty-nine."
Curly: "You all come up here at about the same age, same problems. You spend fifty weeks getting knots in your rope, and you figure that in two weeks you can untie them. None of you get it. Do you know what the secret of life is?"
Billy: "No, what?"
         Curly holds up his index finger. "This"
Billy: "Your finger?"
Curly: "One thing. Just one thing. You stick to that and everything else don't mean nothing."
Billy: *"That's great, but what's the one thing?"*
Curly: *"That's what you have to figure out."*

Billy stares at his index finger in deep thought as the scene fades.

There is only one important thing, and everything else must be submitted to that. For us, this "one thing" is getting our focus on who God is and keep it there.

MB: Understanding this "one thing," the heart issue, brings so much of the Bible together. The reality of the core issue of our relationship with God washes away any trappings of "religious activity," things we do to gain God's favor. God cannot love us more. Once we realize that, then it's easy to give our heart totally to Him. Luke records when one of Jesus' friends discovered this one thing:

> As Jesus and the disciples continued on their way to Jerusalem, they came to a village where a woman named Martha welcomed them into her home. Her sister, Mary, sat at the Lord's feet, listening to what he taught. But Martha was worrying over the big dinner she was preparing. She came to Jesus and said, "Lord, doesn't it seem unfair to you that my sister just sits here while I do all the work? Tell her to come and help me." But the Lord said to her, "My dear Martha, you are so upset over all these details! There is really only one thing worth being concerned about. Mary has discovered it—and I won't take it away from her." (Luke 10:38–42)

Mary's heart was fully given to God. Her only place to be was sitting with the Master. This is the one thing He wants from us: A heart turned fully toward God. This is all He wants from us.

So far, we have seen that God created man to be His partner in managing this planet. Man was not just another creation but rather *God's most favored creation.* Yet the plan derailed when Adam and Eve were deceived in the Garden and rebelled against God. Or so it seems.

God initiated His plan to bring man into His family almost immediately.

Did God know that the plan would derail? Or does He have some greater plan that didn't get off course and is marching on, right on schedule?

This seems to be the case. Along with the words Jeremiah and Ezekiel proclaimed, there was another message, a message of something very significant that was about to happen. It had to do with this character called the Messiah. God Himself was going to take on human flesh and come to Earth give the full revelation of who God is and also to take care of the sin issue once and for all.

Jesus was born in Bethlehem as Micah prophesied. He grew up in Nazareth and more than likely worked as a *tekton,* constructing stone buildings. One of the largest public works projects of that time, the rebuilding of Sepphoris by Herod Antipas, was only a few miles from Nazareth. At about age thirty, He began to proclaim the Good News and a personal relationship with the Living God.

How did one enter into this personal relationship with God? Jesus described the process to a famous rabbi named Nicodemus. It required a spiritual birth.

Nicodemus was confused when Jesus told him that he must undergo another birth. He asked, "Must I crawl again into my mother's womb?"

No, Jesus explains that this is a spiritual birth. He goes on to explain when He is "lifted up," then all who look toward Him and believe will receive eternal life because God is paying the price of sin Himself.

> Jesus replied, "I assure you, unless you are born again, you can never see the Kingdom of God." "What do you mean?" exclaimed Nicodemus. "How can an old man go back into his mother's womb and be born again?" Jesus replied, "The truth is, no one can enter the Kingdom of God without being born of water and the Spirit. Humans can reproduce only human life, but the Holy Spirit gives new life from heaven. . . . And as Moses lifted up the bronze snake on a pole in the wilderness, so I, the Son of Man, must be lifted up on a pole, so that everyone who believes in me will have eternal life. For God so loved the world that he gave his only Son, so that everyone who believes in him will not perish but have eternal life. God did not send his Son into the world to condemn it, but to save it." (John 3:3–6, 14–17)

As I understand it, this spiritual birth happens when you accept Jesus for who He is and His payment for your sin. When you, in faith, reach out to God and say, "I accept the things that you are telling me, I accept who you are in my life, and I submit myself to you," suddenly that spiritual connection that was broken when Adam turned his back on God in the Garden is reestablished as we turn toward Him.

RS: The Greek term "repentance" actually means to turn around. Where is repentance in this birth process?

MB: It is a mental and a physical decision on your part that you will turn away from those things that take you away from God and fill your life with the things that will take you toward God. For all of us, this has different meanings. For me, a former ice cream scooper who was used to eating six to eight scoops daily, it may mean not eating so much ice cream because my focus is on fulfilling myself with food rather than fulfilling myself with God. It could be material things, sensual things, sports, or many of the other distractions that filled our lives before we invited Christ to be Lord of our lives. Do we drop everything? I think that it is a matter of submitting it all to Him as our Lord.

RS: Fundamentally, disobedience is as deep a rebellion as the question, "Who is the real God in my life?" Am I going to live to please myself or live to please Him? I think this is what the ice cream or any other thing is. So there is a sense that when you talk about a new birth, you are also talking about a death. There is a funeral that occurs simultaneous to this new life.

MB: That is just what Paul writes in Romans 6 when he refers to baptism as a form of death and a new life coming forth.

Or have you forgotten that when we became Christians and were baptized to become one with Christ Jesus, we died with him? For we died and were buried with Christ by baptism. And just as Christ was raised from the dead by the glorious power of the Father, now we also may live new lives. (Romans 6:3–4)

It is a process now of death on one side and new life on another. One part of you dies, and God replaces it with something new, something from Him. We put a big word on it: *sanctification*. It is a process where God is changing us from who we were to who He is making us. This process begins the moment we accept Jesus as who He is, the "*kurios*," or "maximum leader," as the original Greek language indicates. A maximum leader to me is the one who has rule over every area of my life.

During the Sandinista War in Nicaragua in the '80s, the Miskito army had many comandantes. But there was only one "*comandante maximo*." He was the ultimate leader, and when he spoke, everybody jumped. I've got the concept.

Jesus is my Comandante Maximo. He is the ultimate leader for me and has rule over every area of my life. But I have to give it to Him, each area, and as I do, He takes the part of Michael Bagby that naturally turns away from Him and replaces it with a new Michael Bagby who has a desire to turn toward Him.

Sometimes, things that happen in the physical world are a reflection of what is happening in the spiritual world. The next scene is a good example.

At noon, darkness fell across the whole land until three o'clock. At about three o'clock, Jesus called out with a loud voice, "Eli, Eli, lema sabachthani?" which means, "My God, my God, why have you forsaken

Michael with Commandante "Jimi"

me?" Then Jesus shouted out again, and he gave up his spirit. At that moment the curtain in the Temple was torn in two, from top to bottom. The earth shook, rocks split apart, and tombs opened. The bodies of many godly men and women who had died were raised from the dead. (Matthew 27:45–46, 50–52)

When Jesus died on the cross, the sky darkened in the middle of the day. Since it was Passover (full moon), it could not have been an eclipse. There was an earthquake. The curtain in the temple that separated the inner court (where the priests gathered to worship) from the Holy of Holies (where God dwelled) tore from top to bottom. Tombs were opened, and many dead believers were resurrected.

Was this an event in the heavenlies or what! Look at what Jesus' death provoked: an earthquake, an impossible "eclipse," a huge, thick curtain being torn, and men and women resurrected. What possible spiritual significance did each one of these events have?

Jesus offered Himself as the payment for our sins. God Himself paid the ultimate price. Why did this have to happen? Because of our sin nature, it was hard, if not impossible, to have true intimacy with our Creator. There really wasn't much of a relationship. There were issues that needed to be resolved: sin issues, justice issues.

For by the power of the eternal Spirit, Christ offered himself to God as a perfect sacrifice for our sins. (Hebrews 9:14)

Because of the death of Jesus on the cross, those issues were resolved! We were "justified and reconciled." It is worth reading what these words mean to your life.

Justified by the Blood of Christ

For all have sinned; all fall short of God's glorious standard. Yet now God in his gracious kindness declares us not guilty. He has done this through Christ Jesus, who has freed us by taking away our sins. For God sent Jesus to take the punishment for our sins and to satisfy God's anger against us. We are made right with God when we believe that Jesus shed his blood, sacrificing his life for us. God was being entirely fair and just when he did not punish those who sinned in former times. And he is entirely fair and just in this present time when he declares sinners to be right in his sight because they believe in Jesus. (Romans 3:23–26)

We are declared "not guilty!"

Reconciled by the Blood of Christ

> But God showed his great love for us by sending Christ to die for us while we were still sinners. And since we have been made right in God's sight by the blood of Christ, he will certainly save us from God's judgment. For since we were restored to friendship with God by the death of his Son while we were still his enemies, we will certainly be delivered from eternal punishment by his life. (Romans 5:8–10)

The relationship is restored. The sin issue was taken care of once and for all. We once again, like Adam and Eve, have free access to God! Thirty-eight years after Jesus' crucifixion, the Roman legions under Titus destroyed the temple in Jerusalem, thus preventing any more sacrificial sin offerings! There have been none for more than 2,000 years.

What is really interesting in all of this is, not only was the relationship restored, there is a whole new level of relationship that God is inviting us into.

Something very culturally significant happened during the Last (Passover) Supper that Jesus had with His disciples that many of us in the twenty-first century have missed.

> And he took a cup of wine and gave thanks to God for it. He gave it to them and said, "Each of you drink from it, for this is my blood, which seals the covenant between God and his people. It is poured out to forgive the sins of many." (Matthew 26:27–28)

RS: Communion (or the Lord's Supper) is a special time for all Christians. Jesus' final celebration of the Passover with His disciples (with unleavened bread and wine) was rich with symbols of God's grace and favor to mankind. But there is more to the story.

When a young Hebrew man decided to marry the girl of his dreams, the first person he went to was her father. He usually began his discussion by saying something like this: "Jacob, I was in the field with my flock the other day when your daughter walked by. She is so ugly that my sheep ran away, and it took me three days to find them all."

To which the father replied: "You are mistaken my son, my daughter is a beautiful girl." Thus began the negotiations for the dowry, the price of the bride. After they had decided how many sheep, goats, barrels of oil, and bushels of wheat she was worth, the girl was called in, and the plan revealed. Wine and bread were brought to the table. The young lady gave bread to the young man and the cup of wine. Without any words, the young man drank from the cup and passed it to her. In his cultural way, he was saying, "I love you and want to spend the rest of my life with you. Will you be my bride?"

The young Hebrew maiden knew what the cup of wine gesture meant, and if she took the cup and drank from it, she was culturally saying, "Yes, I accept your proposal of marriage."

MB: In our culture, we make a different gesture. I remember the day in April 1988 when I asked Laura to marry me. It was at a beach café in La Ceiba Honduras; there was hot, muggy air and loud, blaring music (the song *Push It*). I dropped to my knee, took her hand, looked deeply into her eyes, and said "Laura, will you be my wife?" (It was one of the best moves that I ever made!) She laughed and replied, "Yes, of course!" This kneeling and taking the hand of your beloved is a gesture that makes more sense in our culture.

RS: The groom then left to build a room on his father's *insula* (or courtyard home), and she prepared herself for the wedding. She had to be ready when the groom showed up; if she was not, the wedding was off. When the groom's father de-

Jungle Love Boat cruise 1989

cided that the home was ready (he was the building inspector; sometimes the young boys were in such a hurry they would only put the walls up and leave the lights, door, and air conditioning for later!), the groom dressed himself and went to the bride's village. If he really loved her, he sent someone the day before to tell her he was coming. Once he arrived, the wedding feast began and usually lasted the week.

Jesus used this image of the wedding celebration (John 14, Matthew 25) often in His teaching, since it was an event so familiar to everyone. When Jesus passed the cup of wine to His disciples, they understood the cultural language He was using and realized He was inviting them into the closest possible relationship. Afterward, they referred to themselves (the Church) as the bride of Christ. The marriage relationship is the ultimate in intimacy. This is what God has invited us to be—intimate family members.

In our culture, it is customary to give the girl an engagement ring, so while we are away, she will have something to remind her of the engagement. Jews didn't do that. Instead, Jesus told the disciples, "Do this often in remembrance of me" (don't forget whom you are engaged to!). As a result, we regularily celebrate communion (or the Lord's Supper) in our congregations today.

MB: John spoke of this intimate family relationship that results from the new birth process. Bride? Son or daughter? All of these speak of intimate familiar relationship.

> But to all who believed him and accepted him, he gave the right to become children of God. They are reborn! This is not a physical birth resulting from human passion or plan—this rebirth comes from God. (John 1:12–13)

Paul describes this relationship in his first chapter to the church in Ephesus. It is such a rich passage to go through, just to realize who you are—how God sees us.

> How we praise God, the Father of our Lord Jesus Christ, who has blessed us with every spiritual blessing in the heavenly realms because we belong to Christ. Long ago, even before he made the world, God loved us and chose us in Christ to be holy and without fault in his eyes. His unchanging plan has always been to adopt us into his own family by bringing us to himself through Jesus Christ. And this gave him great pleasure. So we praise God for the wonderful kindness he has poured out on us because we belong to his dearly loved Son. He is so rich in kindness that he purchased our freedom through the blood of his Son, and our sins are forgiven. He has showered his kindness on us, along with all wisdom and understanding. . . . Furthermore, because of Christ, we have received an inheritance from God, for he chose us from the beginning, and all things happen just as he decided long ago. And now you also have heard the truth, the Good News that God saves you. And when you believed in Christ, he identified you as his own by giving you the Holy Spirit, whom he promised long ago. The Spirit is God's guarantee that he will give us everything he promised and that he has purchased us to be his own people. This is just one more reason for us to praise our glorious God. (Ephesians 1:3–8, 11,13–14)

I love the language Paul uses to describe this relationship. He says God has given us every spiritual blessing and has adopted us into His family—and this gave Him great pleasure. I love that line! Paul writes that God has showered His kindness on us (that word *shower* has such an excessive feel to it!) This is obviously God doing something with us that is giving Him great joy.

In this new relationship we have with God, our identity is a very important element for us to understand.

> But you are A CHOSEN RACE, A royal PRIESTHOOD, A HOLY NATION, A PEOPLE FOR God's OWN POSSESSION, that you may proclaim the excellencies of Him who has called you out of darkness into His marvelous light. . . . (1 Peter 2:9 NAS)

How does God see us? Who are we to Him? The Bible says in 1 Peter that we are an order of priests and a holy nation, literally, God's own people.

RS: That is a hard one for me to grab on to—being a priest. I have an image of this celibate person who is tucked away in some remote monastery and out of touch with real life.

MB: I think the picture Peter is giving us here is of a person who has direct access to God. The old priestly order had to go through extensive cleansing procedures before coming before God. In their cleansed state, they were able to represent the others. Since the cross, we are all "cleansed" and have direct and immediate access to God Himself.

This intimate relationship with God and special identity that we have with Him requires a distinctive mindset.

> Since you have been raised to new life with Christ, set your sights on the realities of heaven, where Christ sits at God's right hand in the place of honor and power. Let heaven fill your thoughts. Do not think only about things down here on earth. (Colossians 3:1–2)

Our old frame of reference was ourselves and what was ultimately good for us. Now our values and goals should be centered on God's character and will. After all, Jesus did not say: "If you want to follow Me, then plop down in your La-Z-Boy, and I will take care of all your needs. Keep looking out for yourself, and above all, let personal comfort and convenience be your guide. Then you will find true life in your personal possessions, vacations, and bank accounts."
Instead He stated plainly:

"If any of you wants to be my follower, you must put aside your selfish ambition, shoulder your cross, and follow me. If you try to keep your life for yourself, you will lose it. But if you give up your life for me, you will find true life. And how do you benefit if you gain the whole world but lose your own soul in the process? Is anything worth more than your soul? For I, the Son of Man, will come in the glory of my Father with his angels and will judge all people according to their deeds." (Matthew 16:24–27)

With this new mindset, we are to consider ourselves as condemned prisoners, not having any rights of our own. What does it mean to "take up your cross?" Who was carrying around a cross in first-century Jerusalem? Only condemned prisoners on their way to the place of execution. A modern version of this verse might be "take up your (choose one) 1) electric chair, 2) gas chamber, 3) hangman's noose, or 4) lethal injection."

I have been crucified with Christ; and it is no longer I who live, but Christ lives in me; and the life which I now live in the flesh I live by faith in the Son of God, who loved me, and delivered Himself up for me. (Galatians 2:20 NAS)

Since we are dead to this world, let us let Christ live through us, and let His ways be our ways. *What Would Jesus Do?* Since He is living inside you (Colossians 1:27), then "Let Him Out To Do It!" God is looking for followers who understand that His heart is for others. It is not what you know or what you say, it is how you love and serve others.

After washing their feet, he put on his robe again and sat down and asked, "Do you understand what I was doing? You call me 'Teacher' and 'Lord,' and you are right, because it is true. And since I, the Lord and Teacher, have washed your feet, you ought to wash each other's feet. I have given you an example to follow. Do as I have done to you. How true it is that a servant is not greater than the master. Nor are messengers more important than the one who sends them. You know these things—now do them! That is the path of blessing." (John 13:12–17)

To be successful in ministry, no matter at what level, requires an attitude of servanthood to whomever God places across your path. Paul later described to his disciple Timothy another aspect of this mindset.

Suffer hardship with me, as a good soldier of Christ Jesus. No soldier in active service entangles himself in the affairs of everyday life, so that he may please the one who enlisted him as a soldier. And also if anyone competes as an athlete, he does not win the prize unless he competes according to the rules. The hard-working farmer ought to be the first to receive his share of the crops. Consider what I say, for the Lord will give you understanding in everything. (2 Timothy 2:3–7 NAS)

In addition, we are now to have the courage and dedication of a soldier, the discipline and desire of an athlete, and the patience and faith of a farmer. These are important elements of our mindset dedicated to the Lord.

Above all else, our main objective in this life should be to know Christ in greater and deeper ways. Paul, perhaps the greatest missionary of the early Church, who accomplished more than most of us will, told the church in Philippi that this was his number one goal in life!

Yes, everything else is worthless when compared with the priceless gain of knowing Christ Jesus my Lord. I have discarded everything else, counting it all as garbage, so that I may have Christ and become one with him. I no longer count on my own goodness or my ability to obey God's law, but I trust Christ to save me. For God's way of making us right with himself depends on faith. As a result, I can really know Christ and experience the mighty power that raised him from the dead. I can learn what it means to suffer with him, sharing in his death, so that, somehow, I can experience the resurrection from the dead! (Philippians 3:8–11)

Meditate on this passage for a while. Let it penetrate deep into your spirit. This is the most important thing that we can do here in this life!

Having the intimate relationship, the special identity, and a dedicated mindset gives us the ability to fulfill a particular function that God has created us for.

For we are God's masterpiece. He has created us anew in Christ Jesus, so that we can do the good things he planned for us long ago. (Ephesians 2:10)

We are God's *poema* (Greek)—a work of art, a masterpiece—and He has a definite plan for our lives.

Masterpiece . . . artistic creation . . . a unique piece of majestic work. God has created each one of us in a very special way and planned long ago the things that He has for us to accomplish in His kingdom.

During my years flying in the Navy, one of the most important moments of our day was when we looked at the daily flight schedule to see what type of flights we were scheduled for. This was our purpose in life; this is what wearing the wings was all about.

Usually, the schedule came out sometime after the evening meal. We all hung around the Ready Room to see what our launch time was, what the mission was, what the target was, and who we were flying with. When your name was not on that daily schedule, the time turned "flat," it was a bummer. No excitement. No fulfillment. No satisfaction of a job done well. Just stay on the ship all day and do paperwork.

Coming into God's "air wing," I realized that He had the flight schedule written for me even before I arrived on the planet. God has a specific plan for me; and what excitement, fulfillment, and satisfaction there is in flying with Him.

> "You didn't choose me. I chose you. I appointed you to go and produce fruit that will last, so that the Father will give you whatever you ask for, using my name." (John 15:16)

We are to be fruit farmers, cultivating the fields that He has given us. What field has God assigned you? Your home? Your neighborhood? Your workplace? A "foreign" field through your prayers and financial help?

Along with this higher level of relationship with God, the exclusive identity that we now have in His family, the committed mindset, and the specific functions that He has for us, there is a grand future for all believers.

> "There are many rooms in my Father's home, and I am going to prepare a place for you. If this were not so, I would tell you plainly. When everything is ready, I will come and get you, so that you will always be with me where I am." (John 14:2–3)

Jesus is presently building a place for us. We will be with Him for all eternity.

> For the Lord himself will come down from heaven with a commanding shout, with the call of the archangel, and with the trumpet call of God. First, all the Christians who have died will rise from their graves. Then, together with them, we who are still alive and remain on the earth will be caught up in the clouds to meet the Lord in the air and remain with him forever. So comfort and encourage each other with these words. (1 Thessalonians 4:16–18)

Soon, Jesus will appear in the sky, and we will be taken up to heaven with Him. Can you imagine the chaos that will result when millions of office workers, car drivers, airplane pilots, field workers, factory workers, and people on the street suddenly disappear?

Blessed and holy are those who share in the first resurrection. For them the second death holds no power, but they will be priests of God and of Christ and will reign with him a thousand years. (Revelation 20:6)

One of our next jobs will be to reign with Jesus here on Earth for 1,000 years.

Meanwhile, He has given us a model for living in the present through the lifestyle dedicated to Him and His purposes.

They joined with the other believers and devoted themselves to the apostles' teaching and fellowship, sharing in the Lord's Supper and in prayer. A deep sense of awe came over them all, and the apostles performed many miraculous signs and wonders. And all the believers met together constantly and shared everything they had. They sold their possessions and shared the proceeds with those in need. They worshiped together at the Temple each day, met in homes for the Lord's Supper, and shared their meals with great joy and generosity—all the while praising God and enjoying the goodwill of all the people. And each day the Lord added to their group those who were being saved. (Acts 2:42–47)

Life is truly received and lived as we take time to study the Word, worship God, pray, spend time with other Christians, and help each other. This passage from Acts 2 is the model for our modern church and contains the elements that we all should be involved in.

When I flew in the Navy, we always entered a hostile area in a formation that was based on *mutual support.* If we were two airplanes looking for enemy aircraft, we would be about a mile apart, abeam (even) with each other, and constantly scanning the 6 o'clock position (rear quadrant) of our wingman to protect him from an attack by enemy fighters.

If we were in a four-plane strike formation, we would fly to the target in a loose "finger-tip" formation that gave everybody opportunity to check the 6 o'clock of each other. If we did get attacked, we had pre-briefed tactics that we would employ to defeat the enemy's attack and turn the situation around so we could take the offensive position.

The Christian life is very similar. Mutual support is as vital in the spiritual realm as it was in the air battles I fought over the Indian and Pacific Oceans and training areas in the US (fortunately for me it was all practice, no live bullets!). It's very hard to live outside the circle of your Christian brothers and sisters. Not only do you lose the protection and edification factors, but you miss out on true life itself.

When I was a child, there was a TV show called the *Lone Ranger*. A masked man rode around on his horse, Silver, appeared in towns or places where there was trouble, took care of the situation, often with his silver bullets, and then rode out of town to who knows where. His only traveling companion was an Indian named Tonto. He never had any long-term relationships and was a real loner. Years later, while reading Proverbs in a Spanish Bible one day, I discovered that *tonto* in Spanish means "idiot." *I have come to the conclusion that any one who is a "lone ranger" Christian is traveling with an idiot (himself).* Besides, God commands us to

> Think of ways to encourage one another to outbursts of love and good deeds. And let us not neglect our meeting together, as some people do, but encourage and warn each other, especially now that the day of his coming back again is drawing near. (Hebrews 10:24–25)

Obviously, this dynamic of fellowship is very important to God in our spiritual growth.

An intimate relationship, a special identity, a dedicated mindset, a singular purpose, an extraordinary future, and an exciting lifestyle in the present are all affected by a peculiar process that is happening inside you.

We have mentioned it briefly, this process of sanctification. Understanding this process is one of the most important tools that you have as a member of the kingdom of God.

Paul says: "For this is the secret: *Christ lives in you,* and this is your assurance that you will share in his glory" (Colossians 1:27). Meditate on this concept for a moment. It is profound and the source of many of our next steps.

> Beloved, now we are children of God, and it has not appeared as yet what we shall be. We know that, when He appears, we shall be like Him, because we shall see Him just as He is. (1 John 3:2 NAS)

As children of God, we will grow up to become like our heavenly Father.

Lukas: Be like God? Did I read that correctly?

MB: Yes, you did. Paul explains it well in this passage from Philippians that we talked about in our last session but is worth repeating:

> And now that I am away you must be even more careful to put into action God's saving work in your lives, obeying God with deep reverence and fear. For God is working in you, giving you the desire to obey him and the power to do what pleases him. (Philippians 2:12–13 NAS)

Many believe that once they get "saved," it is all over. They can cruise through life, waiting for their eternal reward. Actually, "it" has just begun, and God uses every experience here Earth to mold you into His character. As you allow God to work in you, you actually begin reflecting more and more of His characteristics. In this sense, you start *"becoming like God."* As we mentioned before, the phrase "put into action" can be better translated "bring to completion." *Salvation is just the first step in a divine process.*

If Christ is living in us (Colossians 1:27), then how can we "let Him out"? I believe by first asking Him to manifest Himself through us is a good starting place. Then we are to take each situation and ask ourselves, "What would Jesus do?," and with the power of the Holy Spirit, do it. As we deny our own nature and put it to rest, then we do allow Christ to come out of us and touch situations and people around us.

> Since you have heard all about him and have learned the truth that is in Jesus, throw off your old evil nature and your former way of life, which is rotten through and through, full of lust and deception. Instead, there must be a spiritual renewal of your thoughts and attitudes. You must display (or "put on") a new nature because you are a new person, created in God's likeness—righteous, holy, and true. (Ephesians 4:21–24)

We should be willing to abandon many aspects of our old nature and put on the new self that God is creating in us. This is the choice that we have in each situation. Do we hold on to our "old self" (thought patterns, habits) or go with the "new self" that God is creating? Do we let Christ out or leave Him trapped inside our own emotions and self-centeredness?

> As we know Jesus better, his divine power gives us everything we need for living a godly life. He has called us to receive his own glory and goodness! And by that same mighty power, he has given us all of his rich and wonderful promises. He has promised that you will escape the decadence all around you caused by evil desires and that you will share in his divine nature. (2 Peter 1:3–4)

God has given us divine power to help us put on the "new self." As we put this new self on, we share in His divine nature. Peter tells us how this divine power becomes available to us: it is as we know Jesus better! This is the reality of Christ living within us. As we let him out, we share in His divine nature.

> When you follow the desires of your sinful nature, your lives will produce these evil results: sexual immorality, impure thoughts, eagerness for lustful pleasure, idolatry, participation in demonic activities, hostility, quarreling, jealousy, outbursts of anger, selfish ambition, divisions, the feeling that everyone is wrong except those in your own little group, envy, drunkenness, wild parties, and other kinds of sin. Let me tell you again, as I have before, that anyone living that sort of life will not inherit the Kingdom of God. But when the Holy Spirit controls our lives, he will produce this kind of fruit in us: love, joy, peace, patience, kindness, goodness, faithfulness, gentleness, and self-control. (Galatians 5:19–23)

The habits or actions of the "old nature" (the flesh) contrast sharply with the actions or fruit of the Holy Spirit in our lives: love, joy, peace, patience, kindness, goodness, faithfulness, gentleness, and self-control.

What is the evidence of being filled with the Holy Spirit? Is it a manifestation of a spiritual gift or a spiritual fruit?

The presence of the Holy Spirit in your life will produce fruit, and if you see any of these fruit appearing and increasing in your life, then know that the Holy Spirit is indeed working.

RS: I constantly go to different churches to teach and have interaction with many different types of local congregations. In many churches I hear a form of the Gospel that includes all these obedient steps that we have mentioned. But can a person come to know Jesus and open his heart to God and not be doing all the right things?

MB: Of course! I doubt that we will ever get to the point where we are doing all the right things. I think this is a process where change is constantly happening or at least should be.

There is a great story of a missionary to an Alaskan Indian tribe. One of his recent converts was an old Eskimo man who one day came to him and said, "Pastor, ever since that day I invited Jesus into my heart, I have felt like there is a war going on inside me."

"What do you mean?" asked the missionary.

"Well, it's like there is this white dog and this black dog, and they are fighting inside," replied the old man.

The pastor asked, "Which one is winning?"

The old Eskimo thought for a moment and then said something very profound: *"The one that I feed the most."*

When we step into Christianity, Paul tells us to "bring to completion your salvation" as it literally says in Philippians 2:12. This is a clue that the Christian life is a divine process, beginning the moment that you accept Jesus as the *"Kurios"* and invite Him in. And as we feed the white dog, then the black dog has less and less power. The cool thing is this passage in Philippians says that actually God will give us the desire to make these changes, and He will also give us the power to make it happen.

Can a believer still be a member of God's family and not be doing all the right things? I think Paul tells us very clearly in 1 Corinthians 8 that we are only responsible for what God has revealed and illuminated to us. In this portion of the letter, Paul is discussing whether the believers should be eating meat that has been offered as a sacrifice to some of the pagan gods. I thought about this recently when we were in Corinth together while I was standing with Laura in the ruins of the butcher shop. Paul was correct in his counsel to go ahead and eat this meat, but he said if he forced his belief on one with a "weaker conscience" and made him eat this meat, then he was sinning against God and this person. In essence, the weaker brother was responsible only for what God has shown him personally.

> And you are sinning against Christ when you sin against other Christians by encouraging them to do something they believe is wrong. (1 Corinthians 8:12)

RS: It is important for us to understand the different ways God looks at people. There is a person who knows Him in his heart, is beginning a walk with Him, has pulled out all the stops to give everything to Him, and has turned his back on all the influences that pull him away.

Then there is this other person who has started on this journey, who for one reason or another, is not walking in obedience to what God has shown him. That person has a struggle all his own.

There is a third person who is walking through the minefield blissfully ignorant that there is such a thing as a mine. Those are the poorly taught. I frequently have people expressing things like, "If a person is pro-abortion, they must not be saved." Well, as I understand it, the Scripture says salvation is by grace through faith in the works that Messiah has done plus nothing! Even if they are poorly taught, even if they believe some things that we might find "unorthodox," even if they are sitting in a church with statues all around, doing things that they shouldn't be doing. They can be poorly taught on the beginning of their journey, and this is not the same as a lost person. A lost person is one who does not have the life of the Spirit of God within him.

MB: We have the opportunity to go as fast and as far with God as we want, or we have the opportunity to hang back. The natural tendency is to hang back on the fringe. We are content and comfortable in the areas that we haven't yet given to God. Often it takes some kind of crisis to get us moving forward; this is God yanking me in. God will always bring us to a point where He will show us how important it is for us to give Him that area. That's when real spiritual growth takes place.

RS: In a way, the death that occurs keeps resuscitating itself. Parts of me are rising up and being slain again. This is the sanctification process.

MB: Most definitely! Gene Edwards gives us a great illustration in his book, *The Inner Journey*. He says God is building a temple and we are the stones. The quarry is planet Earth. God uses huge saws to shape us, smaller saws to trim us, grinders to smooth us, and polishing cloths to shine us. Finally, we get to the point where we are ready to be inserted into the building. All of that work is done here, and what state we are at when we leave here is where we will be fitted in.

For me, this is a good illustration of what God is doing in this process we call sanctification. He is working on us, carving unsightly things out, trimming us, polishing us, and getting us ready to fit into something much bigger than us or what we could even imagine. If we realize what is happening to us, then it is a process that we can get excited about, even though often it hurts. Quite frankly, this is not fun.

RS: It's like surgery—necessary, but not something you want to go through every day.

MB: It's like we are in a hurdle race. I never liked running hurdles in track because when you successfully jumped over one, another one appeared, requiring another jump, and then another, and another! That is what the Christian life is, and if we stop jumping for a while, then God will always bring us around to the place where we are ready to begin jumping again. It's a process I believe occurs until I take my last breath as long as I allow God to work on me.

The hope for me is what Paul writes in 2 Corinthians 3:18: "And as the Spirit of the Lord works within us, we become more and more like him and reflect his glory even more."

This photo, taken in the Bavarian Alps a few months ago, tells it all. It was a cloudy, rainy day as we walked through the woods. When we arrived at the lake, the mountain was covered by the clouds. We ducked into a lakeside café for some coffee, and as we sat there, the sun began breaking through the clouds. By the time we finished, the sky was clear, and we hurried to the shore to get this photo. The reflection in this scene is so real that when I gave one of my first prints to my friend Tony, I accidentally had it turned upside

Near Mittenwald Bavaria

down. He looked closely, and commented: "It's a bit pixilly (*not in sharp focus due to the low resolution of the digital image*)", not realizing that it was upside down.

At some point in this process of spiritual growth, I will be like my heavenly father, although somewhat *pixilly*.

My son, Lukas, is growing up. When people see him, they see me because he is becoming more and more like me. He looks like me (and his mother,) he acts like me, he uses the same words that I do; its scary! I've got to be very careful. God has used these four kids in my life to really fine-tune me! Talk about hurdles to jump over! Development of spiritual fruit! These kids have been a catalyst. People are going to look at him, and, if I am the godly father that I aim to be, hopefully say that Lukas looks just like his father.

Lukas is beginning to look (and act) like his father

RS: I want to take a moment here and just encourage all who are listening and reading. I think when we begin talking of obedience and becoming all that God wants me to be, as well as understanding that He says I have as an inheritance, there is a problem; actually, a rather big problem, and here it is: I realize that in my own growth I am not always doing what I need to be doing, and I am not always putting everything into it, in spite of what I know to be true.

MB: Isn't the realization that it's sometimes three steps forward and two steps backward a natural part of this process?

RS: It's sobering to accept that some of us are growing slower in these areas, and we are not doing what we ought to do. When you get overwhelmed with that, go back to what Paul writes in Romans 7: "That which I should not do, I do. That which I should do, I don't. All the things I am supposed to be doing, I don't do, and the things I am supposed to do, I'm not! O wretched man that I am. Who will deliver me from this body of death?" (Romans 7:15–25)

In the Roman period, if a man killed another man, one of the possible penalties would be to strip the man who was killed bare, strip the killer bare, strap that dead body to his back, and put him in a cage. Slowly, the dead flesh would permeate the living flesh and kill it, like gangrene. It would slowly and horribly take the life of the murderer. Now this was an unusual punishment but a known punishment.

"Who will deliver me from this body of death?"

There is a sense in which as we are moving on in our relationship with God and are aggressively obedient to Him we are seeing victory. But there are times when you will feel like you are strapped to the body of the old you, and the rottenness that was you is coming over and ruining all the great things that God is doing in your life. I am encouraged that if Paul felt like that as he moved from place to place it has to be a normal part of the Christian experience. It has to be something we each experience.

MB: Let's be real here because the Bible has always been real when it comes to examples of godly men and women walking out their walk with God and the total aspect of living in this world. It's not often a rosy picture, and there are some aspects of this dying-to-yourself process that are unpleasant. Our own human nature is often one of them. At least it is for me.

But there are "carrots" that God holds in front of us to encourage us on. The future we have with God is incredible; it goes way beyond our wildest imagination. If we could only catch this concept! This is why Paul was taken to the third heaven and saw this picture, so that He could share his enthusiasm with those of us who haven't been there yet, and encourage us to press on. He said, "forgetting all things, I press on to the upward call of Christ" (Phil. 3:14). He saw it. That was enough to encourage him to really go for it. Because what else do we have?

When Jesus began to give some very hard teaching about being the Bread of Life and His disciples having to eat this bread, many turned away. He asked the twelve,

"Are you going to leave too?" Simon Peter replied: "To whom would we go? You alone have the words that give eternal life." (John 6:68)

It is the same thing for us. Yes, we are going through a process that is sometimes difficult. But knowing what lies ahead, we can persevere and endure whatever is placed before us. Only Jesus has the words of life. So whatever we are going through right now, God is going to be there for us, seeing it through, and we will be better off spiritually as a result.

Maybe this perspective will help wrap this session up.

GETTING YOUR WINGS

Since the beginning of time, men have looked at birds and tried to figure out how they fly. When I was a child, I used to watch the birds and wonder the same. At age five, our family traveled from Germany to the US by air. As I watched Ireland, the North Atlantic, Iceland, Greenland, and parts of Canada pass beneath the wings of the *Super Constellation*, I realized the view of the earth from above was well worth the effort it took to get up there.

I felt very special to see the earth from this perspective. Seeing clouds from the side, from above, and while flying through them was an amazing sensation for a five-year-old. When we flew to Turkey a few years later, these feelings were confirmed, and it was only natural that after graduating from college, I chose to perform my military service in the air.

After reciting the oath of office and committing my next years to defending the United States, I entered Naval Flight School. After months of physical and academic training, we climbed into an airplane and flew it off the ground. Those first few flights were exhilarating, and I realized if I was going to remain a pilot, I must discipline myself to learn all there was to know about flying. After all, getting off the deck of a carrier and back on was going to be a challenging experience. To do it safely required my full attention. After twenty months of flight school, I received my wings of gold and the right to fly.

I learned quickly that there was more to it than just getting up in the air. There was a purpose to flying. Sure, it was great just to soar with the birds and angels, but most flights had a mission to accomplish. Usually, it was getting from point A to point B and delivering something in the process. To do that properly required an extensive knowledge of the aircraft, weapon systems, tactics, weather, geography, and the enemy. One could not survive long in such an unforgiving environment without a handle on all these aspects of accomplishing the mission.

From the beginning, men have looked at the sky and the landscape around and wondered about the One who created it all. Down through the ages men have had a deep longing to know their Creator, to relate to Him, and to not only know about Him, but to intimately know Him. History is full of stories of men reaching out to God; from Icarus, who soared so high that his wings melted, to Paul of Tarsus, who acquired years of great learning about God before he finally knew God. From the Roman emperor Constantine who conquered in Jesus' name, to many kings and presidents who have governed in God's name, men have searched for an understanding and relationship with the Creator of the sunrise and sunset.

Lt. Bagby

God Himself created mankind in His image. In spite of man's rejection of His authority over their lives, He made provision for a relationship between them when He Himself took on human form and paid the price for man's sin. After making it possible for men and women to become members of His family, He gave them the right to soar with Him, and He made it possible to have an intimate relationship when He sent His Holy Spirit to dwell inside them.

The "new man" now was a different species; he could live not only in the physical realm, but he could also interact with the invisible, spiritual realm. Learning about this "new" spiritual environment and the opposing forces arrayed against the kingdom were only the first steps to a longer, more significant journey. This awakening of man's spirit inside was an exciting event. Even more exciting was what this would allow man to actually participate in God's plans for not only this planet, but for the entire universe.

Early Christians learned that involvement in God's mission had a two-fold purpose. God's plan was not only carried out through the actions of members of His family, but in the process something very special was taking place within the spirits of men. They were actually being changed through their involvement with God's mission, more and more into persons who shared God's personality!

The more change that occurred, the more intimate became their personal relationship with the Creator Himself. As I look back now, I realize that receiving those gold wings on April 18, 1975 was really only the first step toward me becoming an effective warrior capable of carrying out a mission to defend my country.

When I committed my life to the Lord in November 1981, it was only the first step in a life-long journey where God would use me as much as I would allow Him to, and in the process, make me into the man that He wants me to be.

Often recognizing the process is the first step toward allowing it to happen. *God says that as we allow it to happen, He will make it happen.*

As we walk in the process of "new things coming," may we be filled with thankfulness, wonder, joy, and awe at things that God has not only allowed us to do, but also given us the privilege to do. May we appreciate even more the God who has graciously invited us into His family to participate in the "divine nature" and soar with Him to the high places.

Personal Reflection

1. What does it mean to you to be created in God's image?
2. Which of the Greek words for sin is most meaningful for you?
3. What was the major benefit to you of Jesus' death on the cross?
4. How does knowing your divine identity help you face problems?
5. What is your major hindrance to the "sanctification" process?

Deeper Water

A. In 1 Peter chapter 1, Peter gives us a description of what happens as we grow spiritually. Read verses 3 through 10 and list these steps.
B. In Galatians chapter 5, Paul contrasts life in the spirit and life in the flesh. Read closely this chapter and meditate on this process that is happening inside you.
C. In Colossians chapters 2 and 3, Paul describes how to live the new life in Christ. What are the important points that Paul make here that apply to your life?

There is so much purpose to our lives in the spiritual world! This has been the life-changing dynamic for many over the centuries, and numerous projects and programs have been birthed as a result. Unfortunately, as these were passed on to the next generation, they often became just that—programs and projects without the life that God intended. Christianity for many became a routine, a religious act that was void of the Spirit. The reality is that once we step into God's presence and realize the opportunities and high stakes, the most important thing that we can acquire is a passion for the mission.

A Passion for the Mission

I urge you therefore, brothers, by the mercies of God, that you present your bodies as a living, holy sacrifice, acceptable to God, which is your reasonable service. (Romans 12:1 LMB)

RS: When I understand the heart of God, I begin to sense the purpose He has for mankind. If His objective is to make me more like Him, if that is what He really wants me to be, then I have to go through a process. That process is first of all an understanding. It has to happen on a mental level before it happens in the heart.

The church at Rome was struggling to understand what God's agenda was, so Paul wrote sixteen chapters of a letter that we call Romans. It was essentially written to say one thing: "If you have really

Truman, David, and Michael baptizing in Nicaragua

185

considered all that God has done, it will be perfectly reasonable for you to lay yourself down on an altar, die, and allow what comes away from that altar to be Messiah living in you, instead of you living in you" (chapter 12:1).

Why is that reasonable? God says *"All I want is everything."* That is not a reasonable position. In negotiation there must be a basis for bargaining. God is not negotiating. He came to the table and said (see the first three chapters of Romans): "I don't care if you are the heathen running out there in loincloth in the middle of the bush, or the moral person in chapter two who says I keep a standard of morality, or the religious person in chapter three. I don't care which of those persons you are, you are condemned. And I will tell you why. Because the heathen is worshipping the tree rather than the God who created it, the moral person doesn't live up to his own moral standard, and the religious person is corrupt in his heart to the very core; and all three of you are condemned."

Now, He could have continued saying: "So, ha, ha, that's it! Let's pack it in." But He doesn't. Chapters 4 and 5 lay out: "But God who is rich in mercy could not let that sit the way it was." So He decided to take care of it, and He left heaven's high place, put on skin, came down, walked on the earth, trained, taught, modeled, and then died as a sacrificial lamb. And gave me an opportunity to receive Him, so that I would have life.

OK. So, having life, why does that make it reasonable for me to lay down my life? He didn't stop there. He went on and justified us, declaring us righteous when we weren't righteous. Justified is not "just as if I had never sinned," it's "I did sin, I'm absolutely guilty, and He paid the penalty."

He gave us chapters 6, 7, and 8 where He says, "Look! There is a whole process of growing." We talked about this in the last session: a process of dying to ourselves and recognizing that He lives in me, yielding myself to the spirit of God, and obeying Him. Chapter 7 is for those who want to cling to ritual, the Law, or the thing that would give them a good symbol that says they were good people. No, that's not where the heart is. In chapter 8 He says, "Spirit, Spirit, Spirit, Spirit"—thirteen times He says, "It's by the power of the gift that I have given you." If I was condemned and He declared me righteous, if I now have this incredible investing of God to carry me through this process we call sanctification, then how does that make it OK for me to lay my life down?

"Wait a minute," God says, "there is one more piece. I want to vindicate my relationship with Israel. I want you to know the pattern that I gave you in the past: I am a trustworthy God. I'm worth laying down everything for. You can trust Me. If you study Israel's past, or present, or future, I'm going to show you, through the history of this people, that I am reliable. Now look, if you were despicably wicked, I did everything to save you, brought you through the process, and you can check My track record against Israel. Doesn't it become reasonable now what I am asking you to do, which is to lay down everything?"

We ask, "How do I do that?" In the next four chapters He tells you what that means. The whole matter is just one issue: *I want you. I want everything about you. I want you, you, you!*

MB: God wants all of us, and we have to give it all to him. This is a mentality that we have to have. Give it all; it's just our reasonable service!

RS: Unfortunately, over and over again in our lives we have seen the consequences of failing to give everything to the Lord. There are so many believers we know and have worked with who, in a moment in their lives, God was really using them, only to find out later they grabbed control of something again. I have seen a pattern in ministry where men and women in their young lives work hard to build a ministry, and in their later lives, destroyed the very ministry they built. Because in the beginning it was God's; in the end it was theirs.

Randy teaching in Jerusalem

It all comes down to an issue of possession. It should be so simple, but it's often hard to pull off. The toughest part of the whole thing is remembering that if God is trying to make me more like Him, what is He like? He is a God who does not stop giving and will go to any length to give you everything possible because He wants to shower on you good things. How does that fit into my life? I need to respond to be like Him. I need to be the same kind of person who will go to any length, give up anything, at any cost.

MB: So what is this "laying down" of our lives? We lay it down on the altar, it's our reasonable service. What does He want us to do? You just said it in a nutshell: He wants us to give. If you look at the Christian Scriptures, there is a passage that directly addresses this issue.

> One of them, an expert in religious law, tried to trap him with this question: "Teacher, which is the most important commandment in the Law of Moses?"
>
> Jesus replied, "You must love the Lord your God with all your heart, all your soul, and all your mind.' This is the first and greatest commandment. A second is equally important: 'Love your neighbor as yourself.' All the other commandments and all the demands of the prophets are based on these two commandments." (Matthew 22:35–40)

Of all the 612 laws God gave Moses, Jesus focused on only two—*Deuteronomy 6:5* and *Leviticus 19:18*. He didn't refer to any dietary laws, or sacrificial laws, or any societal laws, laws that in one sense were easily obeyed. Instead, He brought to attention the two most difficult laws. Why were they difficult?

To fulfill these laws required a heart turned fully toward God. You can't just go through the motions of "loving God" with heart, soul, and mind; by definition this is something that comes from within. Without profound conviction, it is impossible to live a life that reflects love for your neighbors. These are actions that must be rooted deep inside your being. They must reflect a heart condition, a heart turned fully toward God. This "heart turned fully toward God" is something you see over and over again in the pages of Scripture. This is the main thing God wants from us. This is all He wants from us. Everything else will follow this heart condition, which is totally focused and submitted to God. When our hearts are given to Him, then it becomes very natural to give and actively love others.

RS: A few years ago, we were bombarded over the airwaves with "Toyota" love: *"I love what you do for me!"* Madison Avenue sells you something by showing how it will benefit you. God's approach to love is from an entirely different direction. Look at the way He created mothers.

When the baby cries in the middle of the night, the mother doesn't get up to feed the baby simply because she has an overwhelming sense of *emotional* love. She's often groaning as she gets up. But, knowing that the baby cannot care for itself, her getting up in the middle of the night is an act of love; it is an act of meeting a need that the child cannot meet on its own. And she does it only because the need exists, not for any thanks the baby will give her at the moment or even later! The only payoff she gets is a few more hours of sleep while the child sleeps.

Look how this applies to the life of a believer. I am not commanded to like the people in my fellowship. I'm commanded to love them. I'm glad He didn't say "like," because there are some people whom I naturally gravitate to and others whom I never connect with. So how do I deal with that love command? As I walk into a room and look at each one of them, I ask myself, "What does that person need that I can do?" And then I begin to do it. That action is the expression of love. It is *meeting the need because there is a need.*

MB: The funny thing is, when we actively "love" someone that we don't particularly like, eventually there comes genuine "like" feelings. C.S. Lewis mentions this phenomenon in his classic *Mere Christianity* in a chapter titled "Let's Pretend." It is a work of the Spirit that has happened to me over and over again. The feelings came as a result of me stepping out and doing something I was uncomfortable doing because it needed to be done.

There are different words for love in the Bible, different concepts than our society has; yet what God wants from us is very simple. He wants total devotion with all of our heart, all of our soul, all of our mind, and all of our might (Deuteronomy 6:5). The question is how? How did those first-century believers who heard Jesus command this respond? Undoubtedly, they responded in a very functional manner. What was in their hearts was expressed in their actions.

How Do We Love God with "All Our Heart"?

The Hebrew word for *heart* in Deuteronomy 6:5 is *lebab*, which translates "inner man;" the source of the life of the inner person in various aspects, with a focus on feelings, thoughts, volition, and other areas of inner life. We love God "with all our heart" by first worshipping and praising Him. Praise and worship is simply our human response to His divine presence. The Bible is full of examples of humans responding to God's presence by worshipping and praising Him.

When all the people of Israel saw the fire coming down and the glorious presence of the LORD filling the Temple, they fell face down on the ground and worshiped and praised the LORD, saying, "He is so good! His faithful love endures forever!" (2 Chronicles 7:3)

To the Hebrew mind, the heart was the core of their innermost being. An encounter with God usually evokes some sort of emotional response from this innermost part, recognizing God for who He is and what He has done for us. The Book of Psalms provides us with great examples of how to praise and worship God. To really understand what the psalmists were communicating, it's important to realize that where the word *praise* appears in our English Bibles there is actually one of seven Hebrew words (which are translated *praise* in English). Understanding this concept of praise as the early Church

With Roy and Mary Kendal, and Martin Hjalmeby at the spa at Ein Gedi.

190

knew it, will help us as we "worship the Lord with all our hearts." Our dear friend Roy Kendall of the Jerusalem School of Worship offers us the following insights.

The Seven Hebrew Words for Praise

1. *Hallal*: To praise the Lord by celebrating, by dancing, by shining forth, by acting clamorously foolish; A very robust liberating kind of praise.

    Hallal the LORD! Hallal God in his heavenly dwelling; Hallal him in his mighty heaven! (Psalm 150:1)

2. *Shabach*: To praise the Lord with a shout and a loud voice.

    Your unfailing love is better to me than life itself; how I Shabach You! (Psalm 63:3)

3. *Yadah*: To praise the Lord with hands and hand movements.

    I bow before your holy Temple as I worship. I will Yadah to your name for your unfailing love and faithfulness, because your promises are backed by all the honor of your name. (Psalm 138:2)

4. *Todah*: The sacrifices of praise that amplifies a sustained singing; Also refers to praising the Lord as a processing choir or parade, or by giving thanks.

    "He who offers Todah honors Me . . ." (Psalm 50:23 NAS)

5. *Zamar*: To praise the Lord with the playing of an instrument.

    My heart is steadfast, O God; I will sing, I will Zamar. (Psalm 108:1 NAS)

6. *Tehillah*: A praise from your spirit, the pouring out of your heart before God; letting Him know how you feel; being real with Him.

    Yet you are holy. The Tehillah of Israel surround your throne. (Psalm 22:3)

7. *Barak*: To praise the Lord by kneeling or bowing low.

> Prayer also will be made for Him continually, and daily He shall be baraked. (Psalm 72:15 NKJV)

To worship and praise the Lord in these manners is truly *loving Him with all your heart!* We get excited at football and basketball games right? We jump and shout at concerts right? (At least I did.) We get emotional! Why shouldn't we get excited about being in God's presence? There is a progression from this exuberant expression to even deeper emotions. As we do sense His presence, this joy and celebration will naturally lead to intimate, reverent communion with Him.

Lukas: So I can get excited about God!?

MB: Definitely! It's only natural that we would get excited about our Creator who is adopting us into His family! This is better than winning the lottery! And don't forget, as you get to know Him, your sense of awe and reverence will grow. To truly know God is to *hallal*, *shabach*, and this will usually lead to *tehillah and barak*.

Lukas with Michael at Munchenburg castle, Germany

How Do We Love Him with "All Our Soul"?

This word *soul* in Deuteronomy 6:5 is the Hebrew word *nepesh*, which carried the meaning of the inner self, i.e., the essence of life, including thinking, feeling, willing, desiring. Your *nepesh* is the center of your ethics. It is the source of obedience to God's commands. Jesus said:

> "If you love me, obey my commandments." (John 14:15)

Obedience to God has always been a big issue in the Bible. Consider what God said to Moses on Mt. Sinai while He was giving the "big Ten Commandments."

> I do not leave unpunished the sins of those who hate me, but I punish the children for the sins of their parents to the third and fourth generations. But I lavish my love on those who love me and obey my commands, even for a thousand generations. (Exodus 20:5–6)

Samuel gave us a great perspective on the importance of obedience to God in an encounter with a disobedient King Saul.

> But Samuel replied, "What is more pleasing to the LORD: your burnt offerings and sacrifices or your obedience to his voice? Obedience is far better than sacrifice. Listening to him is much better than offering the fat of rams." (1 Samuel 15:22)

The word *obey* is used *360* times in the Bible. That's almost one usage for every day of the year! The obedience the Lord desires comes from the essence of our being, our *nepesh*. It goes beyond our emotions; it is deeper than our intellect. Our heavenly Father wants a relationship of trust with His Children.

Being a father myself, I can grasp the importance of this. There are situations with my four children when I need them to obey me, and I don't have time to explain. Imagine trying to explain to a four-year-old why they should not walk in front of an airplane when the propellers are turning! Or not to drink the water in the Rio Coco when we are swimming and bathing.

I want them to have the trust in me so they will obey me just because they know that "my ways are higher than their ways" (sound familiar?), and often, at this age (twelve, eleven, five, and three), they don't realize the dangers that are lurking in certain situations. I also want them to know that I love them and would lay down my life for them. I hope the level of love and respect between us is so great that obedience, rather than rebellion, would be their natural response to me. This is the ideal for all parents, but reality is different. After all, none of us taught our babies to grab the toy and yell, *"Mine!"* It's the sin nature that's in the genes.

I don't want my kids to obey me because they *have to*, but rather because they *want to*. God wants to have a similar relationship with us. This is loving Him with all our soul.

Arielle: So, we don't obey to gain favor with God, but rather obedience comes from our love for Him.

MB: Exactly! Obedience results from the love relationship!

How Do We Love Him with "All Our Mind"?

I believe this love has to do with letting our mind dwell on Him and always keeping all our thoughts inside the corral that's labeled: "What's good for my relationship with God."

This word used for "mind" in the Greek is *dianoia*, which means reasoning, understanding, thinking. The first way we love God with our mind is by setting our priorities. The Bible is very clear that God is number one, your family is number two, your ministry is number three, and your work is number four. Everything else follows these.

Remember your first girlfriend (or boyfriend)? You probably couldn't get her (him) out of your mind. Your thoughts were always coming back to that special one. How about your present "love"?

When I met Laura and fell in love with her, I wanted to spend all my time with her. The first and last thing on my mind each day was to see her. I wanted to do things that pleased her. I wanted all my thoughts, words, and actions to reflect the love I felt for her. Now we've been married for fifteen years. I have realized Satan will send "distractions" my way. My work is probably my greatest distraction from our relationship. It especially was noticeable when we were given a twin-engine Piper Seneca, which needed a lot of my time and attention. Laura used to joke as I headed out to the airport "Where are you going today? To see your girlfriend?"

I got the message. My priorities had gotten out of line. It is easy for those involved in ministry to get number one and number three confused. After all, when we serve God, we are making Him number one right? As long as we don't neglect our family in the process! I have seen ministers so caught up in their work for the Lord that they leave their families in the dust. I don't think this brings smiles to God's face, quite the opposite. Now I know as I keep Laura above my work, *I am loving her with my mind*. If I don't, I know there can be big problems, and our relationship will suffer as a result.

God also wants us to love Him with our minds. Our thoughts should always be centered on Him and what's good for our relationship. Paul puts it this way in 2 Corinthians:

> We are destroying speculations and every lofty thing raised up against the knowledge of God, and we are taking every thought captive to the obedience of Christ . . . (2 Corinthians 10:5 NAS)

It's important that we bring every thought inside the "sphere of God" in our life. God says that when we do, our relationship with Him will grow. Filling our minds with God's thoughts has a similar effect. Look how the psalmist describes this process:

> How blessed is the man who does not walk in the counsel of the wicked, nor stand in the path of sinners, nor sit in the seat of scoffers! But his delight is in the law of the LORD, and in His law he meditates day and night. And he will be like a tree firmly planted by streams of water, Which yields its fruit in its season, And its leaf does not wither; And in whatever he does, he prospers. (Psalm 1:1–3 NAS)

MEDITATION

Meditation is contemplation, pondering. Unlike other forms of Buddhist or New Age meditation where you try to empty your mind, for a Christian, it is filling your mind with God. When you meditate on God's Word, your spiritual roots will grow stronger; your spirit will be continually nourished; your character will change to reflect more of Christ's character; there will be fruit of the Spirit in greater measure; your intimacy with God will grow! You will be receiving true life!

PRAYER

Prayer is another way to love the Lord with your mind. Prayer is nothing more than talking to God on the celestial telephone. Communication is essential in any relationship that is growing and getting more intimate. It's important to decide that you will communicate with God and set time aside regularly to talk with Him. Jesus gave us some guidelines for our communication with God in Matthew 6:

> "When you pray, don't babble on and on as people of other religions do. They think their prayers are answered only by repeating their words again and again. Don't be like them, because your Father knows exactly what you need even before you ask him! Pray like this:

Our Father in heaven, may your name be honored. May your Kingdom come soon. May your will be done here on earth, just as it is in heaven. Give us our food for today, and forgive us our sins, just as we have forgiven those who have sinned against us. And don't let us yield to temptation, but deliver us from the evil one." (Matthew 6:7–13)

Notice that Jesus says *"when you pray"* and not *"if you pray."* He also says, *"pray like this."* Jesus gave us an outline for prayer. We are to fill in the specifics. How do you like it when you call someone and get a prerecorded message? Or receive a form letter? That's probably how God feels when we begin reciting learned prayers with little or no feeling.

- *Let God know how you feel about Him.* Worship and praise Him.
- *Confess any thoughts and acts that are outside God's character.* This confession clears the slate for further conversation.
- *Thank God for the good things that He is doing in your life.* Even those things that may not be pleasant, but are working for God's purposes (James 1:2).
- *Ask God to give you the things you need in this life.* Ask Him to specifically help others who need Him in their life; ask Him to intervene in situations beyond your control. How can we expect anything to happen before we have talked to our heavenly Father? It usually doesn't. With this connection we have to the spiritual world, our prayers can impact areas in far corners of the globe. That is an amazing fact!

Consider this testimony of the far-reaching power of prayer.
A missionary on furlough told this true story while visiting his home church in Michigan:

While serving at a small field hospital in Africa, every two weeks I traveled by bicycle through the jungle to a nearby city for supplies. This was a journey of two days and required camping overnight at the halfway point. On one of these journeys, I arrived in the city where I planned to collect money from a bank, purchase medicines and supplies, and then begin my two-day journey back to the field hospital.

Upon arrival in the city, I observed two men fighting, one who had been seriously injured. I treated him for his injuries and at the same time witnessed to him of the Lord Jesus Christ. I then traveled two days, camping overnight, and arrived home without incident.

196

Two weeks later, I repeated my journey. Upon arriving in the city, I was approached by the young man I had treated. He told me that he had known I carried money and medicines. He said, "Some friends and I followed you into the jungle, knowing that you would camp overnight. We planned to kill you and take your money and drugs. But just as we were about to move into your camp, we saw that you were surrounded by twenty-six armed guards."

At this I laughed and said I was certainly all alone out in that jungle campsite. The young man pressed the point and said, "No sir, I was not the only person to see the guards. My five friends also saw them, and we all counted them. It was because of those guards that we were afraid and left you alone."

At this point in the sermon, one of the men in the congregation jumped to his feet and interrupted the missionary and asked if he could tell him the exact date that this happened. The missionary told him the date. And the man who interrupted told him this story:

On the night of your incident in Africa, I was preparing to play golf. I was about to putt when I felt the urge to pray for you. In fact, the urging of the Lord was so strong I called men in this church to meet me here in the sanctuary to pray for you. Would all those men who met with me on that day stand up?

The men who had met that day and prayed for their missionary brother in far off Africa stood to their feet. The missionary wasn't concerned who they were, he was busy counting how many men were standing. There were twenty-six.

Prayer is a mysterious thing. Why would God want us to ask Him to do something that He can already do if He wants? Could it have something to do with our free will? Or is it to prepare the bride of Christ for the future? One thing is certain: God commands us to pray and in a way that goes beyond rattling off superficial sentences. He wants us to be real with Him!

This "being real" is one of the most important aspects. When we get detached and impersonal, we are talking to a wall. Praying is as much listening as it is talking. Any conversation with some one you love is a two-way street. Prayer is taking the time to align ourselves with God, and in essence, agree with things that He is doing or wants to be done.

Prayer is a time to pour your heart out to God. He already knows what you are thinking and feeling anyway. It is also a time to hear from Him. Prayer is not something we should do a few minutes a few times a week. Paul says that we should pray without ceasing (1 Thessalonians 5:17). I believe we should be in an attitude of always talking to God and listening for His voice during the course of our days.

Prayer is one of the most effective means to get close to God. That's really the bottom line: God wants an intimate relationship with you—not a casual relationship, but one that goes deep. Loving Him with all your heart, soul, and mind is the only way into this intimacy.

Fishing off Maui

Mikaela: Intimacy? God wants that kind of relationship with me?

MB: Yes, more than anything else. This is what it is all about: relationship with God on the most intimate level! Now let's move on to the second most important commandment:

Jesus replied, "'You must love the Lord your God with all your heart, all your soul, and all your mind.' This is the first and greatest commandment. A second is equally important: 'Love your neighbor as yourself.' All the other commandments and all the demands of the prophets are based on these two commandments." (Matthew 22:37–40)

Luke records that when Jesus was asked, "Who is my neighbor?" Jesus told the story of the Good Samaritan—which showed that "our neighbor" is any fellow inhabitant of this planet who needs help (Luke 10:25–37).

In the pages of the Christian Scriptures, we often see the phrases, "one another" and "each other." The New Testament gives us at least twenty-one practical ways to love "one another." Study each of the passages listed below to fully grasp the importance God places on loving one another.

198

The Twenty-One Commandments for Interpersonal Relationships

1.	Romans 12:10	Be devoted . . . Give preference . . .
2.	Romans 12:13	Contribute to the needs of . . .
3.	Romans 14:13	Do not judge . . .
4.	Romans 14:19	Build up . . .
5.	Romans 15:7	Accept . . .
6.	1 Corinthians. 12:25	Care for . . .
7.	Galatians 5:13	Serve . . .
8.	Galatians 6:2	Bear one another's burdens . . .
9.	Ephesians 4:2	Be patient . . .
10.	Ephesians 4:32	Be kind and tenderhearted . . .
11.	Ephesians 4:32	Forgive . . .
12.	Colossians 3:16	Teach and admonish . . .
13.	1 Thessalonians 4:18	Comfort . . .
14.	Hebrews 3:13	Encourage . . .
15.	James 4:11	Do not be against . . .
16.	James 5:9	Do not complain . . .
17–18.	James 5:16	Confess your sins . . . Pray for . . .
19.	1 Peter 4:8	Keep fervent in your love . . .
20.	1 Peter 4:9	Be hospitable . . .
21.	1 Peter 5:5	Submit . . .

Why is God so intent on making sure that we know how to practically love one another? There are many reasons.

First, we need to feel love from others. God has designed us in a manner that requires feelings of acceptance, love, and affection. When that is happening in a healthy manner, our contentment and satisfaction levels are high. When there is an absence of love in our lives, there are serious consequences that affect all levels of society. Just ask any social worker or psychologist. Our jails and institutions are full of people who never received the proper amount of love as a child or young adult.

Second, we need help in this life. We need help from each other. Anyone who says otherwise is a true "lone ranger" and travelling with "Tonto" (Spanish: *idiot*). Loving and serving one another is God's practical solution to many of life's problems. He doesn't have to send a legion of angels if He has a few willing servants who will respond to the needs of others around them.

A third reason is that God knows that as we involve ourselves in the lives of others we grow spiritually and become more intimate with Him. Loving one another in these practical ways allows God's character to come forth more and more. Asking ourselves, "What would Jesus do," in each interpersonal situation will always result in a practical expression of love. When we serve others, in effect we are partnering with God in a work that will have profound affect. That other person will benefit from your love, but perhaps the greatest beneficiary will be you.

Lukas: Me? How can that be?

MB: Remember the movie *Karate Kid*? Daniel was a guy who wanted to learn karate. He showed up for lessons eager to learn some karate moves. His teacher, Mr. Miyagi, told him on the first day to go "paint fence." The boy was surprised and reluctantly spent all day with a brush moving it up and down over the boards.

The next day the boy arrived tired but still eager to learn some karate moves. Mr. Miyagi told him to go "wax car." Disheartened, yet obedient, he went with rags and spent the day moving the cloths in circular motions over not one but a whole fleet of classic cars owned by his teacher—"wax on . . . wax off."

The next day Daniel arrived for lessons, and Mr. Miyagi assigned another mundane chore, sanding the deck. Another day passed in "mindless physical labor." He arrived the next day ready to begin his lessons. When he was assigned another "chore," the boy protested. "I came here to learn karate," he screamed in frustration. It was then that his teacher said "Show me 'paint fence.'" The boy stared with a puzzled expression. "Show me 'wax car'!" Still no reaction. The teacher suddenly moved forward and with his hand tried to hit the boy while crying out "Show me 'wax car.'" Daniel reacted quickly and naturally with a circular sweeping motion, preventing his teacher's hand from striking him. Then Mr. Miyagi moved in with another punch, this one a little higher. "Show me 'paint fence.'" The boy again moved naturally and quickly. With a smooth up motion of his hand, he easily deflected the blow.

Suddenly, the light went on. Daniel realized the previous hours of "painting fence," "waxing car," and "sanding deck" had trained his hands to move in a natural karate-style motion. Through these mundane chores, he had learned to defend himself.

We have seen how the Bible tells us to "love one another" and "serve one another." Yet in the Book of Ephesians, Paul tells us of a deeper purpose of these commands:

He gave some (gifts) as apostles, some as prophets, some as evangelists, and some as pastors and teachers, for the equipping of the saints for the work of service, to the building up of the body of Christ; until we all attain to the unity of the faith, and of the knowledge of the Son of God, to a mature man, to the measure of the stature which belongs to the fullness of Christ. (Ephesians 4:11–13)

According to Paul, God has gifted men to train the members of the body of Christ in works of service (ministry to "one another"), which will build up the body of Christ. These works of service will lead to greater spiritual maturity on the part of individual members and the body as a whole. Involvement in ministry is a means by which spiritual growth occurs.

When I was a younger Christian, I was deeply affected when I read Ephesians 2:10. Realizing I was "created in Christ for good works," I, like many other Christians, latched on to this concept as my *raison d'etre*, the thing that now gave my life purpose. I focused on these works, not realizing there was a deeper purpose for these works.

Let's face it, any problems the Church is now tackling through the various established ministries could be solved with a snap of God's fingers if He wanted to. For some reason, He doesn't. Many times He chooses to work through us. He wants us involved in the process of actively loving and helping others. To me, *that alone is a clue that there is a deeper purpose here.*

The attitude that the average Christian has toward the "works of the Church" directly affects his spiritual well-being. Some are so focused on the work that they ignore things like developing relationships, family priorities, and an attentive relationship with the Lord. "Works" become their ticket into the heavenly realm. They forget the basic "salvation by grace message." "Religion" and "legalism" dominate.

On the other hand, many of those holding fast to the saved-by-grace theology are not very active in the various programs and ministries of the church. They never get involved in any of the programs of the church (except perhaps on the receiving end). They often become lazy Christians who want nothing more than to be fed on Sunday morning.

Both these groups suffer from a false understanding of the purpose of being involved in the ministry of the Church, of loving one another in practical ways. For those obedient to these twenty-one commandments of interpersonal relationships, many can look back and see when they involved themselves in the lives of others, something happened inside. *It is a spiritual dynamic.* You can't help but be affected when you pray for someone with a terminal disease. Holding a dying, malnourished baby in your arms for the first time touches something deep inside. Working with a single parent or a person with a sexually transmitted, deadly disease causes something to change in your spirit. Seeing children respond to teaching on the Word of God or to a family rebuild their relationships on godly principles is exciting. Both bring a growth in your faith in the power of the Word.

It is a spiritual dynamic: when we involve ourselves in the lives of others by loving them and serving them, growth in our spiritual character occurs, and we become closer to God.

Why?

Because it is *what Jesus would do*. When we "let Him out" to touch others around us, we become more and more like Him. Working with God in ministry is a means to spend time with Him. Any time you work with others on a project, you finish that project being better friends with your workmates. Ministry is an opportunity to co-labor with God here and now. That's one of the reasons why Jesus, Peter, James, and Paul commanded the people in the early Church to be involved in ministering to one another.

> "Let us be glad and rejoice and honor him. For the time has come for the wedding feast of the Lamb, and his bride has prepared herself. She is permitted to wear the finest white linen." (Fine linen represents the good deeds done by the people of God.) (Revelation 19:7)

The Bible says there will be a wedding in the future, and Christ will join with His bride, the Church. Through our involvement in the "work" of the kingdom, the ministry of the Church, we will be well known to the Groom as we walk down the aisle. If we don't get involved in the work of the kingdom by serving others, we might be like a veiled bride in an arranged Middle Eastern wedding, who is a stranger to the groom. *Ministry is our opportunity to get to know God better and be spiritually changed in the process.*

Another reason we should actively love "one another" is most important! Jesus told His disciples:

> "So now I am giving you a new commandment: Love each other. Just as I have loved you, you should love each other. Your love for one another will prove to the world that you are my disciples." (John 13:34–35)

God wants our belief "in Him" as *Kurios* (or Maximum Leader) to have a practical expression and not be just empty words. James (the leader of the Jerusalem church) puts it this way:

> Now someone may argue, "Some people have faith; others have good deeds." I say, "I can't see your faith if you don't have good deeds, but I will show you my faith through my good deeds." (James 2:18)

Loving one another is the most important way that we can express our faith in Jesus. It is more personal than simply handing a tract to a person and more valuable than leading such a "sanctified life" that we don't want to be "soiled" by contact with "sinners."

Loving one another is the mark of true spirituality. What keeps us from loving others? Maybe it is fear of extending ourselves. Perhaps it is our pride holding us back. Maybe it's because we have made judgments against *those people*." Remember that we are not commanded to like them, just to love them!

What is the number one reason that people don't come to church? It is the hypocrites, the actors, the ones who simulate being followers of Jesus. These show little or no love to others and reveal themselves as people who are far from the heart of God.

RS: God has given us two heavenly bodies in the sky that help us on a regular basis. The Sun and Moon. The Moon has no light of its own, it only reflects the Sun. To the extent that it reflects the Sun, it lights the earth in the night. My greatest desire is for each of us to be like the Moon, to understand that it's not about what we are; it's about what we reflect. Did Jesus say: "By this all men will know that you are My disciples . . . if you can discuss intelligently theological concepts on a high level?"

No! What He really said was "*By this all men will know that you are my disciples if you love one another*" (John 13:35).

Randy in his backyard in Jerusalem.

You reflect who Jesus is, and as a reflection of the light that is not yours, you are just like the Moon. If you reflect the character of God in your life, you become Christlike.

Where will that reflection first be seen? It has to be first in the household of faith—to other people who are brothers and sisters. How can you tell me that you are a godly person, but you can't get along with other believers?

MB: How can we obey the second great commandment if we haven't obeyed the first? How can we love our brothers, sisters, and neighbors if we haven't loved God first and are "reflectors?" If we can't receive God's love, we can't reflect it. God tells us to love Him with all our heart, soul, and mind, and to love our neighbor. He doesn't want us to be theoretical lovers or hypocritical lovers. He wants us to be very practical lovers. As we do these two things, people are attracted to Him.

This third aspect leads us to the next big commandment.

Lukas: Would that be to "make disciples"?

MB: Exactly! The plan that God set forth when Adam and Eve rebelled against Him continues on today. I believe that we are indeed living in the twenty-ninth chapter of the Book of the Acts of the Holy Spirit. Chapter 28 ends so abruptly that either we have lost the end of the book Luke wrote, or in fact God is writing the "rest of the story" in the lives of His modern-day disciples. I think that is the case.

God's plan is simple. He wants to bring all men into His family.

> This is good and pleases God our Savior, for he wants everyone to be saved and to understand the truth. (1 Timothy 2:3–4)

Jesus told us in the Great Commission that wherever we happen to be going, we should be making disciples, baptizing them, and teaching them all He told us.

> "Go therefore and make disciples of all the nations, baptizing them in the name of the Father and the Son and the Holy Spirit, teaching them to observe all that I commanded you; and lo, I am with you always, even to the end of the age." (Matthew 28:19–20 NAS)

There has been some confusion over what this passage of Scripture actually means. When I was a young believer, there was a famous Christian singer who made an album titled "Jesus Commands Us To Go." I got the feeling that I should be on the next plane out of Maui going somewhere to tell people about the Lord.

My cousin, Kean, who had initially invited me to church and is responsible for much of my early discipleship, saw my zeal and asked me one day: "Mike, how would you like to go to an island in the Pacific where only five percent of the people go to church on Sunday and evangelize?"

"Let's go!" I replied. "Where is this place anyway?"

"You are standing on it," he said with a big smile.

The message was clear. I didn't have to go anywhere else to be an evangelist and disciple maker.

As I took a close look at the Great Commission, I realized that a more accurate translation gives this message very clearly. *Young's Literal Translation* gives of Matthew 28:19 gives us this understanding:

> having gone, then, disciple all the nations, (baptizing them—to the name of the Father, and of the Son, and of the Holy Spirit . . .)

Of the four verbs in this passage—go, make, baptize, and teach—only "make" is in the command form. This is the emphasis of the passage. Wherever we happen to be going in our daily lives, God wants us to be about the business of making disciples. If we are going to work tomorrow or to the beach, our primary focus should be to encourage people in their relationship with the Lord.

Mikaela: Then how can I make disciples?

MB: First of all, you must be a disciple. Obey the first two commandments—love God and love your neighbor. You will find that if you are successfully doing these first two, then making disciples will naturally follow. If you try to make disciples without loving God and loving your neighbor, you are going to be frustrated; there won't be much fruit, and it won't be much fun. Be a disciple! Develop the disciplines of prayer, reading the Word, meditation, fasting, praise and worship, and being "others-centered."

Arielle: Discipline? Does this mean I get spanking?

MB: No, we are not talking about correction here, although God will be showing you a "better way." To develop a discipline means simply to "gain control by obedience or training." Self control is one of the fruits of the Holy Spirit. God wants you to be an effective learner, one who is putting into action what you are receiving from Him. That's what being a disciple is all about!

As you are a disciple, you will notice things around you will be changing. Your friends and family will notice a difference, especially as they are more and more on the receiving end of your love. Some of your friends will accept this with joy. Others who don't know the Lord may be skeptical; some will even be hostile. Your lifestyle changes are sometimes threatening to others, especially to those who are living a life that they themselves are not necessarily pleased with. Expect these reactions. And take some action!

Lukas: What sort of action? Tell them to stop sinning or they will go to hell?

MB: There may be a time for that. But first, begin praying for them. Ask God to come into their lives. *Look for ways you can love them.* Ask Him to give you opportunity, at just the right moment, to share the Good News of relationship with the Creator. Ask for them to be receptive. God wants everybody to be included in His family. We are the ones who deliver the invitations. Consider what Paul said in the Book of Romans:

For "Anyone who calls on the name of the Lord will be saved." But how can they call on him to save them unless they believe in him? And how can they believe in him if they have never heard about him? And how can they hear about him unless someone tells them? (Romans 10:13–14)

Think about all the relationships you have. Not just your family, but what about the guy who works on your car? How about that person who cuts your hair? Your dentist? Your doctor? The guy at the hardware store who helps you find what you need? The person at the checkout counter where you buy your groceries? Your aerobics teacher?

You have relationships with all these people and more. Think about it. With these relationships come ample opportunities to be used by God in this mission that He has given you—to reach out to the lost and needy. Take a moment to go beyond the immediate business needs—move into a more personal level. "Love them" in the course of your daily events. Try it. After all, *What would Jesus do* in the same situation?

This past summer, I was preparing for a trip to Nicaragua. On our final day in Florida, Laura asked me to go to K-Mart and buy a trashcan that was on sale. I had many things on my list for that day, but it was a savings of three dollars, and we needed a new container.

I went to the store, found the big, black plastic trashcan with wheels and went to the checkout. A young girl with a nametag that read "Candice" took my credit card and began to check me out. I casually asked her if K-Mart was still in bankruptcy. She replied that she didn't know and didn't care. That began a conversation that went something like this:

"So you are not a K-Mart career employee?"

"No, I'm a sixteen-year-old single mom with a new baby."

"That must be challenging. Is your family helping?"

"No, the father is black, and they are racist."

"Are you involved in a church anywhere?"

"I've gone to a few, but there was nothing there for me."

"You definitely need God's help now."

"Why?"

"Because there is a devil out there called Satan who is out to steal from you and destroy your life."

At this point, Candice took out a piece of paper and began writing.

"How do you spell that?"

"S-a-t-a-n"

She wrote it down. I realized that I needed to tell her more.

"But there is another that you need to know about. His name is Jesus."

She wrote that name down alongside the first name.

At that point, we begin to have a conversation about Jesus. I could tell by the way that she was looking over my shoulder that the other cashiers were also listening. Fortunately, there were no other customers in any checkout lines. After about five minutes, I said, "Candice, I think that you might find help at a church. Please try to find one. If you like, come to ours."

I gave her directions, noticed the time, and hurried out the door, dragging the big, black, rolling garbage can. In a few moments I was at the van and opened the back door, having to first move a discarded shopping cart that somebody had left there. Lazy people!

Much to my dismay, the back was filled with boxes. I remembered that four weeks earlier Laura had placed some of her clothes and Moselle's baby clothes in the van to take to the Salvation Army. With these boxes in the back, there was no space for the big, black, rolling garbage can. I felt the temperature rise as I realized that now I was going to have to put the big, black, rolling garbage can in the middle seat, which looked to be almost impossible due to its size. This was getting too much. After all, why had Laura not followed through and taken these boxes of clothes to the Salvation Army weeks ago? Now I was really getting ticked as I tried to push the big, black, rolling garbage can over the seat into the middle space, but it wouldn't go; it was too big.

I had approached my meltdown point when I looked down into one of the boxes and saw one of Moselle's (and Arielle's) infant outfits on top of one of the boxes. I looked and saw another. Then I saw one of Laura's dresses in another box. By this point, it had begun to sink in, and I began to melt. I pulled out the big, black, rolling garbage can and set it down beside the now not-so-abandoned shopping cart. My knees got weak as I realized how God had began a month earlier to orchestrate a plan to meet Candice's needs. It was a complete plan, down to the strategically-placed shopping cart. I was almost in tears as I paused to tell God how sorry I was that I almost blew His plan.

I quickly loaded four boxes of clothes into the shopping cart and hurried back into K-Mart. As I entered, Candice asked me if anything was wrong. I told her that these boxes of clothes were from my family and were for her and her baby and explained what had just happened. As I walked out the door, I heard her let out a shriek as she called out to the other cashiers *"Look, I just got some boxes of baby clothes."*

It's not too difficult to bring the conversation from business to more personal subjects, especially if people sense you are genuinely interested in them. That's what loving them is all about: taking a personal interest. As you love them, there may be opportunity to reach out to them. Perhaps they have a need you can pray for. Or maybe they might accept an invitation to lunch, or dinner, or church. Even if they initially refuse, they will know you are a person who is genuinely concerned about them. Business relationships become friendships. At some point in their lives, *they will* need to know someone like you who knows the truth and who is walking in relationship with God.

What this means is that those who become Christians become new persons. They are not the same anymore, for the old life is gone. A new life has begun! All this newness of life is from God, who brought us back to himself through what Christ did. And God has given us the task of reconciling people to him. For God was in Christ, reconciling the world to Himself, no longer counting people's sins against them. This is the wonderful message he has given us to tell others. We are Christ's ambassadors, and God is using us to speak to you. We urge you, as though Christ himself were here pleading with you, "Be reconciled to God!" (2 Corinthians 5:17–20)

The mission that He has for us is to be His ambassadors to our families, to our neighbors, to all the places we happen to be "going." It's really a *lifestyle of evangelism.* God will bring people across our paths whom He is inviting into His family. We are the ones who will extend the invitation.

It's important to remember that most people are brought into relationship with the Lord through a series of divine encounters with many members of the family of God. Statistics show that it takes an average of 5.7 such encounters before a person accepts Jesus as Lord.

At a recent baptism on the beach in Maui, a young lady named Danielle who was about to be baptized told her pastor, Craig, about the chain of encounters that led her to Christ. It all began when she was in a second-hand furniture store and picked up a Bible that was lying on a table. She had an impulse to ask the owner of the store "How much is this Bible?" The owner, Shelly, told her if she wanted the Bible, it was free. That conversation ended in an invitation to a Bible study. Eventually, Danielle went to that study and was touched by God as well as by many in the group. She decided to give her heart to Jesus.

Craig asked her who it was that gave her the Bible. Danielle didn't know her name, nor had she seen her since. Craig noticed Shelly, the owner of the furniture store, sitting a few feet in front of Danielle at that moment on the beach. She was totally unaware of how her kindness was the first step in a divinely orchestrated effort that resulted in eternal life for Danielle.

We are responsible only to love the one that God brings across our path at that moment, just as Shelly at the furniture store did, and give any words that the Holy Spirit may want to give them—*words of encouragement, words of hope, but rarely words of con-demnation.* That's why it is important to rely on the leading of the Holy Spirit, especially when we are using a "canned" evangelism program. The Holy Spirit knows exactly what a person needs. If we follow His lead, we will see fruit from our efforts. If we don't, we may "bruise" the fruit He is cultivating.

What is the message that we are to give in these situations? Paul says we are to tell them that: "God was in Christ, reconciling the world to Himself, no longer counting people's sins against them" (2 Corinthians 5:19).

This is a message of repentance and hope, an opportunity to wipe the blackboard clean, to make a fresh start. Do you think people will respond to such a simple message? I did!

It's all really simple: Love God, number one; love each other, number two. Only then can we fulfill the third great commandment in the Christian Scriptures—to go and make disciples. This is a simple divine recipe for evangelism and discipleship.

RS: There is a really tender image in the last part of John's Gospel. It's the final call of a disciple, Peter. In that final call, Jesus is going to challenge him to leave an old lifestyle and enter into a new one. I use it in my mind as a picture of what the whole process of outreach really is.

Peter had last been seen and heard from in a very definite way in John 18, where he denied knowing Jesus three times. Peter had basically flunked Discipleship 101. After three years in school, he really failed. At Jesus' appearance in the Upper Room, you don't hear Peter say anything. That silence is deafening! Peter always has something to say.

In chapter 21, Peter says, "I'm going fishing," and some of the other disciples went with him. There they are, on the lake at night when the fishing is normally good. They catch nothing, and this has bad memories for Peter, another all-night failure.

On the shore appears a figure who calls out, "Hey, did you catch any fish?"

"No," is the reply. "We haven't caught anything."

The person on the shore says, "Cast your nets on the other side."

The disciples have heard this before. John looks at Peter and says, "*I think it might be Jesus.*"

So Peter jumps into the water and gets to the beach, where he finds a single, solitary figure sitting with a fire and fish. He's already got His meal. The important thing to understand is that in the Middle East you don't eat a meal with someone unless there is a relationship. The relationship is everything. Sharing a meal is having a relationship. That's why Jacob and Laban ended up having a meal together, and the prodigal son's older brother refused to eat with him.

What is Jesus doing in front of the other disciples? He's telling Peter: "I want you to know that it's OK. I know you failed Discipleship 101, but Discipleship 201 is about to begin. Let me give you the ground rules. Peter, do you love Me?"

"Lord, You know that I love You."

"Then feed My sheep."

"Peter, do you love Me?"

"Lord, You know that I love You."

"Tend My lambs."

"Peter, do you love Me?"

"Yes, Lord, I love you."

"Feed My sheep."

"Peter, you have been a fisherman. Now I want you to stop being a fisherman, and start being a shepherd."

Randy teaching on the Sea of Galilee

Mentally, there has to be a shift in Peter's mind. To be a fisherman, you don't have to build a relationship with fish, you just have to catch them and get them in the boat, then to the market, and you are done. But to be a shepherd is to see the birth process all the way through until they are giving birth again and to nurture them along every stage of life.

I think some people are running around with evangelism as an idea like catching fish. "There's one over there, hook him, and reel him in. Notch my belt for Jesus!" There are others who are saying: "Wait a minute. That 'I will make you fishers of men' was an early command, but the later one was stop being a fisherman and start being a shepherd."

What does that mean? Certainly the birth process is there for the fisherman, but there must be the nurturing, loving relationship of a shepherd with his sheep for the process to be complete. You must win the respect and love for the sheep. For them to call you shepherd, there is a whole process of building relationship. And this must be an overflow of our relationship with God, which leads to an overflow of our relationship with people.

MB: Without these two overflow elements, you will not be successful, and it will just be another program. There will be frustration, knocking our heads against a wall, and we will not see any fruit. Yet if we love God and actually spend time loving other people, then the whole process actually becomes pleasurable. *Let me let you in on a secret: God wants us to have fun while we bring people into His Family.* It has to be an enjoyable experience! We forget this.

RS: You can only get into a legitimate conversation with a person if you are willing to listen to them and to learn. If I'm just in the conversation to nail them with Jesus, I am doing a disservice to them.

MB: Not only that, you have also done a disservice to God. That person may have the idea that the next person who talks to them about God is going to try to manipulate them and make them feel guilty. We miss the whole point! They are not going to accept anything you say until they first feel God's love coming through. It's a basic part of the recipe. The bread will not rise unless you have the soda and yeast. It will not happen. Many of us are eating flat, stale, tasteless bread, and we are seeing that in our ministry because we have forgotten those vital ingredients. *We forget the most important moment of a witnessing encounter in the evening with our neighbor is the morning time that we spend with our God.* From my own experience, I know the days I begin by taking time with God are the days that my relationships with others go well, and I have opportunities to nudge and encourage.

RS: It's important for us to realize that people all over the world want to be loved and appreciated for who they are. No one wants you to drop into their life with the answer they are looking for. They are getting hit left and right with every advertiser out there telling them if they use this toothpaste, the women will love them. If they go to this place, they will find happiness.

All across America and around the world today, people are in vans moving to "happy land." They truly believe if they can pack up their problems and move, they will be happy. They are running all over the globe, and they are not happy. The problem is that they are taking their problems with them!

Ultimately, if you are going to reach that person and give them the message of this incredible thing God has given to you, it needs to be because you are truly concerned about the house on fire around them.

Somebody asked me recently, "What gives you the right to come into another country and tell them how they should live or believe?" My reply was in a word, "God." You are a believer, and you are doing this because He told you to! The problem is that their house is on fire, and what kind of neighbor am I if I let them burn without warning them? I don't twist arms, and I don't make people do anything. If you truly do start to love the other person, share their needs and take care of them, then you begin that process of liking. As a believer, God is such a natural part of who you are. How could He not come out?

MB: You are doing it because of what Paul said in Romans chapters one through twelve: You are presenting "your body as a living sacrifice" because it is only your "reasonable service."

RS: It has to be more than just a mission. I like the word *passion* much more than I like the word *mission*. *Mission* has a sense of duty. *Passion* has a sense of "*I get out of bed in the morning because this is what I live for!*" I want to see all of my children get to the place where they have a passion to love God, love their neighbor, and to share with everyone around them because they can't *not* share. It would be unthinkable not to share! There are people with a passion from automobiles to soap products. How is it that we have to put on a program for people to muster passion for the Living God? Something is wrong. It means that we are programming our evangelism and not understanding that it is a simple overflow. It is a passionate overflow of a love for God and what He is doing in us.

MB: Relationships are eternal. They are the only things we take with us when we die. Think about that for a moment. Right now we are building relationships with God's people that will last for eternity. Of all the things I have done in my life, from flying fast jets, to skiing powder slopes, to eating delicious ice cream, this is what I enjoy the most! This is where the richness of life really is.

God has given us a *mission*, and I use that word because it defines my activities and my goals. *But God wants us to have a passion for the mission.* That only comes when we step back and see the big picture and realize what is really important in the long run. And the cool thing is, God makes it fun in the meantime! It is such an adventure! He sends me to interesting places, provides all I need and want, and I watch Him do incredible things. Incredible! People's lives are changed, and it's really not because of anything that we are doing! I am actually able to see God move right in front of me! And people's lives are affected for the good.

I was on an airliner flying to Honduras in 1987. There was a girl sitting beside me. In those days, when the war was going on in Nicaragua, you had to have a good reason to go to Honduras. I asked her finally: "Why are going to Honduras?"

She replied, "I'm going to Roatan on the Bay Islands for scuba diving. What about you?

I said a quick prayer, hoping God would give me something interesting to say. I said simply, "I work there."

"Really, doing what?"

"I work for a great company. We have undoubtedly the best Boss ever who runs the company. He knows how to do His job very well."

"I wish my boss was like that."

"He sends us to interesting places to work, and whatever we need for our job, He provides it. Really. It's amazing some of the things we get. The best part of it all is that my company has a retirement plan that is literally out of this world!"

"That sounds like a company I should be working for."

Surprised at her response I quickly replied, "Funny thing you should say that because we are taking applications right now."

I then gave her the details of going on a two-week mission trip and staying on to work with the Miskito Indians. We talked about God, and I could not help but share what an adventure I was having in this life of service.

People in this world are looking for adventure, and the greatest adventure available is getting involved with the Living God and doing what God is doing. You face risks and challenges, and you see things happen that would never happen. You see God take you beyond what you would normally be able to do—because it's God who is doing it all. There is nothing more powerful in this life.

God's adventure is something He wants us all to be a part of wherever you are, whatever you happen to be doing. When we stand before the Lord, there will be nothing greater than for Him to come up to us, give us a hug or whatever He will do, and say "You know, you did well."

What more could we ask for? It's only reasonable then that we give it all to Him now.

Arielle: So what's the bottom line, Pops?

- *Be a disciple.* Love and obey God. Take time to talk with Him. Take even more time to listen! Read the Word often (daily if possible). Ask the Holy Spirit to be your teacher as you read (this is very important!). Meditate on what you read. Ask God to show you the personal application.
- *Love other people.* Be "others-centered." Ask God to give you love for others when you don't feel it. Pretend until He does. Often, as we decide that we are

going to be kind, patient, gentle, etc., the real feelings come! Try it. Serve them just as Jesus did. Remember that love is an action, not just a feeling!

- *Get involved in a church* (or Bible study, or care group) where you can interact with other brothers and sisters. Give of yourself. Be a friend. Look for ways to meet their needs. As you do, God will provide you with friends, and your needs will be met as well.

- *Keep your priorities straight*: Number one is God; number two is your family; number three is your job. Never allow number three to become number one or two.

- *Look for the ways that God will use you* in your circle of family, neighbors, friends, and acquaintances. Pray that God will use you. Pray for them. They are your mission field. As Francis of Assisi said: "Go out today and preach the Gospel, and if you have to, use words."

- *Take time to tell your friends about the great things God has done* and is doing in your life. Ask them if there are any specific things that you can pray for them (since you are praying for them anyway). Listen to them. Love them. Be ready to share some Scripture at the appropriate time. You may want to give them a booklet, tract, or even a Bible again at just the right time. If they are ready to be introduced to Jesus personally, pray with them to receive Christ as their Lord. Invite them to your church or group. At first, they will probably be more comfortable talking with you. Good. Schedule some time to read the Word and pray together. Eventually help them

On the job in Honduras 1987

plug into the church or small group.

- *Pray that God will give you greater vision for your mission.* Pray for a world vision. Get involved in outreach outside your own neighborhood, either through your prayers, personal involvement, or financial partnership. Pray that God will use you in a mighty way.
- *Pray for greater intimacy with God.* Pray that He would gift you with greater gifts of the Spirit and that there would be greater fruits of the Spirit in your life.
- *Look forward* with great joy and anticipation for the great things that God is going to do in your life and in your mission.

Personal Reflections

1. How do you love God with your emotions, obedience, and priorities?
2. What is your biggest area of challenge in being obedient to God?
3. How do you best practically "love your neighbor?"
4. In your weekly rounds to stores, gyms, schools, and other places in your community, who are you evangelizing and discipling?
5. Are you enjoying the mission that God has given to you?

Deeper Water

A. Why does the second line in Psalm 136 repeat itself over and over?
B. What is the goal of Paul's ministry as he defines it in Philippians 3?
C. What Psalms display a deep passion for God?

Addendum: In the following pages is a Bible study guide designed to help you understand the organization and themes of God's Word. Included are thumbnail sketches of each division and book, as well as some perspectives that will help you extract practical principles for daily living.

Every able spiritual warrior is dressed and ready for battle. He has his helmet, body armor, weapons, and is walking in

The Shoes of the Gospel
A Bible Study Guide

Stand firm therefore, having girded your waist with truth, having put on the breastplate of righteousness, and having shod your feet with the preparation of the gospel of peace; (Ephesians 6:15–16)

Lukas: I know that the Bible is one big book, but why are there sixty-six little books inside? What do they all mean? Do they fit together in some way? What is the message of the Bible, and what do I do with it?

MB: The Bible is a big book with sixty-six different parts. They are organized into two major divisions (the Old and New Testament) and nine sub-divisions. This may sound confusing, but these small "books" do fit together in a very nice way. Many people have a hard time understanding the individual messages of the various books. They sometimes feel that there is nothing there that is relevant for our time. Nothing could be further from the truth!

Mikaela: OK. We are ready to jump into the Bible if you can help us!

MB: Don't worry. I can show you an easy way to get into it but not get buried. The books are organized in a logical order, and there are some strings that tie them all together. *The main thing is to begin your reading by first asking the Holy Spirit to guide you and teach you.*

Reading the Bible is like digging a ditch, something that I have lots of experience in. You dig one shovelful

Lukas and Mikaela
at the dig at Tell Dan, Israel

and then another. You don't try to take it all out at one time—just one shovelful, and when you are ready, the next. We will look at some thoughts, or themes, that run throughout the books of the Bible. These will help you keep your thoughts focused. Remember to take into account the context of the passage. It is only then that you can discover the principles that God is communicating for your lives today. Let's take a look at the Hebrew Scriptures. Here are the seven major themes, or

Seven Shoestrings of the Hebrew Scriptures

There are seven "strings" that run through the Hebrew Scriptures. You can tie almost any passage to one of these strings.

1. *God is a good God.* Unlike the Hindu or Greek-Roman gods who are out to trick man and use him or the god of Islam who wants only "submission," our God is one who defines the word *good.* There is nothing bad about Him.

    Give thanks to the LORD, for he is good! His faithful love endures forever. (1 Chronicles 16:34)

2. *Man has the free will to choose his fate.* God loves us so much that He will never force us to do anything. He created us for relationship—it's hard to personally relate to a "robot."

    "Today I have given you the choice between life and death, between blessings and curses. I call on heaven and earth to witness the choice you make. Oh, that you would choose life, that you and your descendants might live!" (Deuteronomy 30:19)

3. *God blesses those who follow Him.* All the good things that we want in this life (peace, joy, good relationships, and spiritual growth), God wants for us too, and as we are obedient to Him and His principles for living, we receive.

    "This book of the law shall not depart from your mouth, but you shall meditate on it day and night, so that you may be careful to do according to all that is written in it; for then you will make your way prosperous, and then you will have success." (Joshua 1:8 NAS)

4. *God's ways are higher than man's ways.* God's point of view is radically different from ours.

    > For just as the heavens are higher than the earth, so are my ways higher than your ways and my thoughts higher than your thoughts. (Isaiah 55:9)

5. *Man, when left to follow his own instincts, will rebel against God and follow his own desires.* Man is generally "self-centered" while God is always "other's-centered."

    > In those days Israel had no king, so the people did whatever seemed right in their own eyes. (Judges 21:25)

6. *God has a plan to redeem man from his sinful state.* God created us for intimate relationship with Him. At the moment of mankind's rebellion against Him, God put into action a plan to bring all men and women into His family.

    > And He will redeem Israel from all his iniquities. (Psalm 130:8 NAS)

When I was a child living in North Carolina, I used to look for Coke bottles along the road. If I found any, I could take them down to Lud's filling station and "redeem" them for money. Five bottles would get me a cold RC Cola, and another three would get me a Moon Pie. I was in heaven! I had taken something that was worthless and littering the highway and turned it into something very valuable—an RC Cola and a Moon Pie! God is in the same business—taking a creation that rebelled against Him and making him a member of the royal family.

7. *There is a war occurring between the forces of Satan and the forces of God, with man in the middle.* The force of rebellious angels is constantly trying to win mankind over to their side and thwart God's plan for humanity.

    > This was the horn that seemed greater than the others and had human eyes and a mouth that was boasting arrogantly. As I watched, this horn was waging war against the holy people and was defeating them. . . . (Daniel 7:20–21)

Arielle: How can I remember the order of all those books of the Hebrew Scripture?

MB: Here is an easy way to remember how to find the books. Look at your hand. Just as you have five fingers, the Hebrew Scriptures have five divisions. You will find this a handy way to locate every one of the thirty-nine books of the Hebrew Scriptures. Just begin remembering your thumb as the Books of Moses, your index finger as "History," your middle finger as "Poetry And Wisdom," your ring finger as "Major Prophets," and your pinkie as "Minor Prophets." We will use the spaces between the fingers to remember the Christian Scriptures, but let's not jump ahead. Now is the time to take a closer look at each "finger."

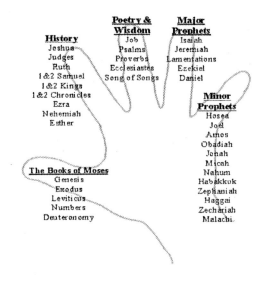

Division 1 (Thumb)

The Books of Moses: five books by the "man who knew God" (also referred to as the Torah).

MB: In the Hebrew Scriptures, God reveals Himself in a way that shows His heart toward mankind. We see the care in which God did the creation thing in Genesis and how He interacted with the characters from Adam and Eve to Joseph in such a loving manner.

Then we have the Law presented to us, and through this we see so much of God's character. God shows us that He is a just God. He is a merciful God. That's important for you and me. When mankind doesn't meet up to His standards, there is a way to deal with his sin. God gives man a prescription for living a life that will be good for him. "Don't eat these foods (many for health reasons) because I didn't design your body that way. You may have health problems if you eat these animals. Don't covet your neighbor's wife because this will get you into trouble. Take a day off each week for rest and reflection; you need it." What I used to think were just a bunch of thoughtless rules and regulations are actually good principles for me to live my life by.

Here is God saying, "I want to give you a gift. It's called life. I want you to experience it to the fullest." Jesus later said, "I came to give you abundant life." God revealing Himself through His Law to me is a beautiful thing.

RS: It is always worth remembering that the Scripture doesn't begin with Adam—it begins with Moses and goes backward in time. The story of Adam, the story of Noah, and the story of Abraham are all written much later, at the time of Moses. It is God revealing the past, just to get you to the children of Israel and to a place to appreciate what God was doing.

God reveals Himself in the text and His character all through a historical brushstroke of what He did. It is a very brief brushstroke, and from Genesis 1 to 11, He's only trying to get you to understand that He created the world, walked with man, and man fell and sinned. Then He began to work within the framework of governments, and then He decided to work within the framework of a specific people to reach the rest of the world. But throughout, the heartbeat is the same—God choosing to reach a world, caring about man, seeing man walk away from Him, and doing everything to draw him back to Himself.

Genesis is the story of beginnings. Creation, the fall of man, the Flood, and God's redemptive work through Abraham and Joseph, are the themes of this book. When reading the Creation account, realize that more and more scientific evidence is supporting biblical creation than ever before. Remember, it takes much greater faith to believe in the *theory* of evolution than what Moses describes in Genesis. *Read 1:1–31, 2:1–21, 7:1–23, 12:1–4, 45:3–15.*

Exodus describes the Hebrews exit from Egypt. Some of the events recorded are the birth of the nation Israel and the giving of God's Law. In this book, God gives a good description of Himself through *His* laws, signs, and miracles. *Read 12:1–13, 20:1–18.*

Leviticus contains God's direction for His priests and laws for the Hebrew people. There are many principles in this book that apply to our lives today. *Holiness* is the key word, and the word *holy* appears 152 times in this book. What does holy mean? "Distinct." It's important to understand that God wants His family to be distinct from the rest of mankind. *Read 4:1–8, chapters 18, 19, and 20.*

Numbers is about the wanderings of the Hebrews in the desert of Sinai after they refused to enter the land. The principle theme is that God's people must live by faith. We see many examples of men and women who did and were blessed in the process and many who didn't and suffered the consequences of wandering in the desert and never entering the Promised Land. This is a book for our culture and times. *Read 13:25–14:10, 21:4–9.*

Deuteronomy is in essence the constitution of the new nation of Israel. It means literally the "second telling" of the Law that Moses gave to the nation before they entered the Promised Land. This book is so important that Jesus and the apostles quote from Deuteronomy over eighty times in the Christian Scriptures. This book contains much wisdom for families and many principles for our time. *Read 6:4–9, 8:2–7, 30:11–20.*

Division 2 (Index Finger)

The historical books: twelve books written by leaders of Israel.

MB: We see examples of interaction between God and men and women in the twelve history books—people like Samson, Gideon, Deborah, Samuel, David, Solomon, Nehemiah, Esther, Hezekiah, and others. Paul later writes that

> these things happened to them as an example, and they were written for our instruction, upon whom the ends of the ages have come. (1 Corinthians 10:11)

I think that we can pull principles for our lives and everlasting truths from these accounts of men and women in the Hebrew Scriptures. Remember that there is a difference between a narrative and an instruction in Scripture. This is important. We see this in the life of Gideon, whom the angel found threshing grain in a winepress, hiding from the Midianites. The angel calls Gideon a valiant warrior and tells him to go smite the Midianites. But Gideon is anything but valiant at this point and has to see an impressive display from the angel before he was willing to do anything. Later, when given another command to go fight, he does the famous fleece test—another sign of his unbelief. So I can draw a lot from this story. God's view of me may be different than my view—I may be able to do more than I think with His power. I should trust God at His word and not have to ask Him again and again.

There is David, who has a passion for God, and who also is involved in lies, adultery, and murder. I catch the profile of one who turns God's head, and this I want to incorporate into my own life. David is a faithful, patient warrior who understands it's all about relationship with God, not necessarily obeying the letter of the Law. Luke records in Acts that "David was a man after God's own heart." I want to be that type of man as well. Yet I also see the pitfalls and consequences of indulging the flesh (the Uriah and Bathsheba events), and this I want to avoid.

In the Kingdom period, we see God revealing Himself as it's described in Psalm 136 where every other line declares "His lovingkindness is everlasting."

There were so many kings (nineteen in a row at one point) who turned their backs on God, and many did despicable things, very offensive to God, yet God's mercy was there for them, waiting for them to turn back. This is good for me, because I know that whenever I turn my back on God, mercy will be there for me as well. I still have a chance because "His lovingkindness is everlasting."

Nehemiah was a very special individual who was called by God to a very important task. He teaches me spiritual warfare and godly leadership principles through his experience of rebuilding the walls of Jerusalem. There is so much for us in these twelve books, and each story has many principles for our lives today.

Let's look a the thumbnails sketches:

Joshua is about the conquest and division of the Promised Land. Joshua was a great military leader, but more importantly, he was a man of faith, courage, and obedience. Joshua had an ear that was very sensitive to the voice of the Lord. With God, he was able to accomplish some incredible things. *Read 1:1–9, 2:15–24, 6:1–26, 9:2–16.*

Judges tells what happen when people forget about God and "do their own thing." God placed His people in a very strategic spot—literally on the freeway between the great powers of that era. Whenever the Egyptians, Hittites, Assyrians, or Babylonians wanted to expand their kingdoms, they usually had to march through Israel to get to their enemies. When the people of Israel were faithful to God, there were no expansionistic tendencies in any of those nations. However, when they turned their backs on God, there arose a pharaoh or king who suddenly desired more territory. We see in the Book of Judges many cycles of waning devotion to God. The great lesson from Judges is that obedience to God brings peace, while disobedience brings oppression and death. *Read 6:11–7:25, 13:1–16:31.*

Ruth is the story of redemption. Ruth was a foreigner who was not only allowed into God's family but was made part of the royal line of the Messiah. The real inside story here is Naomi, a woman who declared in chapter 1 that God "had turned His hand against her." In the next three chapters, we see how that was not true (*a difference between narrative and instruction*) and how much God's hand was reaching out to her, restoring her. *Read 2:1–3:18.*

First Samuel tells how Israel rejected God as their king and asks the last "judge" to appoint one. God chose a man who looked very good from the outside but was lacking in his spirit. Saul's life is a great example of the consequences of partial obedience. Meanwhile, we see a young shepherd boy named David defeat a nine-foot giant with a sling. *Read 15:1–29, 16:6–13, 17:1–52, 26:2–25, 30:1–25.*

Second Samuel tells how the shepherd David became king, won great military victories, murdered one of his best soldiers, and then married his wife. We see consequences of sin, and God's grace over and over. Still, God made a covenant with David that is still in effect (Luke 1:31–32). *Read 6:6–11, 7:8–17, 11:1–12:24, 15:1–18:18.*

First Kings begins with Solomon, describes the building of the temple, and then the division of the kingdom into two separate nations—the northern ten tribes, called Israel, and the southern two, called Judah. The success of each king was directly linked to the closeness of his relationship with God. The ministry of Elijah is a highlight of 1 Kings. *Read 3:6–28, 6:1–38, 8:54–61, 11:1–13, 12:1–24, 18:16–46.*

Second Kings traces the decline of the kingdoms of Israel and Judah until the Assyrians and the Babylonians, who conquered the land and deported large portions of the population, finally take them away into captivity. Two kings, Hezekiah and Josiah, and two prophets, Isaiah and Elisha, are the spiritual heroes of 2 Kings. *Read 4:1–37, 6:8–23, 18:1–20:11, 23:1–25, 25:1–11.*

First Chronicles is a mini-Hebrew Scriptures that begin with Adam and end with the death of David. It was probably written by Ezra to help build the spiritual foundation of the returning refugees. *Read 11:1–26, 16:8–36, 20:4–8.*

Second Chronicles continues the mini-Hebrew Scriptures with the reign of Solomon and "chronicles" the reigns of the kings of Judah. Over and over we see that the reason God allowed the nation to be exiled was because of their disobedience to God. *Read 5:7–14, 7:1–14, 20:14–25, 31:1–32:33.*

Ezra was a priest who led a group of refugees from Babylon back to Jerusalem. Ezra knew that the Word of God would be an essential element for rebuilding the nation. Ezra showed us the three-step process to becoming a teacher of the Word. First, he "set his heart" to study God's Word, then to put it into practice in his own life, and only then to teach it to the people in Israel. You can't teach what you don't already know. When it comes to spiritual things, you can't effectively share with others if you haven't heard from God and been obedient in your own life. *Read 3:8–13, 5:1–6:12, 7:6–10.*

Nehemiah was the security chief to the king of Persia. He returned to Jerusalem and led the effort to rebuild the city walls and gates, finishing in only fifty-two days. Nehemiah was a man of prayer, an effective manager, and one of the greatest leaders mentioned in the Bible. The book is both a leadership manual for the body of Christ and a practical guide to spiritual warfare. *Read 1:3–2:18, 4:1–23, 8:1–12.*

Esther is a story of God's sovereignty and love for His people, even though the name of God is not mentioned in the book. Esther shows us how God places people in specific situations for His purposes. Through her obedient response, God rescued His people. *Read 1:1–3:11, 6:1–11, 7:1–10.*

Division 3 (Middle Finger)

Five books of poetry and wisdom.

MB: The books of wisdom and poetry have become foundations of my life. God gives me wisdom on how to relate to my family and neighbors, how to raise my children, and how to run my business. He shows me more of who He is and how to relate to Him. He shows me through Solomon's experience what happens when I indulge myself and stray away from Him. This is all found in this one little section.

Job is perhaps the oldest book in the Bible and deals with the age-old question of why righteous men suffer. The cause of Job's suffering was Satan and his pride (the open door). Job expressed prophetic insight in 19:25 by declaring, "My Redeemer lives." This book is also significant for it's personal narrative account of the creation. *Read 1:7–22, 4:17–20, 38:1–36, 40:1–5.*

Psalms was the hymnbook of the Hebrew people. We have the lyrics to the songs, but unfortunately the music was lost. The Hebrew word for psalms is *tehillam*, which means the praise that comes from pouring out your spirit in a frank and open manner. There is intimacy with God and power when we praise the Lord. *Read 1:1–6, 8:1–8, 37:1–26, 91:1–16, 103:1–12, 119:1–105.*

Proverbs was mostly written by Solomon and is one of the most practical books of the Bible. Almost every area of life is covered. Proverbs has thirty-one chapters. Each month of the year has thirty-one days or less. Coincidental? Or did God mean for us to begin each day with a chapter of His wisdom for dealing with the situations that we will encounter in the course of our days? *Read 1:1–31:31. One chapter per day! Start with today's date and get on cycle.*

Ecclesiastes, written by Solomon, describes his full pursuit of all the pleasures and accomplishments available in this life. This is a story for our materialistic—and pleasure-seeking times. In the end, however, Solomon declares that the most important things one can do is obey God and enjoy the days that He has given you. *Read 1:12–2:25, 3:1–14, 4:9–12, 12:1–14.*

Song of Songs (Song of Solomon) is a romantic love story. This book establishes the rightful place of physical love within marriage and describes the intimate relationship between Christ and His bride. This book is a great source for Valentine's Day readings. It is also a good book to read to your children when as they are maturing into adults. It's important to let them know that God invented sex and gave it to us to enjoy within the context of marriage. *Read 1:1–4, 2:3–6, 7:1–12, 8:6–7.*

Division 4 (Ring Finger)

The Major Prophets: books by God's messengers.

MB: There are seventeen books of prophets in the Hebrew Scriptures. These were men who heard God's heart for His people and communicated specific words for the times. Traditionally, the prophets were the spokesmen for the common people outside the royal, political, and religious circles. Their messages addressed issues in society and situations where God's help and influence was needed. Yet in the midst of each of these short books, we see in such a grand fashion the heart of God for His people. We hear God expressing deep and profound feelings for His family.

In all five of the Major Prophets and the twelve Minor Prophets, God speaks through individuals to their societies with specific messages, yet their messages are full of relationship-with-God nuggets for me in the twenty-first century. Man hasn't really changed all that much, and God certainly hasn't, so the message of Micah to "do justice, love mercy, and walk humbly with your God" still works for me. There is so much here for the modern-day believer, and yet most of us rarely crack these pages in our Bibles.

Let's take a look.

Isaiah gave many prophecies about the coming Messiah and gives us a thorough portrait of Jesus and His ministry. He was a contemporary of Kings Hezekiah and an effective prayer warrior in the battle against the Assyrian king, Sennacherib. *Read 6:1–8, 14:12–17, 40:28–31, 53:1–12, 55:6–11.*

Jeremiah gave warnings of the impending destruction of Jerusalem. In the midst of impending doom, he also foretold of God extending Himself in man in a very special way. One of the most significant passages in all the Old Testament (31:31–33) tells of the coming New Covenant. *Read 1:5, 17:5–10, 18:1–6, 29:10–14, 31:31–33.*

Lamentations, also written by Jeremiah, mourns the fall of Jerusalem in five poems. Despite this, the prophet declares God's lovingkindness and faithfulness. *Read 3:1–25.*

Ezekiel reminds his fellow refugees why God judged them and why they were in captivity in Babylon. Still, Ezekiel gives a strong message of restoration and hope. *Read 22:30, 28:11–19, 36:25–27, 37:1–10.*

Daniel was an official of the king of Babylon whose courageous stand for the one true God caused many around him to know the Lord. Even the king, Nebuchadnezzar, gives his testimony in chapter 4. Daniel shows us how to live in the midst of a culture that does not know the Lord. Is this a book for our times? Daniel also received many visions of end time events, and this book is an important source for understanding the Book of Revelation. *Read 1:3–19, 2:1–49, 3:8–30, 4:2–37, 10:1–21.*

Division 5 (Pinkie)

The Minor Prophets: twelve books not "minor" by any means

Hosea was a prophet to the Northern Kingdom who married a harlot named Gomer, who was symbol of Israel's unfaithfulness to God. As Hosea kept going after his wayward wife to bring her back, so God pursues us with His love. Hosea gives us a great picture of God's love for His bride. *Read 1:2–7, 2:9–20, 6:1–6, 10:12, 14:9.*

Joel urged the people of Judah to turn their hearts toward God. Joel spoke about the Day of the Lord. Peter used this famous passage on the day of Pentecost to describe the "*xenolalia*" (speaking in known tongues) that was heard by the crowds. *Read 2:1–17, 2:28–32.*

Amos was a shepherd from Judah who traveled to Israel and urged the people to repent and return to the Lord to escape the coming judgement. He spoke of the plumb line that God would use to measure His people. God does give fair warning and opportunity for repentance. *Read 4:13–5:8, 5:21–24.*

Obadiah is a short book that predicts the fall of the region known as Edom because of her joy in Jerusalem's destruction. God does judge those who have harmed His people. *Read 1:1–4, 1:15–16.*

Jonah traveled from Joppa to the capital of the Assyrian Empire, Nineveh, via the belly of a whale. The Assyrians were the Nazis of their era and were hated by many, yet God sent Jonah to save them. What compassion our Lord has, even for evil people! His obedience resulted in the great revival of his day. *Read 1:1–4:11.*

Many believe that to be swallowed by a big fish and survive seems pretty far-fetched. I did too until I read about a fisherman who, in the early 1920s, fell off his boat (off of Marseilles, France) and was swallowed by a huge fish. The next day this same fish was caught by another fishing boat and hauled aboard. Imagine their surprise when they cut the fish open to discover a live human being in the stomach of the fish. He had survived on trapped air inside the fish, but his skin was white from the stomach acid, and he had lost much of his hair. What do you think would be the reaction to a bleached, hairless man showing up in your city preaching repentance and relationship with God?

Micah spoke out against oppression and false worship of God. He warned of the coming judgment on Judah and urged the people to have true relationship with God. Micah spoke of the Messiah (he predicted Jesus' birthplace) and gave us a definition of true religion. If there is any doubt how the Jews in the Hebrew Scriptures were saved, read Micah chapter 6. *Read 2:1–3, 3:1–8, 4:1–8, 5:2, 6:6–8.*

Nahum declares that God is awesome, and He is the one who rules and judges, even (*especially*) those who don't acknowledge Him. Nahum predicted accurately how Nineveh would be destroyed. *Read 1:1–13, 2:4–13.*

Habakkuk questioned why God would allow evil to go unpunished and how a holy God could use a more wicked people to punish the Jews. Isn't this a book for our times? Verse 2:4 is what Martin Luther read that caused him to start the Reformation, and verses 3:17–19 are guidelines for adverse situations. *Read 1:2–13, 2:4, 3:17–19.*

Zephaniah predicted judgment for Judah because of their indifference toward the Lord and calls for the people to seek the Lord. He describes the "Day of the Lord" and ends with a great promise of restoration. *Read 1:7–18, 2:1–3, 3:12–20.*

Haggai encouraged the returning exiles to get their priorities right and obey God by completing the task that He had placed before them—to finish rebuilding the temple in Jerusalem. He gives a practical message to put your faith in action. *Read 1:3–11.*

Zechariah also encouraged the former refugees to rebuild the temple. He also gave more prophecies about the coming Messiah than any other prophet except Isaiah. There are some great principles for ministry in chapter 3. *Read 4:1–7, 3:1–7, 7:8–14, 9:9, 11:10–13, 14:1–8.*

Malachi rebuked the people for not truly worshipping God. He spoke against the corrupt priests who were leading the people astray and against husbands who were divorcing their wives and marrying younger (and often pagan) women. Malachi asks twenty-three questions, and the answers provide some pointed insight into some of the spiritual issues of his day as well as ours.

MB: As I read these thirty-nine books, even though they were written by at least twenty-four different individuals over a 1,000 year time span, all of this comes together very cohesively. It is like God saying: "Hey Mike, you want to know about Me? Do you want to know My ways? Do you want to know how to relate to Me? Do you want to know how to live your life successfully? It is all right here in the pages of the Hebrew Scriptures."

Laura and Michael at the Dead Sea covered with "mud therapy"

RS: One of the problems is that the way that we learn the Scriptures is usually through preaching and teaching—in twenty—, thirty—, or forty-minute chunks. The problem with this is that you are looking at a natural process. Take, for example, the process we call life, which includes conception, birth, early-toddler stage, grade-school years, adulthood, old age, and finally death. We don't look at a person's life in portions. We wouldn't say for example: "Today we are going to look at the life of Mike Bagby, just his birth, and here is a picture . . ."

MB: It wasn't a pretty picture, Randy. My mother would never let that one go public.

RS: What's important is that it is unnatural to view a person's life in the context of just a snapshot, but that is the way that we have to teach the Bible. We can't start every message with "in the beginning" and start from there. It is like taking an ingredient—an egg—out of the recipe of a cake. It is an important and distinct ingredient, but it really only works because it is part of the cake. I am interested in the taste of the chocolate cake, not the egg.

MB: Exactly! We want the taste of the cake and to be able to enjoy that. That's why we have to read the Hebrew Scriptures as a unit, in light of each other. Then these thirty-nine ingredients form a delicious and nutritional cake!

Here is another perspective from Laura that might help.

PHOTO ALBUMS

A few days ago, we were looking through some old photos from the Hjalmeby family collection. It was fun to see them in a different light and in many different scenes in their native Sweden. It gave us a good feel for where they came from and what their history and family were all about. We felt like we knew them a lot better. It also drummed up more questions regarding their family and lives prior to coming to America. It certainly made us appreciate them so much more knowing all that they've been through and had accomplished over the years.

The New Testament is a giant photo album of Jesus Christ. It is an album with photos taken by Matthew, Mark, Luke, John, and others; and by looking through the pages, it is obvious that Jesus is the center attraction. There are many snapshots of Jesus teaching by the lake; Jesus talking to a woman by a well; Jesus at a wedding; Jesus at a party; Jesus having a meal with His friends; Jesus with sick people; Jesus with spiritually-troubled people, Jesus with priests, Jesus with a Roman soldier; Jesus with children. . . .

As each photographer has his or her own style, we see these four portraits of Jesus through four different lenses.

Matthew was a Jewish photographer, capturing the image of Jesus as the King—the Messiah. He wrote in a way that Jews would understand how the Hebrew Scriptures pointed to this remarkable person Jesus, who fulfilled many prophecies given for the Messiah. Matthew quotes more from the Hebrew Scriptures than any of the other evangelists.

Mark was a Jew who was working with Peter in Rome. His portrait of Jesus was one that a Roman could relate to. Jesus was captured in many photos as a man of action—a Roman ideal. Mark took the time to explain to his Roman audience things about Jewish culture. Matthew didn't have to do this; his audience already knew these things.

Luke was a Greek, and he took photos of Jesus that a Greek audience could understand. Jesus was portrayed as the "perfect man," an ideal of Greek society. Luke also ordered Jesus' life into a logical procession from pre-birth to post-resurrection so that his logical Greek readers could fully comprehend the significance of this singular man.

John was an intimate friend of Jesus, and his photo gallery shows Jesus as the Son of God—literally, God in the flesh. He wrote in a way that Jews and Greeks alike could receive this portrait of God Himself.

Every good photo album comes complete with captions, explanations of what is happening in each photo. This "New Testament photo album" has captions too. *They are called the Epistles.*

Friends and followers of Jesus wrote explaining the significance of the various elements of His life and how they apply to our lives.

Paul, with his Hebrew heritage and Greek education, was perhaps the perfect person to communicate the Gospel to the Greek-speaking world. His evangelism efforts resulted in the planting of many churches, and his nine letters to these churches and four letters to his disciples provide much practical application of Jesus' message to mankind.

James and Jude were brothers to Jesus. James was the leader of the church in Jerusalem. He wrote a very practical application of the Gospel that reflects his Hebrew attitude of function.

Peter was Jesus' friend who had a few years to meditate on the meaning of all he was taught by the Master. His letters reflect a deep understanding of practical elements of Jesus' teachings.

John lived the longest of the original twelve disciples, and his three letters reflect a loving, yet orthodox, application of the Gospel. His Revelation paints a unique picture of the coming Jesus.

As we view Him in His various roles, we begin to appreciate Him more. We see how He frequently handled opposition and get a good picture of who He is and the depth of security He had as a person, knowing exactly where He came from and certainly where He was headed. Indeed He was a picture of perfect security.

He becomes a quick hero to anyone looking through His album.
Unique is His character; Admirable are His ways.
We ourselves often become like who we are with;
We ourselves emulate those we look up to.
We do well to look into the album of the Living Life
sent to inspire all those who open His Book.

MB: Now let's get to the strings that tie it altogether. Here are the seven major themes or

The Seven Shoestrings of the Christian Scriptures

1. *God in the flesh:* Jesus Christ. After telling us about Himself in the pages of the Hebrew Scriptures, He came to live among us so that we could truly know Him and relate to Him. *Read John 1:1–4; Colossians 1:13–20.*

And the Word became flesh, and dwelt among us, and we beheld His glory, glory as of the only begotten from the Father, full of grace and truth. (John 1:14)

2. *Redemption through the blood of Jesus Christ.* What was required in the Book of Leviticus, what was prophesied in Psalm 22, and described in Isaiah 53 was fulfilled. *Read Romans 3:23–25, 5:6–11; Hebrews 10:1–22.*

   But God demonstrates His own love toward us, in that while we were yet sinners, Christ died for us. Much more then, having now been justified by His blood, we shall be saved from the wrath of God through Him. (Romans 5:8–9 NAS)

3. *Man and woman's identity as a member of God's family.* We are not just friends but intimate family! We are no long estranged from God but called to the closest possible relationship with Him. *Read Ephesians 1:3–14.*

   But as many as received Him, to them He gave the right to become children of God, even to those who believe in His name. (John 1:12 NAS)

4. *How Christians are to walk in this world.* If we have a new spirit within, we should live a new way. By living in this new way, with a renewed mind and set free of the sins of the past, we become more intimate with God and more effective in the mission that He has assigned us. *Read Galatians 5:16–25; Philippians 2:12–13.*

   So I advise you to live according to your new life in the Holy Spirit. Then you won't be doing what your sinful nature craves. (Galatians 5:16)

5. *The future of all disciples of Jesus.* Despite all the adverse things that may happen in this life, Jesus tells us: "Relax, Paradise awaits you." *Read 1 Thessalonians 4:13–18; Revelation 19:1–21:8.*

   There are many rooms in my Father's home, and I am going to prepare a place for you. If this were not so, I would tell you plainly. When everything is ready, I will come and get you, so that you will always be with me where I am. (John 14:2–3)

A few years ago, our friend Ralph, a hardcore Oakland Raiders fan, was traveling in Japan and anxious to get the score and some details of the Raiders/Broncos Monday night football game. After searching many papers, he finally saw a score only and was relieved to see that the Raiders had won 34–32.

A few days later, he arrived back in Honolulu and on the way home asked his wife about the game. She just smiled but didn't say anything. When they arrived home, she marched him to the television, made him sit down, and popped a video into the VCR. Ralph was pleased to see that it was the Raiders/Broncos game.

The Broncos scored quickly, followed by another score. The Raiders couldn't get on the scoreboard, but the Broncos were rolling, scoring more field goals and touchdowns. The half ended with the Raiders scoreless. Ralph began wondering if he had read the score correctly or if it was possible that the Japanese newspaper had misprinted the results. No, it had to be the correct final score.

The second half began, and the Raiders came on the field a different team. They were fired up and began to score—and score they did! Touchdowns, field goals—one after another. Finally the Raiders scored and went ahead. Denver never caught up. The final score was 34–32.

Ralph later said that as he watched the first half, knowing the final score of the game, he actually enjoyed seeing Denver score in such a way that they were sure that the game was in the bag. He knew that a big disappointment was in store for them and great joy was waiting the Raiders and their diehard fans. It is much the same for Christians. We know the final score.

6. *The reality of spiritual warfare.* Our environment here on planet Earth is a battle-ground with the forces of darkness arrayed against the kingdom of light. *Read John 10:10; 1 Peter 5:6–10; Ephesians 6:10–18.*

> Be of sober spirit, be on the alert. Your adversary, the devil, prowls about like a roaring lion, seeking someone to devour. (1 Peter 5:8 NAS)

On Maui, along the road from Kihei to Lahaina, is Maalaea Harbor. This harbor is where many of the diving, fishing, and other "tourists" boats are docked, and every morning, it is a hot bed of activity. I used to work as crew on the Sea Sport, and I really enjoyed seeing all the visitors arrive at Maalaea, excited with the anticipation of the adventure that lay ahead. They were smiling, laughing, and generally having a lot of fun, most without a care in the world (except a few who were dreading the thought of "feeding the fish" when the waves got a little rough). It is amazing how jolly people can be at 6:30 A.M., even before they board their "pleasure craft!"

Many Christians remind me of the tourists that gather at Maalaea each morning. They have just been saved and have entered into relationship with the Lord. Everything is great! They believe that all ahead is smooth sailing—a bowl of cherries without the pits and vanilla frozen yogurt on top! They are awaiting their Lord to pull up on a giant white Love Boat and take them away from the cares of this world.

As they are standing there on the dock laughing and scratching, they see the ship on the horizon, heading in to pick them up. Anticipation grows as the ship gets closer and closer. They strain to see the details of this approaching ship, and finally it comes into full view.

Some begin to shriek and others begin to moan as they realize that this "pleasure craft" is not white but rather has a dull, gray paint. The "promenade" decks on each side are lined turrets with protruding guns.

This is not the Love Boat. This is a battleship! The captain motions them to board and assigns each a battle station. Reality begins to set in. There is a war to be fought, and the stakes are the lives of each human being in this world.

7. *The final chapter of this world.* Things often don't make sense unless we understand the big picture. With this understanding, we can persevere through any crisis, holding on to the promise of victory. *Read Matthew 24:1–48.*

> And I saw a new heaven and a new earth; for the first heaven and the first earth passed away, and there is no longer any sea (chaos). (Revelation 21:1 NAS)

MB: Now let's get into the exciting twenty-seven books that make up the Christian Scriptures.

Arielle: Twenty-seven books?! How can I remember all these?

MB: You can divide the New Testament into *four divisions,* and let's take a look at our hand again to help us remember. For the Old Testament, we used the fingers to place each book. *For the New Testament, we will use the spaces between each finger to help us remember.*

Look at the space between the thumb and index finger. These are the "His-Story" books—five books about Jesus and His disciples. The space between your index finger and middle finger is where Paul's epistles (or letters—fourteen of them) are placed. The space between the middle finger and ring finger is where the General Epistles fall. These are seven books written by relatives and friends of Jesus. The last space by your pinkie is for the one book of Prophecy—Revelation.

Remember, look at your hand as we go through these books and lock each one into its place. It will save you a lot of time the next time your pastor says to turn to the Book of Philemon.

Division 1

The Gospels and Acts: four portraits of Christ.

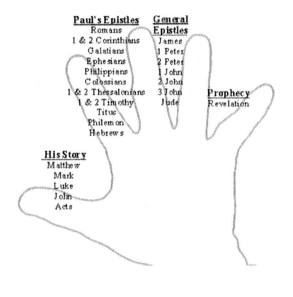

RS: The New Testament, or better put, *the Christian Scriptures*, gives us four distinct views of Jesus.

Matthew records for us *Jesus' words*. The book is a series of sermons with some narrative tying them together. *Mark* describes for us *Jesus' works*. Jesus is a man of one action after another. *Luke* puts everything in order and gives us a *chronology*. *John* tells us about the problems that Jesus had with the religious authorities. We read Matthew, Mark, and Luke and ask ourselves, "Why did they crucify Him?" John tells us why. John is also trying to describe Jesus to an audience who is Hebrew-thinking and Greek-thinking. To the Hebrew-thinker, it's not what you say that's important, it's what you do. To the Greek-thinker, however, it's how you describe yourself. John gives us seven "I Am's" (the Door, the Way, the Good Shepherd, the Resurrection, etc.) and gives us seven signs of what Jesus does (heal the blind, feed the multitudes, raise the dead, etc.) so that both sides of the audience can soak up the message in their own cultural terms.

MB: *Matthew* was a former tax collector and one of Jesus' disciples. He was an eyewitness to most of the events of Jesus' ministry. Since Matthew's ministry was probably to the Jews, he wrote a biography that would appeal to his own people.

How? By quoting fifty-three times from the Old Testament (which all Jews would be familiar with) and using seventy-six other references to the Old Testament. He referred to many prophecies and used the title "Son of David" for Jesus. Obviously, David was one historical figure that every Jew knew. Matthew presented Jesus to his Jewish audience as their promised King and Messiah. Study Matthew if you want to read the words of Jesus. *Read 5:1–7:29, 10:5–42, 13:1–58, 18:1–25:46.*

Mark was around during Jesus' ministry (see Mark 14:51–52—the naked guy was probably Mark!). He was a traveling companion of Peter, and most of Mark's Gospel was the gospel of Peter (since Peter probably couldn't read or write). Since Peter was ministering in Rome, Mark was written with the Roman culture in mind.

The ideal Roman citizen was a man who served the State in a very effective way. Mark and Peter portrayed Jesus as the "perfect servant." Just in the first chapter the word *immediately* (in the NAS) is used ten times. Jesus was man of action! *Read 1:14–2:13, 4:35–5:43, 8:1–9:29, 14:1–16:13.*

Luke was a Greek and a doctor. Although he probably didn't personally witness Jesus' ministry during His years before the cross, he had access to excellent primary sources—most of the disciples. Luke was a first-rate historian, and he gives us an excellent chronology of the life and ministry of Jesus. This is a cultural reflection of his logical Greek background, and as he traveled with Paul in the Greek world (Greece, Asia Minor), it is very natural that Luke wrote an account of Jesus that his people could relate to.

When you think of Greek culture, what images come to mind? I see statues of men and women, perfectly sculpted, perfectly formed. I see groups of men debating, learning, and involved in drama and other arts. I think of the athletic competitions, the Olympics, and the Greeks "being all that men could be." Luke presents Jesus to this culture as someone to whom they could look up to—the Man who was perfect in all His ways. *Read 1:5–2:40, 4:1–5:39, 10:1–12:59, 14:1–19:27, 20:1–38, 24:1–53.*

John was a dear friend (and possibly cousin) of Jesus and of the original twelve disciples was probably the youngest. John gives us (all cultures) a very personal account of Jesus' life, which focuses on His divine nature. From the very first verse, John identifies Jesus as none other as God in the flesh and in chapter after chapter gives us declarations and evidence of Jesus' true identity as the "Son of God." Remember that the term "son" in the Hebrew world was not used to necessarily denote a biological offspring but was often understood as "exact replica of."

John, who enjoyed a place of intimacy with Jesus (John 13:23), understood the essence of God in the flesh. This gospel and his later letters continually refer back to this all-important characteristic—love. Whether is was Jesus weeping over the death of a friend, talking to a Samaritan adulteress, healing a paralytic, or washing His disciples feet, we see Jesus as a man of compassion and love. John used the word *love* more than all the other Gospel writers combined (thirty vs. eleven plus five plus twelve [NAS]). *Read 1:1–18, 3:1–21, 4:3–5:47, 6:15–71, 8:1–11:46, 13:1–17:26.*

The fifth book in the "His-Story" division is the *Acts of the Holy Spirit*, which is sometimes referred to as Acts of the Apostles. It is obvious in reading this book that it was the Holy Spirit doing the work, sometimes in spite of the apostles!

RS: With these pictures of who Messiah is, we see in the Book of Acts the application of what this all means to us personally. We don't really see the "Acts of the Apostles," but rather we see the "acts of the Risen Lord" through the apostles. It is God putting on human skin, showing us His character in another dynamic way, and then demonstrating what that does for me. Ultimately, I intersect with the Living God, I understand who He is, and I begin to see it lived out in my life. The first pattern for that is Peter, John, Phillip, and then Paul, who carries the rest of the book, along with others.

MB: We see a sudden ending to this book. Chapter 28 ends with Paul preaching the Gospel, "with all openness, unhindered." Period. I feel like the Holy Spirit did this. Luke got to this part and laid down his pen and never picked it up again because he knew that chapter 29 was being written right before his eyes in the succeeding years. We are living in chapter 29 right now, writing of the "acts of the Risen Lord" through our own lives. This is exciting! Another exciting thing is to look at fallible guys like Peter, who failed the big test, and Paul, who was so lost that he was actually killing early believers, and see how God used them. I think, *Wow, if He can use these guys like He did, what can He do with me?* I am living in Acts 29. We are writing those verses right now that will be read later. Those verses that describe how the Miskito Indians got discipled, how many Arabs got converted and discipled, how many in need felt the love of God through our hands!

The things that the Holy Spirit is playing out thorough us will be remembered when we stand before the Lord on that final day. That is exciting!

Division 2

Paul's epistles: fourteen letters to churches and individuals.

MB: The epistles give us explanation and application of the truths presented by Jesus. These were written by men who knew Jesus intimately: His buddy, Peter; His possible cousin, John; his brothers, James and Jude; and finally, by Paul, who with his rabbinical training and his Greek scholastic training was the one most able to take this Good News to a broader audience.

RS: I'm fascinated by the pattern that the apostle Paul gives us. When he goes into a town, there is either a riot or a revival! Here is a man who is barely five feet tall, yet his reach goes all the way up to the stars. I see the man, warts and all. I see the power of God in spite of the person, and I also see the mass of contradictions that is Paul (and also Peter and David), who really wanted to do the right thing but kept doing the wrong thing.

I think that we look at these guys in a way that Church history and Christian art has—with halos on their heads and their feet not quite touching the ground. It's unfortunate, because it's unreal. These were real men like you and me. The truth is that Paul leaves an area and rest comes to the churches: "Thank God, he's out of town; we can get on with our lives." There is a tremendous emphasis on all their accomplishments because we are accomplishment-oriented. But their accomplishments were not really what the story is about, rather it is the story of a loving God who, in spite of these hardheaded, tough individuals, gets things done. God is doing the impossible through the unlikely.

Here are the thumbnail sketches:

Salvation through Christ is the theme of *Romans*. In this letter to the church at Rome, Paul expresses in a very Greek logical manner the message of the Bible. Chapter 8 is an excellent summation of the message in Romans. It's Christ only, not Christ plus something else that gets you into the kingdom. *Read 1:18–32, 3:1–31, 5:1–21, 7:14–8:39.*

First Corinthians is one of the most practical books in the Bible. Corinth was a busy seaport and a town where there was a huge temple of the love goddess Aphrodite and statues everywhere of men and women in various sexual postures. Can you imagine what struggles the people in Corinth had when they came believers? The word *korinthaizomai* in classical Greek means "corrupted" or "fornication!" It is a word taken from the name "Corinth" that describes the lifestyle. As a result, many morality problems were addressed, as well as some basic spiritual issues. Does this sound like a book for our generation? *Read 1:18–31, 2:14–16, 6:1–9:27, 12:1–15:58.*

Second Corinthians is a book that teaches us much about the life and ministry of Paul. Other themes included are authority, giving, and spiritual warfare. In this book, we are also given an account of Paul's trip to heaven. *Read 4:1–18, 5:10–20, 12:1–13.*

Freedom in Christ is the theme of *Galatians*. In one of his earliest letters, Paul states that salvation is the result of faith only and not works. This letter resulted from some Jewish believers who told the new Greek Christians that they needed to follow the Jewish law to be "complete." We see in this letter what happened when the two cultures (Greek and Jewish) clashed and how we are to separate the truth of the Gospel from our own culture. Let's not make the mistake of many earlier missionaries who tied Christianity to their culture. *Read 1:6–3:2, 4:4–7, 5:1–6:10.*

Ephesians is one of the definitive books in the Bible. Our identity in Christ, how to walk in this world and interact with the invisible, spiritual world, are the themes of this book. Some of the most personally meaningful passages in the Bible are found in this letter to the church at Ephesus. Through each chapter, Paul lays a foundation for the next. So, before you begin to do spiritual warfare (chapter 6), make sure that you are compliant with chapters 1–5. The message of Ephesians is essential for every Christian! *Read 1:3–14, 2:8–10, 3:8–11, 4:4–6:18.*

The focus of *Philippians* is attitude. Writing from prison, Paul explains the *kenosis* (pouring out) of Christ from His Divine nature into His human nature and the resulting goal of His life. If God is reaching out to us by becoming a human, then Paul wants to know this God intimately. Paul sets our highest priority in this life—knowing Him. *Read 2:1–16, 3:1–15.*

Colossians presents a clear picture of the supremacy of Christ above all other "roads to God." Believers are complete with Christ and nothing else. There were two extremes that had sprung up (and continue to) in the Church—mysticism and legalism. Mysticism says that experiences and "special knowledge" are needed in addition to what Christ did on the cross. Legalism says that you must obey certain codes of conduct to maintain your relationship to God. These codes usually go beyond the "love God," and "love your neighbor" laws that Jesus gave us in Matthew 22:37–40. And the codes change according to the times and culture. Yet the Gospel message is simple and clear and is trans-cultural and timeless. As a retail businessman says "location, location, location" for success in business. Paul says "Jesus, Jesus, Jesus" for a successful spiritual life. *Read 1:13–23, 2:8–4:6.*

First Thessalonians is one of Paul's earliest letters, written to a materialistic society in an important Roman town. Christian conduct, the Day of the Lord, and Paul's integrity are the main themes of this very practical book. *Read 4:1–5:22.*

Second Thessalonians was written by Paul to correct a possible misunderstanding about the Day of the Lord resulting from his first letter. In addition, Paul defines the Christian work ethic to this "yuppie" church. *Read 2:1–12, 3:6–15.*

First Timothy is a discipleship manual to a young pastor filled with practical instruction on how to handle the affairs of church life. This book is a great encouragement to any young person involved in any ministry. *Read 2:1–3:13, 4:6–6, 6:3–19.*

Second Timothy continues the discipleship for a young soldier of Christ. Paul gives much practical and personal counsel on how we are to work as ministers of the Gospel. *Read 1:6–14, 2:1–26, 3:12–4:7.*

Titus is another pastoral letter to another young disciple who was planting churches. Paul gives a set of attitudes and a code of conduct for all Christians to adopt and teach. *Read 1:5–3:8.*

Philemon, written to a friend of Paul's on behalf of an escaped slave and new Christian, teaches us to look at the big picture and forgive, love, and get involved in ministry. *Read 1:6–19.*

Hebrews is the most important link between the Christian and Hebrew Scriptures. Using twenty-nine direct quotations from the Old Testament, Hebrews proclaims the sufficiency and supremacy of Christ and Christianity. A study of Hebrews will make the Torah come alive. A reading of the Torah will make the explanation in Hebrews and the value of Christ and His death on the cross all the more clear. *Read 4:1–16, 5:1–6:12, 8:6–9:15, 10:11–25, 11:1–12:13, 13:8.*

Division 3

The General Epistles: seven letters written by close friends of Jesus.

James is another book of practical theology. Written by the brother of Jesus, who was the leader of the Jerusalem church, James gives us very practical advice on Christian conduct. He also gives the balance to Paul's "saved by faith" message in Romans. You cannot take into your conscience the principles of Romans without also taking in the principles in James, even though at first they may seem to conflict. Instead they reveal a deep harmony of the Christian life. *Read 1:2–15, 2:14–26, 4:1–17, 5:13–16.*

First Peter gives encouragement to Christians who were being severely persecuted for their faith. Peter gives us insight into our identity, conduct, prayers, trials, and spiritual warfare. This book is another discipleship manual; this one from the leader of Jesus' disciples. *Read 1:3–7, 1:13–19, 2:1–10, 3:19, 4:12–19, 5:6–10.*

Second Peter tells us how we are to grow spiritually. Peter also warns us about false teachers and reminds us about some of the things that will be happening in the last days. In this book, Peter also demonstrates an understanding of celestial physics. He also validates Paul's letters as Scripture. For a short book, there is an amazing amount of content! *Read 1:2–21, 3:3–16.*

First John is one of the most profound and essential books in the Bible. John, who used the word *love* more than any of the Gospel writers, defines to us the nature of God. He also tells us how to test the spirits. Perhaps the most profound passage in the Bible is found in first two verses of chapter 3. John, who had a very intimate relationship with the Lord, reveals much of his understanding of living in the spiritual world in this book. *Read 1:1–2:10, 3:1–2, 3:9–24, 4:1–12.*

Second John is a short letter that reminds us to "love one another" and commands us to "close the door" to false teachers.

Third John is the shortest book in the Bible, yet contains an all-important message. John tells us to support traveling ministers (missionaries), so that we may be partners with them in their work. David said it another way in 1 Samuel 30:28: "For as his share is who goes down to the battle, so shall his share be who stays by the baggage. They shall all share alike." The writer of Samuel goes on to say in the next verse: "And so it

239

has been from that day forward, that he made it a statue and an ordinance for Israel to this day." Prayers, hospitality, financial support, and giving of our time are great ways to help missionaries.

Jude reminds us to be vigilant in the faith and to oppose heresy. Jude, who was a brother of Jesus, also gives us some understanding of the fall of angels and an encounter between the angel Michael and Satan.

Division 4

Prophecy: one book, written by a friend of Jesus
Revelation begins with letters from Jesus to seven first-century churches that contain timely messages for our times. John goes on to received a unique portrait of Jesus and a detailed account of the coming and final events of this world. The Book of Daniel has a strong connection with this book. *Read 1:9–3:22, 12:1–17, 19:11–16, 20:1–21:8.*

MB: There are many messages that are given in Revelation. Many great and glorious things are revealed and many events explained. There are also many warnings given. One of the most shocking images is found in chapter 3.

> "I know your deeds, that you are neither cold nor hot, I would that you were cold or hot. So because you are lukewarm, and neither hot nor cold, I will spit you out of My mouth." (Revelation 3:15–16 NAS)

The word translated "spit" in this passage is actually the word *vomit*. I think that this word gives us a better picture of what Jesus was trying to communicate.

Mikaela: "Vomit? That doesn't sound like something Jesus would say!"

MB: Laodicea was a town located in Asia Minor. Close by was the town of Heropolis, which was famous for an extensive system of natural hot springs. People from all over the Aegean world came to Heropolis for the medicinal healing effects of these mineral baths. On the other side of Laodicea was Colossae, a city know for the cold mountain spring that provided refreshing drinking water to its residents. Although we in the twenty-first century have speculated what exactly Jesus meant by this illustration, to the members of the Laodicean church it couldn't have been more clear: "If you are neither "healing" or "refreshing" to my body, I will expel you."
Though this illustration may seem strange (to us who are not familiar with the geographical features of the region), Jesus is probably saying two things. That He doesn't

want anyone whom is "lukewarm" in relationship with Him. He also doesn't want members of His body who are neither *healing* nor *refreshing* in their relationships to others. When we become too concerned about our own comfort levels, as the Laodicean church had, we often become indifferent to the needs of those God has places around us. If we arrive at this state, then He will *vomit* us out of His mouth.

Jesus is serious when it comes to relationships, especially the one that we all have with Him. Remember He paid a great price to make the relationship possible. When we reject relationship with Him or take it lightly, then He reacts in a way that displays His emotions. I had an experience that happened a few years ago that might help explain.

One weekend, the *U.S.S. Kitty Hawk* was in San Diego. We had been out to sea for three weeks, so we were ready for some action. I went with three of my fellow aviators to the beach. We spent all day there, and since it was hot, we drank a lot—hey, we were thirsty! After weeks out at sea, flying, and defending the Pacific Ocean, we had a lot of catching up to do!

Next, we went to a Mexican restaurant for tacos and more drinks. The next event was the Jimmy Buffet concert at San Diego State. Finally, after midnight, we were ready to go "back ship" (as we used to say to the Philippino taxi drivers at Subic Bay Naval Station).

I was driving. We were on the freeway heading south to Coronado, and my friend Dan was sitting behind me, apparently passed out, with his head leaning back. I was cruising in the fast lane, and traffic was light.

Above the music blaring out of the radio, I heard Dan mumble, "Poouull over."

"What did you say?" I asked.

Dan again mumbled, "Poouull ooover."

I began changing lanes. "Pull over!" came the command, now urgently!

Now it was more than a mumble. I moved into the right lane and began to decelerate.

"Pull over now!" Dan moaned.

Suddenly, I heard a gurgling sound. What followed was a multi-sensual experience.

Following the gurgle, there was an explosion in the back seat. As I heard the sound of a human in agony, I saw a liquid substance splatter the windshield in front of me. The entire inside of the windshield was covered except for an outline that matched the shape of my head.

At the same moment, I felt a warm substance hit the back of my ears and the back of my neck. A pungent odor filled the car. The sound, visual, feel, and smell sensations all hit me at the same moment.

Then I felt the liquid substance dripping off my ears and head on to the collar of my shirt.

"I'm pulling over Dan," I said as I stopped the car on the shoulder.

Dan stepped out and deposited the remainder of his tacos, beers, and tequila beside a road sign.

Let's not be lukewarm about our relationship with Jesus. Let's take the time to get to know Him through these books of the Bible. Let's dedicate time to be with Him in our prayers and quiet time.

Let's be healing and refreshing in our relationship with the people that He places around us. Let's not get ourselves into a place where we become the liquid substance that was dripping off my ears.

Finally, let's look at a practical way to study the Bible.

RS: The truths of the Bible are wrapped in the context of where, to whom, and why the various books of the Bible were written. The Bible is meant to be a timeless message to all peoples and cultures, filled with principles for our lives. Our challenge is to extract these truths and principles, not necessarily through our own cultural perspectives, and apply them to our lives. *The question is: How do we actually study the Bible and extract these truths?*

MB: The key to understanding the Bible is an intimate walk with the Holy Spirit. He is the ultimate teacher. He is the one who makes the words jump off the page. *Cultivate your relationship with Him.*

RS: Let me offer another suggestion that may be fun to try. The Bible is made up of several genres of literature. Rather than studying all of them, let me offer some keys that have helped me put a lot together.

Read a Gospel (or an historical book like 1 Samuel). When you follow the story from beginning to end, imagine there are no verses or chapters dividing the text. *Read the whole book* or listen through to it on cassette. When you are listening, follow with your eyes on a Bible.

Break the text at every drama "scene change" (i.e., "The next day Jesus went . . ."). For instance when you are finished with the Gospel of Luke, you will see seventy-two scene changes. Some scenes are long (Jesus is at a Pharisee's house from 14:1–17:10), and others are a few verses. Some are narrations of events to get to the story (Luke. 1:1–4), and others are the story of what Jesus did and said. When you are finished, you have the basic "scene frames."

Inside the scenes are smaller "purpose portions" (called "telics"), which teach an independent lesson. *Write next to each what timeless truth is communicated by that portion.* When you have a string of them done, ask why one follows the other. Is there any connection between the first and the second lesson? Let me give you an example.

Luke 14:1–17:10 is set in one wealthy Pharisee's house on a Sabbath evening. There is a large dining hall where the disciples, Jesus, and a number of wealthy Pharisees are reclining. There is an adjacent hall (normally with three doors to an open atrium) where a large number of poor and locals are gathered to watch the banquet and listen to the discussion. This was allowed in ancient times. *Within the scene are nine events, each teaching a timeless truth.* Let's look at them:

A. *14:1–6:* Jesus healed a man of dropsy. The Pharisees sat silently after Jesus questioned if it would be right to do this on the Sabbath, for they were shamed by that question in 13:10–17.

B. *14:7–11:* Jesus turned to the invited guests (the wealthy), who all wanted the best seats, and told a parable: *Don't exalt yourself, but humble yourself to become truly important in the kingdom.*

C. *14:12–15:* Jesus turned to the host and told him next time *not* to call the influential but rather *to become an influencer* by calling in those who cannot repay you in this life.

D. *14:15–24:* Someone called out "God is preparing a feast for (we that are) the righteous!" This prompted another lesson from Jesus who said, "When those who are called don't come, others are invited!" *This veiled warning was to show that God was calling out to others,* for they were hardening their hearts!

E. *14:25–35:* Jesus turned to the crowd in the atrium as they pressed into the doors to hear Him. He cautioned them, "Count the total cost of commitment to Me. Some want to listen!"

F. *15:1–32:* The response to His hard words included some (publicans and sinners) to draw nearer but others (Pharisees) to back off and criticize! He heard their criticism and answered them with a three-part parable. In each part, something was lost, something was found, and the person that found it (a sheep, a coin, a son) had *joy.* In the end of the "son" parable, the elder brother criticized the joy of the father that found his lost son. The elder brother was the Pharisee group that was listening and murmuring about Jesus. The theme: When that which is lost is found, *joy* should be the result!

G. *16:1–13:* Jesus then turned to His disciples in front of the Pharisees and the crowds, telling them: "Don't respond to wealth as the Pharisees have! You need to learn to be as wise as the world about use of assets, but use them always to build kingdom ends!"

H. *16:14–31:* Jesus then addressed the covetous Pharisees to tell them, "Bad priorities lead to bad choices!" He attacked the choices they made concerning their lack of defense of John (vs. 16) and defending John's stand against the illegal remarriage of Herod Antipas, on which they had been silent on (vs. 18)! He followed with the story of the rich man and Lazarus to make the point that "You should know better, you have the Torah and that is all you need to make good decisions!"

I.   *17:1–10:* Finally, Jesus turned to His disciples and reminded them, "You must learn to be humble! Settle your differences between you (vs. 1–6) and become like servants!" (vs. 7–10). This lesson connects all the above, from beginning to end. In the end, the whole scene is to teach one godly character trait—humility. What does humility look like? How does one with humility act? God gives us this story to clearly illustrate this principle.

This is one suggestion on how to study the Gospels; Acts is the same. The writers had a story to tell that gives a message of life to the reader. When we step back and look at the work as a whole, the chapters and verses become connected in a cohesive way. As we look at the Scriptures through first-century eyes, the message that the writers were communicating becomes more apparent.

Our efforts to discover the message of the Bible are richly rewarded through experiencing His divine presence and power in our lives. This is really the point to Bible study: to know Him better, to understand His plans and purposes for our lives, and to live in a manner that is pleasing to Him.

Michael Bagby and Randy Smith

SEEK THE LAMB MINISTRY PROFILE

Christian education, Bible-training seminars, evangelism, and relief in Central America, Europe, North America, the Middle East, Pacifica, and the Far East.

Primary Education in Nicaragua

Our school system, Project Ezra, is located in sixteen Miskito Indian villages along the Rio Coco in Nicaragua, one of the most isolated regions of the Western Hemisphere. We began classes in 1986. Now we have over 2,000 students grades Kindergarten through sixth, with seventy-six Miskito teachers—*and over half of these are our former first-grade students.*

We teach the Bible in Miskito each day to our Project Ezra students and believe that a relationship with the Living God is the most important thing that we can give them!

Discipleship

We believe that the most important focus of our lives is to be disciples of Jesus Christ. Our second most important focus is *making disciples.* We believe that understanding what the Bible has to say on these subjects is of the utmost importance to every follower of Jesus. As a result, we have developed training seminars for equipping believers in understanding the Scriptures and applying God's principles and truths to our lives.

- *Echoes into Eternity* looks at the process of discipleship and practical biblical steps for spiritual growth.
- *Living in the Spiritual World* takes a fresh look at aspects of life as a spiritual being through the eyes of the first-century Church. It is amazing what simplicity is brought about by stepping back to the beginning of our faith.
- *Cultural Connections* presents the lessons of many years of cross-cultural ministry in an effort to equip the potential mission team or missionary for work in foreign cultures across the ocean or around the block.
- In addition to these seminars, we have also developed books, videos, and audio tapes for discipleship training in English, Spanish, Miskito, Arabic, and Hebrew. *The Life of Jesus, Living in the Spiritual World, The Acts Project, The Mission Work of Paul, Just Another Lump of Clay,* and *In The Search Mode* are among the resources currently available.

A new video series, filmed on location in Israel, by Dr. Randy Smith is now available. The titles include *Jesus on Jesus, How Jesus Taught,* and *The Shepherd and His Sheep.*

Missions

Seek the Lamb provides opportunities for hands-on experience in third-world missions in Central America. Our summer cross cultural ministry course, called Deep Water Discipleship, offers individual discipleship as well as ministry training in a very challenging environment where Christianity is relatively new. In addition, we also directly support projects and mission workers in Thailand, England, Nicaragua, Israel, and the United States.

Make a Disciple

Project Ezra is largely funded through our Make A Disciple child-sponsorship program. *For $24 a month, you can provide Christian education to a special Miskito child.*

You will receive a current photo of your special child, a biography, and frequent reports on their academic achievement, health, and spiritual needs. Many have sponsored children from the first grade all the way to the sixth grade. More than thirty of our former first graders are now serving as Project Ezra teachers. Child sponsorship is a great way to get involved in the life of a needy Miskito child and help them with an opportunity that will serve them in this life as well as the next!

For more information about Seek The Lamb and to sign up for a free subscription to our newsletter, "The Conchshell Chronicles," please contact us at:

Seek The Lamb P.O. Box 2151 Vero Beach FL 32961 USA
Tel./Fax 772-770-9772 email: *Lambagby@cs.com*
www.seekthelamb.com

To order additional copies of

Living in the Spiritual World

A Study of the Other World We Live In

Have your credit card ready and call:

1-877-421-READ (7323)

or please visit our web site at
www.pleasantword.com

Also available at: www.amazon.com
and www.seekthelamb.com

Electronic Book Offer

Living in the Spiritual World Full Color Version

If you would like the electronic expanded version of this book complete with numerous color photos taken on location in many of the biblical sites in Israel and Greece, please contact our Seek The Lamb office at the address below:

Seek The Lamb P.O. Box 2151 Vero Beach FL 32961 USA
Tel./Fax 772-770-9772 email: *Lambagby@cs.com*
www.seekthelamb.com

Printed in the United States
25723LVS00004B/1-60

9 781414 101132